POLITICAL IDEAS

for A-level

Liberalism, Conservatism, Socialism, Feminism, Anarchism

Neil McNaughton
Richard Kelly

SERIES EDITOR:
Eric Magee

HODDER
EDUCATION
AN HACHETTE UK COMPANY

The Publishers would like to thank the following for permission to reproduce copyright material.

Acknowledgements

p.178, Rudolf *Rocker, Anarcho-Syndicalism* (1938), Martin Secker and Walburg; **p.182**, Murray Rothbard, *Man, Economy and State* (1962), The Ludwig von Mises Institute.

Photo credits

Photos reproduced by permission of: **p.9** Ian Dagnall/Alamy Stock Photo; **p.11** North Wind Picture Archives/Alamy Stock Photo; **p.26** matteogirelli/Fotolia; **p.27** Georgios Kollidas/Fotolia; History collection 2016/Alamy Stock Photo; **p.41** Bob Daemmrich/Alamy Stock Photo; **p.44** pixs:sell/Fotolia; **p.45** (top) Stephen Mulligan/Fotolia; **p.45** (bottom) Gang/Fotolia; **p.56** GL Archive/Alamy Stock Photo; **p.68** colaimages/Alamy Stock Photo; **p.69** dpa picture alliance/Alamy Stock Photo; **p.78** Sueddeutsche Zeitung Photo/Alamy Stock Photo; **p.82** dpa picture alliance/Alamy Stock Photo; **p.95** age fotostock/Alamy Stock Photo; p.97 vkilikov/Fotolia; **p.104** World History Archive/Alamy Stock Photo; **p.108** Keystone Pictures USA/Alamy Stock Photo; **p.110** Jeff Morgan 12/Alamy Stock Photo; **p.120** Maggie Sully/Alamy Stock Photo; **p.129** Pictorial Press Ltd/Alamy Stock Photo; **p.139** Geraint Lewis/Alamy Stock Photo; **p.143** Mike Goldwater/Alamy Stock Photo; **p.149** Marco Secchi/Alamy Stock Photo; **p.162** Mark Richardson/Alamy Stock Photo; **p.173** Pictorial Press Ltd/Alamy Stock Photo; **p.179** AF archive/Alamy Stock Photo; **p.180** Bettmann/Contributor; p.186 Cliff Hide News/Alamy Stock Photo.

Hachette UK's policy is to use papers that are natural, renewable and recyclable products and made from wood grown in sustainable forests. The logging and manufacturing processes are expected to conform to the environmental regulations of the country of origin.

Orders: please contact Bookpoint Ltd, 130 Park Drive, Milton Park, Abingdon, Oxon OX14 4SE. Telephone: (44) 01235 827720. Fax: (44) 01235 400454. Email education@bookpoint.co.uk

Lines are open from 9 a.m. to 5 p.m., Monday to Saturday, with a 24-hour message answering service. You can also order through our website: www.hoddereducation.co.uk

ISBN: 978 1 4718 89462

© Neil McNaughton, Richard Kelly and Eric Magee 2017

First published in 2017 by

Hodder Education,
An Hachette UK Company
Carmelite House
50 Victoria Embankment
London EC4Y 0DZ

www.hoddereducation.co.uk

Impression number   10 9 8 7 6 5 4 3 2

Year   2021 2020 2019 2018 2017

Typeset by Aptara, Inc.

Printed in Italy

A catalogue record for this title is available from the British Library.

Get the most from this book

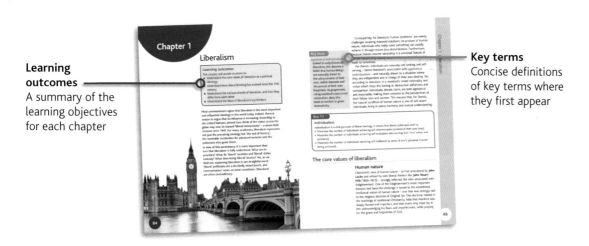

Learning outcomes
A summary of the learning objectives for each chapter

Key terms
Concise definitions of key terms where they first appear

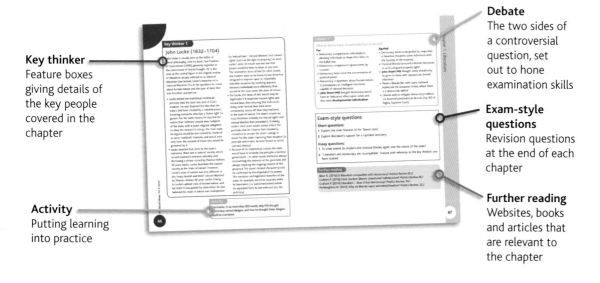

Key thinker
Feature boxes giving details of the key people covered in the chapter

Activity
Putting learning into practice

Debate
The two sides of a controversial question, set out to hone examination skills

Exam-style questions
Revision questions at the end of each chapter

Further reading
Websites, books and articles that are relevant to the chapter

Contents

Introduction   **5**

Chapter 1   **Liberalism**   **9**
Introduction: a pervasive ideology 9
The origins of liberalism 10
The core ideas of liberalism 13
Different types of liberalism 22
Tensions within liberalism 39
Conclusion: liberalism today 40

Chapter 2   **Conservatism**   **44**
Introduction: the 'politics of maintenance' 44
The origins of conservatism 46
The core ideas of conservatism 47
Different types of conservatism 57
Tensions within conservatism 76
Conclusion: conservatism today 77

Chapter 3   **Socialism**   **82**
Introduction 82
The origins of socialism 83
The core ideas of socialism 85
Different types of socialism 91
Tensions within socialism 115
Conclusion: socialism today 116

Chapter 4   **Feminism**   **120**
Introduction 120
The origins of feminism 121
The core ideas of feminism 123
Different types of feminism 135
Tensions within feminism 145
Conclusion: feminism today 147

Chapter 5   **Anarchism**   **149**
Introduction 149
The origins of anarchism 150
The core ideas of anarchism 152
Different types of anarchism 171
Tensions within anarchism 184
Conclusion: anarchism today 186

Index   **188**

Answers to the exam-style questions at the end of each
chapter can be found at **www.hoddereducation.co.uk/
PoliticalIdeasFA**

ntroduction

Four aspects of the course are considered here:

1   This part of the Government and Politics course is entitled 'Political ideas'. While this may seem self-explanatory, it is vital to understand what is actually meant by the terms 'ideas' and 'ideologies' and to distinguish them from political policies.

2   Each section is divided into four dominant themes: human nature, the state, society and economy. Answers to questions should take into account these themes wherever they are relevant.

3   The specification requires you to have knowledge about the beliefs of a number of key thinkers. Below is information on how you should use this knowledge.

4   It is important to employ appropriate vocabulary. The study of political ideas will challenge students to come to terms with new language, but it is important to meet that challenge in order to add clarity to your meanings.

Ideas and ideologies

We are used to discussing specific political policies but these refer largely to short-term, pragmatic decisions made by politicians, parties and pressure groups. Policies are developed to deal with particular problems which arise from time to time. Ideas and ideologies, meanwhile, look at longer-term issues and consider fundamental solutions to such questions. Furthermore, they are based on strongly held principles rather than pragmatic responses to short-term issues. Two examples can help here.

Let us consider the levels of taxation in a society. A policy to reduce income tax may be a short-term method of pumping more money into the economy, increasing spending and boosting economic growth. It cannot be undertaken permanently but it solves a problem in the meantime. Meanwhile, a party or group of politicians might believe that tax levels are generally too high, are a threat to people's economic liberty and individualism, and are a disincentive to work and enterprise, so they should be kept to as low a level as possible in the long term. A low-tax society is therefore a political idea.

Political ideologies are a stronger phenomenon altogether. Ideologies are sets of related political ideas which come together to create a vision of some kind of idealised society. Ideologies are based on strongly held, permanent principles and interlocking doctrines. In our example, the idea of a low-tax society connects with related doctrines such as opposition to high levels of welfare which, like high taxes, may be a disincentive to hard work, and free, unregulated markets which foster business enterprise. Put these three aims together — low taxation, low welfare and free markets — and we have an ideology, usually known as neo-liberalism.

We can now apply the same analysis to another set of ideas. These concern dealing with poverty and inequality:

■ Raising the minimum wage is a short-term policy to reduce poverty.
■ Reducing the gap in living standards between the rich and poor in the long term is a political idea.
■ Creating a more generally equal society with equal rights, empowerment for the working classes, intervention by the state to avoid the 'excesses' of capitalism and public ownership of major industries to spread the fruits of their production more evenly are interlocking ideas, forming an ideology, which we know as socialism.

Put another way, policies come and go, while political ideas and ideologies have more permanence.

This book deals with political ideas and political ideologies but not with policies. There are three 'core' ideologies and five 'optional' ideologies. Apart from the fact that students must study all three core ideologies to be able to tackle the examination questions but have to study only one of the options, there is another distinction to be borne in mind:

■ The core ideologies — liberalism, conservatism and socialism — have dominated western civilisation for more than 200 years. Political discourse and conflict therefore have largely been based on these three. However, they are largely based on western civilisation. Today we must look further afield in our study of political ideas, taking a world view and also considering those ideas that shape the relationships between minorities and the perspectives of alienated sections of society.
■ The optional ideologies — nationalism, feminism, anarchism, ecologism and multiculturalism — have generally shorter histories than the core ideologies but often take their inspiration from different forms of consciousness of the world, ranging from eastern mysticism to gender awareness

to modern scientism. Some aspects of the optional ideas have also challenged the traditional ideas associated with liberalism, conservatism and socialism and as such can also be described as post-modern.

Four themes

These are guides as to how we can analyse and compare political ideas and the beliefs of the many key thinkers presented in this book. You do not have to apply them but you are advised to do so where you can. As a starting point they should be considered in the following ways:

- **Human nature.** This concerns beliefs about the fundamental nature of mankind's relationship with other people and with the world. In the political ideas presented here we will see that various thinkers have described human nature in enormously varied ways, from egocentric to social, from fundamentally good to fundamentally competitive, from gender obsessed to androgynous (having no gender identity), or from dominant over the natural world (anthropomorphic) to claiming to be only an equal part of nature.
- **State.** Nearly all people live under the jurisdiction of one state or another. Political ideas and ideologies therefore have adopted principles about the nature of the state, what part (if any) it should play in society, how it should be controlled and whether it is a force for good or evil.
- **Society.** All societies have a particular structure which has either evolved naturally or been imposed by the state and those who govern the state. Most ideologies therefore have developed some kind of vision of what their ideal society would look like. Sometimes this is very specific, as is the case with socialism, some multiculturalists and certain types of collectivist anarchism; sometimes it is more vague, as is the case with conservatism.
- **Economy.** Not all political ideas and ideologies contain a strong economic perspective, but some do and this should be reflected in analysis where it applies. Again, socialism is a clear example, while neo-liberals, as described above, base most of the ideas on economics and economic principles. Even some socialist feminists have been able to link most of their analysis to economic relations between the sexes. Many ecologists also see capitalism as the main culprit in the degradation of the natural environment and so propose to control or even abolish it.

Key thinkers

There are usually five key thinkers specified for each of the political ideologies in the specification. This book describes their main work, beliefs and importance in the development of political ideas. They are not exhaustive and you should also have knowledge of other key thinkers, but you are certainly advised to refer to them in your examination answers. Directly quoting them is not necessary, though you should do so if you can and if it helps to illustrate your analysis.

Every ideology comprises different themes and variations. Often the different thinkers in the text illustrate these variations most effectively. Thus the distinction between, for example, the liberals John Stuart Mill and John Rawls tells us a great deal about how liberalism evolved between the nineteenth and twentieth centuries. Similarly, Marx's fundamental version of socialism tells us much of how dramatically the ideology has been transformed by more recent left-wing thinkers such as Anthony Crosland and Anthony Giddens.

Political vocabulary

As we have said, you should use accurate and appropriate political vocabulary wherever possible. Fortunately, both this book and the examination specification contain key terms with their meanings. You should take time to understand these and practise using them wherever you can. They can also save you time in your writing as they have specific meanings, which will reduce the need for lengthy explanations.

You are strongly advised to learn those aspects of vocabulary with which you are not already familiar and to ensure that you are able to use them in the correct context.

Chapter 1

Liberalism

Learning outcomes

This chapter will enable students to:
- understand the core values of liberalism as a political ideology
- understand how liberal thinking has evolved since the seventeenth century
- understand the various strands of liberalism and how they differ from each other
- understand the ideas of liberalism's key thinkers

Introduction: a pervasive ideology

Most commentators agree that liberalism is the most important and influential ideology in the world today. Indeed, there is reason to argue that its influence is increasing. According to the United Nations, almost two-thirds of the states across the globe may now be classed 'liberal democracies' — a seven-fold increase since 1945. For many academics, liberalism represents not just the prevailing ideology but 'the end of history', the inevitable destination for advanced societies and the politicians who guide them.

In view of this ascendancy, it is more important than ever that liberalism is fully understood. What are its priorities? What do 'liberal' societies and 'liberal' states embody? What does being 'liberal' involve? Yet, as we shall see, explaining liberalism is not straightforward: 'liberal' politicians are a decidedly mixed bunch, and commentators' views on what constitutes 'liberalism' are often contradictory.

In the UK, the USA and much of western Europe, being 'liberal' usually denotes being at odds with the values of conservatism, while being closer to the values of socialism (hence the much-used term in politics, 'liberal-left'). This would explain why a self-proclaimed American liberal, such as Hillary Clinton, found herself seeking the same party's presidential nomination as a self-proclaimed socialist, Bernie Sanders, while strongly opposing aggressive conservatives in the Republican Party.

Yet if one turns to the states of the southern hemisphere and western Pacific, the term 'liberal' has rather different connotations. In Australia, for example, it is the Liberal Party that offers the main opposition to that country's Labor Party, while providing a home for many of Australia's self-styled conservatives.

Clearly, liberalism is not just hugely influential; it is also complex and potentially confusing. So, to make sense of it, let us examine the origins and core beliefs of this pre-eminent ideology.

The origins of liberalism

In many ways, the roots of liberalism lie in the Reformation, a religious movement affecting much of northern Europe in the late fifteenth and sixteenth centuries. Led by religious protestors such as Martin Luther, these founders of 'protestant' Christianity argued that individuals seeking to communicate with God, and to understand His commands, need no longer rely on priests, popes and other intermediaries. With the advent of the printing press and the printed word, and the wider literacy this promoted, Luther argued that Christianity could now assume a more individualistic character, with each man and woman undertaking their own private prayers and undertaking God's work in their own way.

However, it was the Enlightenment that sought to extend these religious ideas into the political and secular spheres.

John Locke: Enlightenment icon and classical liberal

The Enlightenment was an intellectual movement that emerged in the mid-seventeenth century (coinciding with the English Civil War and the subsequent overthrow of King Charles I), and one that had an especially profound effect upon politics in the eighteenth century (influencing, among other things, both the creation of an independent American republic after 1776 and the French Revolution of 1789). The Enlightenment was defined by a belief in reason rather than faith, and thus promoted relentless debate and inquiry, questioning and scrutinising almost anything that, hitherto, was unthinkingly accepted.

Among the radical ideas that emerged from the Enlightenment were that each individual is someone with free will, that each individual is the best judge of their own interests, and that each individual's life should be shaped by that individual's actions and decisions. More specifically, writers such as **John Locke** (1632–1704) (see 'Key thinker 1' box) — widely regarded as the 'father' of liberalism — began to question the relationship between individuals and governments, seeking to define just why and how individuals should defer to those who governed them.

Today, such an exercise may seem routine. But in the seventeenth century it had revolutionary potential. Until then, it had been assumed — by both rulers and ruled — that the natural form of government was monarchical; that a king (occasionally a queen) had been put in place by God; and that a king's decisions should be instinctively accepted by a king's 'subjects' — a doctrine later termed 'the divine right of kings'. Underpinning this agreement, of course, were a society and culture dominated by faith, religion and superstition.

Yet the Enlightenment was to challenge and eventually destroy such medieval attitudes. For Locke and other Enlightenment philosophers, human beings were uniquely endowed with the power of logic, calculation and deduction. And it was logical, they argued, that human beings should create, by themselves and for themselves, a political system based upon reason (a principle that political scientists now describe as mechanistic theory).

Key term

Mechanistic theory Linked to the writings of John Locke, this argues that mankind is rational and therefore capable of devising a state that reflects mankind's needs. It was a pointed rebuff to notions like the 'divine right of kings', which argued that the state reflected God's will and that obedience to the state was a religious duty.

John Locke (1632–1704)

John Locke is usually seen as the father of liberal philosophy, with his book *Two Treatises of Government* (1690) generally regarded as the cornerstone of liberal thought. He is also seen as the central figure in the original version of liberalism, usually referred to as classical liberalism (see below). Locke's importance to classical liberalism lies in the questions he raised about human nature and the type of state that was therefore appropriate.

- Locke denied the traditional, medieval principle that the state was part of God's creation. He also disputed the idea that the state had been created by a celestial power, involving monarchs who had a 'divine right' to govern. For the same reason, he rejected the notion that 'ordinary' people were 'subjects' of the state, with a quasi-religious obligation to obey the monarch's rulings: the 'true' state, he argued, would be one created by mankind to serve mankind's interests and would arise only from the *consent* of those who would be governed by it.

- Locke asserted that, prior to the state's existence, there was a 'natural' society which served mankind's interests tolerably well. Borrowing a phrase coined by Thomas Hobbes 40 years earlier, Locke described this natural society as the 'state of nature'. However, Locke's state of nature was very different to the 'nasty and brutish' version depicted by Hobbes. Owing to Locke's upbeat view of human nature, and his belief that it was guided by rationalism, he also believed the state of nature was to be underpinned by 'natural laws', 'natural liberties' and 'natural rights' (such as the right to property). As such, Locke's state of nature was not one that people would be keen to leave at any cost. The alternative 'state of law' (in other words, the modern state as we know it) was therefore designed to improve upon an essentially tolerable situation, by resolving disputes between individuals more efficiently than would be the case under the state of nature.

- For Locke, the 'state of law' would be legitimate only if it respected natural rights and natural laws, thus ensuring that individuals living under formal laws were never consistently worse off than they had been in the state of nature. The state's structures must therefore embody the natural rights and natural liberties that preceded it. Similarly, Locke's ideal state would always reflect the principle that its 'citizens' had voluntarily *consented* to accept the state's rulings in return for the state improving their situation (a principle which later became known as 'social contract theory').

- Because of its 'contractual' nature, the state would have to embody the principle of limited government — in other words, limited to always representing the interests of the governed and always requiring the ongoing consent of the governed. The state's 'limited' character would be confirmed by the dispersal of its powers. The executive and legislative branches of the state, for example, would be separate, while its lawmakers (i.e. parliamentarians) would be separated from its law enforcers (i.e. the judiciary).

Activity

Summarise, in no more than 200 words, the type of state John Locke prescribed.

The core ideas of liberalism

Human nature

Liberalism's view of human nature — as first articulated by John Locke and refined by later liberal thinkers such as **John Stuart Mill** (1806–73) (see 'Key thinker 3' box) — strongly reflected the view associated with the Enlightenment. One of the Enlightenment's most important features had been the challenge it issued to the established, medieval notion of human nature — one that was strongly tied to the religious doctrine of original sin. This doctrine, rooted in the teachings of traditional Christianity, held that mankind was deeply flawed and imperfect, and that man's only hope lay in him acknowledging his flaws and imperfections while praying for the grace and forgiveness of God.

Drawing upon the writings of Locke and other Enlightenment philosophers, liberalism has always denied this bleak view, offering instead a more optimistic view of human nature. Liberalism duly argues that human nature has a huge capacity to bring about progress, and an unending ability to forge greater human happiness. At the heart of this optimistic view is a belief that individuals are guided principally by reason or rationalism, and thus are able to calculate answers to all sorts of problems.

Liberals believe that mankind's innate reason is manifested in debate, discussion, peaceful argument and the measured examination of ideas and opinions. Rather than meekly accepting whatever life offers — perhaps on the grounds that it is the 'will of God' or simply 'fate' — individuals have the capacity to plan their own future and effect a preconceived outcome. Indeed, the concepts of both planning and the subsequent 'plan' itself are central to the rationalist idea and the cheery liberal belief that human nature allows us to shape our own destiny.

Consequently, for liberalism, human 'problems' are merely challenges awaiting reasoned solutions; on account of human nature, individuals who really want something can usually achieve it through reason plus determination. Furthermore, because liberals assume rationality is a universal feature of human nature, they usually assume that reasoned discussion leads to consensus.

Key term

Egotistical individualism
Linked to early (classical) liberalism, this denotes a belief that human beings are naturally drawn to the advancement of their own, selfish interests and the pursuit of their own happiness. Its proponents, citing mankind's concurrent rationalism, deny this leads to conflict or gross insensitivity.

Activity

Explain, in approximately 200 words, why liberalism is said to have an optimistic view of human nature.

For liberals, individuals are naturally self-seeking and self-serving — hence liberalism's association with **egotistical individualism** — and naturally drawn to a situation where they are independent and in charge of their own destiny. Yet, according to liberalism, it is mankind's innate rationality and virtue that stop this leading to destructive selfishness and competition. Individuals, liberals claim, are both egotistical *and* reasonable, making them sensitive to the perspectives of their fellow men and women. This ensures that, for liberals, the natural condition of human nature is one of self-aware individuals, living in peace, harmony and mutual understanding.

Society

Liberalism's optimistic view of human nature, particularly our capacity for reason, informs the liberal view about whether 'society' can ever exist without a state. In his classic work *Leviathan* (1651), Thomas Hobbes argued that human nature is so brutally selfish that no society could possibly arise, or survive, until human nature is restrained by a strong, formal authority — in short, a state. But early liberal philosophers like Locke offered a very different view, citing the existence of 'natural' society, with 'natural laws' and therefore natural rights (including the 'right' to life, liberty, property and happiness), all of which preceded the state. So, for liberals, life before the state was created was not 'nasty, brutish and short' (as Hobbes famously asserted) but potentially pleasant, civilised and long.

This liberal belief in a 'natural society', where certain 'natural rights' are enjoyed, helps explain why liberals place so much importance upon the individual (see Box 1.1). Indeed, as John Stuart Mill emphasised during the mid-nineteenth century, the main purpose of any civilised society — 'natural' or manufactured — is to facilitate individualism. In making this claim, Mill and other liberals argued that each individual has a unique personality and peculiar talents; that individuals are rational in pursuit of their self-interest; and that individuals are egotistical, driven by a wish to fulfil their potential and a desire to be self-reliant and independent. In view of all this, each individual therefore seeks freedom. For Mill, in his critical work *On Liberty* (1859), this specifically meant freedom from any dependency on others and the freedom to live one's life in a way that maximises self-reliance and self-fulfilment.

For this reason, liberals believe that the 'default setting' of any society is a focus upon individual freedom and that any society which seeks to deny individualism is dysfunctional.

Activity

Explain, in approximately 200 words, why individualism is central to liberalism.

In this respect, the 'right' to property — defined by Locke as 'that with which Man has mixed his labour' — is regarded by liberals as particularly important, as it is seen as the tangible expression of an individual within society. Furthermore, for later liberals like Mill, property is also the 'prism' through which individuals develop their potential, providing an opportunity, within civilised communities, for men and women to nurture their taste and judgement.

Box 1.1

Individualism

Individualism is a vital principle of liberal ideology. It means that individual needs should be at the heart of political thought, economic life and social organisation, and that society should prioritise the improvement of diverse, individual lives. Its implications are that liberal politicians seek to:

- maximise the number of individuals achieving self-determination (control of their own lives)
- maximise the number of individuals achieving self-realisation (discovering their 'true' selves and potential)
- maximise the number of individuals attaining self-fulfilment (a sense of one's 'personal mission' being achieved).

The economy

In addition to shaping its view of society, liberalism's devotion to private property informs its approach to the economy. Given its belief that property is a natural right, it is inevitable that liberalism should support an economy that puts private property at the heart of all economic arrangements. In short, it is inevitable that liberals should support capitalism.

Ever since the liberal economist Adam Smith enunciated his theory of markets in his seminal work *The Wealth of Nations* (1776), liberalism has been strongly associated with private enterprise and private ownership of the economy. Indeed, this explains why capitalism is routinely described as **economic liberalism**, and provides a key difference between liberalism and many forms of socialism. Although liberals and socialists share many assumptions and objectives, and criticise many of the same things, liberals will still ultimately defend a market-based economy and stridently refute the anti-capitalist message of 'fundamentalist' socialism (see Chapter 3).

Key term

Economic liberalism This is another term for capitalism, an economic system that emerged in Europe in the late seventeenth century. The liberal aspect of capitalism stems from three factors. First, it involves private property, which early liberals like John Locke considered a 'natural right'. Second, it is individualistic in theory, involving individual traders cooperating and competing. Third, it is thought to be of ultimate benefit to all — thus revealing liberalism's eternal optimism and belief in progress.

Activity

Explain in approximately 200 words (and with reference to the chapter on conservatism) how John Locke's view of the state of nature differed from that of Thomas Hobbes.

Key term

State of nature This was a philosophical device used in the seventeenth century by both Thomas Hobbes and John Locke to justify the very different types of political state they were proposing. It referred to what life might have been like before laws, formal rules and governments came into being.

As with the stress on individualism, liberalism's endorsement of capitalism is strongly linked to its positive view of human nature. In making the case for free-market economics, Adam Smith had asserted that if obstacles to free trade were swept away, the 'invisible hand' of market forces would guide traders towards success, resulting wealth would 'trickle down' to everyone, and 'the wealth of nations' would be promoted globally. In making these confident assertions, Smith was clearly reflecting the optimistic tone of liberalism's core values — and, in the view of many non-liberals, being rather naïve about the efficacy of market forces.

The state

Although individualism and capitalism are central to liberalism's view of society and the economy, it is important to remember that this does not render liberalism unique among political ideologies — this also applies, for example, to several branches of anarchism (known as 'individualist anarchism').

What makes liberalism distinctive is that whereas anarchists see the state — any state — as the eternal enemy of individualism, liberals, from John Locke and Adam Smith onwards, believe that individualism and capitalism work best when accompanied by a certain kind of state. But to understand why, it is necessary to explain how liberals think the 'ideal' state originates, what it seeks to achieve and how it should be structured.

The liberal state: origins

To appreciate liberalism's belief in a state, it is important to remember that, while liberalism takes an optimistic view of human nature, it still accepts that, within the state of nature, there would have been clashes of interests between individuals pursuing their own, egocentric agendas. Locke was especially worried that without the sort of formal structures only a state can provide, the resolution of such clashes — particularly clashes concerning property — might not always be swift and efficient. As a result, individualism in the state of nature could have been impeded by stalemated disputes between competing individuals. So a mechanism — a state — was required, to arbitrate effectively between the competing claims of rational individuals.

To provide a sporting comparison, most footballers would accept that, in the absence of a referee, some kind of football match could still take place, with both teams self-regulating on an ad hoc basis (think in terms of a 'kick-around' among friends). Yet, even though it would result in their restriction and occasional punishment, most footballers would also accept that the match would be fairer, more efficient and more rewarding for individual players if a referee was present — especially if the referee officiated according to pre-agreed rules. For liberals, this is analogous to their argument that the state of nature, tolerable though it may be, is still inferior to the particular 'formalised' state liberals recommend.

The liberal state: objectives

Although their root justification for the 'liberal state' was that it allowed the more effective resolution of disputes between individuals, Locke and later liberals were also keen to show that the kind of state they wanted embodied wider and grander principles. These principles were to be significantly developed by England's Bill of Rights of 1689, the American Constitution of 1787 and the first French Republic of 1789. From these historical events emerge various objectives, which are central to any understanding of what the liberal state seeks to achieve.

Rejection of the 'traditional' state

The liberal state is founded upon an explicit rejection of the type of state common in Europe prior to the Enlightenment — a state marked by monarchical, absolutist and arbitrary rule. In other words, the liberal state renounces the sort of state where power is concentrated in the hands of one individual and where that power is exercised randomly. The liberal state would be especially contemptuous of any government that claimed a 'divine right' to govern, according to a subjective and thus irrational perception of God's will.

Government by consent

Following on from its rejection of 'the divine right of kings', liberalism insists that the state is legitimate only if those under its jurisdiction have effectively *volunteered* to be under its jurisdiction: in other words, governments must have the consent of the governed.

This doctrine has a profound effect upon the relationship between politicians and people. Far from being the 'subjects' of the government — as the traditional state had asserted — the people in the state would now have ultimate control over it. As Locke maintained, 'government should always be the servant, not master, of the people'.

Social contract Linked
to Enlightenment
philosophers such as Locke
and Rousseau, this term
denotes that the state
should be a 'deal' between
governments and governed.
It states that in return for
submitting to the state's
laws, the governed should
be guaranteed certain
rights and that, if these
rights are violated, so is the
citizen's obligation to obey
the state's laws.

Tolerance/harm principle
Within liberalism, these
twin terms refer to the
belief that particular
views and activities —
particularly those we might
frown upon — should be
tolerated, just as long as
they do not 'harm' the
freedom of others. Both
concepts are strongly
linked to the liberal belief in
individual freedom.

For this reason, 'government by consent' can be linked to
the notion of 'government by contract' — what Enlightenment
theorists such as Jean Jacques Rousseau (1712–78) later dubbed
a **social contract**. In simple terms, individuals who 'contract
out' of the state of nature and 'contract in' to the formal state
of law agree to accept the latter's authority and restrictions, but
are promised something in return. But *what* are they promised
in return? This leads us to the remaining objectives of the liberal
state.

Promotion of natural rights/individualism

Liberals always assume that, before any formal state was created,
individuals enjoyed 'natural rights' that enabled self-realisation,
self-determination and — therefore — individualism. So it would
be irrational for individuals to abandon both natural rights and
individualism by submitting unconditionally to any state. The
only rational reason to submit to the state would be if it not
only respected but promoted natural rights, ensuring they were
more safely and easily exercised than in the state of nature.

Promotion of tolerance

Linked to its devotion to natural rights, the liberal state is also
concerned to ensure tolerance towards all those individuals who
exercise their natural rights in various ways. Obviously, tolerance
was closely linked to individualism — how could an individual
seek self-determination if his actions and opinions were to be
forbidden by others? It was with this dilemma in mind that
the French philosopher Voltaire (1694–1778) issued his famous
clarion call for freedom, claiming 'I detest what you say but will
defend unto the death your right to say it.'

This notion was to be developed a century or so later by
John Stuart Mill, who insisted that the state should tolerate
all actions and opinions unless they were shown to violate
the **harm principle** — the principle that individuals should be
free to do and say anything unless it could be proved that this
'harmed' the rights and freedoms of other individuals within the
state.

Although liberalism is an individualistic creed, it has usually
recognised that individuals do not necessarily seek isolation
and detachment from their fellow men and women (thus
creating an 'atomised' environment) but are instead drawn
to societies that accommodate their individualism. So, when
emphasising tolerance, for example, early liberals were aware
that individuals were inclined to congregate into religious
communities. It was therefore important that the state should

show tolerance towards such communities, especially those representing the religious views of a minority. So, in the wake of the Glorious Revolution of 1688, which cemented the Protestant supremacy in England, Locke was particularly keen that the post-Revolution state should extend tolerance towards Roman Catholics.

Since then, tolerating minorities has been an ongoing passion for those seeking to support and advance the liberal state. Since the mid-twentieth century, American liberals such as the feminist **Betty Friedan** (1921–2006) (see 'Key thinker 5' box) have sought to update Locke's belief in the tolerance of minorities, campaigning for the state to improve the lot of individuals allegedly hindered by ethnicity, sexuality, physicality or (in the case of Friedan's campaigns) gender.

Activity

Exemplify, in approximately 100 words, how the liberal state promotes tolerance.

Meritocracy

Given the liberal state's stress on individualism, the next principle of a liberal state is that political power should be exercised only by those who show themselves worthy of it. In other words, government should be conducted by individuals who, through their own efforts and talents, have won the trust of the governed. Consequently, there is no guarantee that such responsibility will be conferred upon the descendants of those who govern — unless they, too, can demonstrate competence and integrity.

In this respect, the meritocratic liberal state again stands in contrast to the traditional state. In pre-Enlightenment regimes, power was largely hereditary and aristocratic, with circumstances of birth trumping individual ability. As Thomas Paine (1737–1809) remarked, when justifying the French Revolution's overthrow of the nobility in 1789, hereditary rule was 'beyond equity, beyond reason and most certainly beyond wisdom'. Aristocracy thus had no place in the meritocratic liberal state commended by Locke, Mill and other liberal thinkers.

Equality of opportunity

For liberals, it is an article of faith that all individuals are born equal, have equal natural rights and are of equal value — a belief often referred to as **foundational equality**. Within the liberal state, all individuals must therefore have equal opportunity to develop their potential and achieve control of their own lives. If an individual fails to fulfil their potential, they must be able to assume total responsibility for this failure — and not somehow attribute it to the state.

Key term

Foundational equality/ legal equality This refers to the liberal belief that every individual is born equal, with equal natural rights. Such individuals are therefore entitled to legal equality in a liberal state. This would involve equality before the law and an equal recognition of individual rights.

19

Equality of opportunity
Liberals believe that all individuals should be allowed similar opportunities to develop their potential. Unlike for socialism, however, equality of opportunity for liberalism does not necessarily exist alongside greater equality of outcome.

Limited government
This involves government being 'limited', in terms of how it can act, by a constitution's formal rules and procedures. It is therefore the opposite of arbitrary rule, as practised in medieval, monarchical states.

Justice

Linked to **equality of opportunity** is a belief that the state should embody justice: there must be an assumption that it will treat individuals fairly, or justly, without regard to their 'identity' (as defined, for example, by their occupation, religion, gender or ethnicity). As a result, individuals within the liberal state must be able to assume a just outcome from any complaints they express and therefore a satisfactory resolution to any grievances they have with other individuals.

The liberal state: methods and structures

Having clarified the aims of a liberal state, it is now important to examine the methods whereby such objectives are guaranteed. For liberals, the structure of the state must embody three features:

- constitutional/limited government
- fragmented government
- formal equality.

Constitutional/limited government

Consistent with its faith in government by consent, liberalism holds that the 'contract' between government and governed (see above) should be cemented by a formal constitution. Furthermore, in keeping with its faith in rationalism, this constitution should be preceded by extensive discussion and consensus over what government should do and how it should do it. In this way, constitutional rule is in stark contrast to the arbitrary rule characteristic of monarchical states, where rulers often did whatever they pleased, using whatever methods they wished.

For this reason, constitutional government may be described as **limited government**, with a liberal constitution imposing upon government two broad limitations. First, it ensures that governments must govern according to prearranged rules and procedures, and not in a random, ad hoc fashion. Second, a liberal constitution is designed to prevent governments from eroding the natural rights of their citizens — a restriction often brought about via mechanisms like a Bill of Rights (see Box 1.2).

Fragmented government

The focus on limited government produces another key feature of a liberal state's structure, namely the dispersal or fragmentation of state power. Again, this was brought about largely as a reaction against pre-Enlightenment states where power was concentrated in the monarchy. As Lord Acton (1834–1902) famously observed, 'power tends to corrupt...and absolute power tends to corrupt absolutely'. Fragmented government also reflects liberalism's belief in the rationality of mankind: if individuals are generally reasonable, and inclined to self-determination, it seems logical to empower as many individuals as possible in the exercise of a state's functions.

This idea of fragmented political power has its most celebrated embodiment in the Constitution of the United States. Heavily indebted to the ideas of Locke, it introduces a series of 'checks and balances', designed to avoid power being concentrated. Since then, such checks and balances have become common in liberal states across the world, and are exemplified in Box 1.2.

> **Activity**
>
> Explain, in approximately 100 words, why liberals believe in the fragmentation of political power.

Box 1.2

The liberal state: how is power dispersed?

- A formal 'separation of powers', between the executive, legislature and judiciary.
- A separation of powers within the legislature itself, so as to produce a 'bicameral' (two-house) legislature.
- A Bill of Rights, immune to the short-term decisions of governments.
- A Supreme Court, to uphold any Bill of Rights, and whose decisions override those of elected governments.
- A federal system of government, whereby many of the state's functions are delegated to various regional governments.

Formal equality

Given the liberal belief in foundational equality (that all individuals are born with equal rights), it would be illogical for a liberal state not to reflect this in its own structures. As such, the liberal state strives for formal equality, where all individuals have the same legal and political rights in society. It places significant emphasis on the doctrine of the 'rule of law', which holds that laws passed in a liberal state are applicable to everyone, with no exemptions granted on the basis of status. In short, no one should be outside the law, but no one should be above it either. Likewise, the procedures whereby the law takes its course — as prescribed by a liberal constitution — will apply to all citizens.

Formal quality is also linked to the idea of equal political rights — for example, the equal right to petition a parliament, the equal right to invoke a Bill of Rights before the courts, or the equal right to criticise the state while exercising the 'natural' (and legally protected) right to freedom of speech and publication.

> **Activity**
>
> In no more than 200 words, outline the aims, structures and procedures of a liberal constitution.

Different types of liberalism

As indicated at the start of this chapter, liberalism may be seen as an ambiguous ideology. To see why, and to understand how liberals can differ, it is helpful to look at its two principal strands: classical liberalism and modern liberalism. It is important to remember, however, that both strands uphold the core values of liberalism examined earlier in this chapter. The variations occur merely in respect of how these values might be applied.

Classical liberalism (late seventeenth–late nineteenth centuries)

Given its timespan of two centuries, classical liberalism (or original liberalism) is itself somewhat ambiguous, and includes a diverse cast of politicians and philosophers. For this reason, it is helpful to divide it into two sections: early classical liberalism and later classical liberalism.

Early classical liberalism (late seventeenth century and eighteenth century)

Early classical liberalism represents the attempt, during the late seventeenth and the eighteenth centuries, to relate the ideology's core beliefs to the political and economic climate of the time. It had four distinctive features:

- revolutionary potential
- negative liberty
- minimal state
- laissez-faire capitalism.

Revolutionary potential

As we have seen, Locke's argument for government by consent, and the notion that a state should be driven by the representatives (not masters) of the people, is one of the most important 'core' principles of liberalism; it therefore applies to all strands of liberal thinking. Yet, in the context of the seventeenth and eighteenth centuries, it needs to be emphasised that such Lockean ideas — now commonplace in western democracies — required vigorous argument and sometimes revolutionary upheaval.

In repudiating the twin pillars of the traditional European state (absolute monarchical power and the 'divine right of kings'), Locke's philosophy became associated with England's Glorious Revolution of 1688, which duly secured constitutional government and the end of concentrated political power. Locke's blueprint for representative government also inspired both the American revolt against the British crown after 1775 and the subsequent American Constitution of 1787 — both of which reflected his insistence upon natural rights, the separation of powers and the principle of government by consent.

Similarly, the core liberal idea of rationalism — that humanity's prime characteristic was a capacity for reason and logic — was far from firmly accepted in the eighteenth century; neither was the central liberal idea that society should be geared to maximum individual freedom. Other key thinkers within classical liberalism, such as **Mary Wollstonecraft** (1759–97) (see 'Key thinker 2' box), argued that the treatment of women during this period was a general affront to reason and a particular affront to the individual liberty of half the adult population. Wollstonecraft duly contested that English society in the eighteenth century could only conceive of women as emotional creatures, suited to marriage and motherhood but little else. As Wollstonecraft observed, instead of developing their individual potential, Hanoverian society contrived to 'keep women in a state of listless inactivity and stupid acquiescence'.

Wollstonecraft's subsequent argument — that individual men *and* women required a formal education to release their innate powers of reason — would later be seen as indisputably liberal; yet during the eighteenth and early nineteenth centuries, such arguments were considered dangerously radical by most in authority.

Negative liberty

Early classical liberals, such as Voltaire (1694–1778) and Charles-Louis Montesquieu (1689–1755), were conscious that individual liberty — a crucial 'natural right' — was vital to self-determination and self-reliance, as well as being the condition of government by consent. In England, early 'liberal-feminists', like Wollstonecraft, also tried to relate such ideas to the individual liberty of women. However, early classical liberals were also conscious that 'liberty' was a somewhat vague term, which needed clarification if individualism were to be protected. So what was meant by 'liberty'?

The definition that emerged from classical liberal thinking would later be termed **negative liberty**, one which saw freedom as the absence of restraint. Individuals should therefore assume that they were 'naturally' free until something or someone put a brake on their actions. According to this definition, therefore, a man alone on a desert island might be lonely, but he could still exercise a high degree of personal freedom: an assumption complementing one of liberalism's core beliefs that individuals were potentially autonomous, atomistic and self-reliant. For early classical liberals, this definition would have consequences for both the size of the state and the emerging 'science' of economics.

Key term

Negative liberty A key feature of classical liberalism, this is a notion of freedom that involves individuals being left alone to pursue their destiny. Any attempt to interfere with individual actions may therefore be judged an infringement of liberty.

Mary Wollstonecraft (1759–97)

While John Locke laid the foundations of liberal thought in the seventeenth century, one of those who developed classical liberal ideas in the eighteenth century was Mary Wollstonecraft. Her most important publication, *A Vindication of the Rights of Woman* (1792), remains a classic of political thought and is still strongly linked to feminist ideology. Yet, though gender was crucial to her work, her arguments were actually rooted in liberal philosophy.

- Wollstonecraft's primary claim was that the Enlightenment's optimistic view of human nature, and the assumption that it was guided by reason, should apply to all human beings, male and female. She went on to argue that in eighteenth-century England, both society and state implied that women were not rational, and they were thus denied individual freedom and formal equality. Women, for example, were rarely allowed land ownership or remunerative employment and sacrificed what little individualism they had in order to become wives. Once married, a woman had little legal protection against violence inflicted by her spouse, and no recourse to divorce. Furthermore, women could not vote for those who governed them — a blatant violation, Wollstonecraft pointed out, of 'government by consent'.
- Yet Wollstonecraft was not simply a spokesperson for women's interests. She argued that as a result of fettering female individualism, nations like England were limiting their stock of intelligence, wisdom and morality. As Wollstonecraft observed, 'such arrangements are not conditions where reason and progress may prosper'. She asserted that the effective denial of liberty to an entire gender left society vulnerable to doctrines that threatened the whole spirit of the Enlightenment.
- Like many upholders of 'classical' liberal ideals, Wollstonecraft welcomed both the American Revolution of 1776 and the French Revolution of 1789. Indeed, her other major work, *A Vindication of the Rights of Men* (1790), attacked Edmund Burke's critique of the French Revolution and his related defence of custom, history and aristocratic rule (see Chapter 2). Wollstonecraft thus stressed her support for republican government and formal equality, involving a constitutional defence of individual rights. But such formal equality, she restated, must be accorded to all individuals, and not just to men. For that reason, she applauded the French Revolution's emphasis upon 'citizens' and its apparent indifference to gender differences.
- Wollstonecraft conceded that women themselves were complicit in their subjugation, generally desiring only marriage and motherhood. For this to be corrected, she argued, formal education should be made available to as many women (and men) as possible. Without such formal tuition, she contested, individuals could never develop their rational faculties, never realise their individual potential and never recognise the 'absurdity' of illiberal principles such as the divine right of kings.

Activity

Summarise, in no more than 200 words, how Wollstonecraft's early feminism relates to liberalism's core values.

Minimal state

The notion of negative freedom defined the answer to another key question facing early classical liberals: just how much governing should the new constitutional states undertake? Given that liberty was now seen as the absence of restraint, the answer became obvious: governments should not just be limited in terms of how they could act, but also limited in terms of what they would do. In other words, the limited state should co-exist with the **minimal state**.

The case for the minimal state was perhaps best summarised by Thomas Jefferson (1743–1826), one of the USA's Founding Fathers, who noted:

> 'The government that is best is that which governs least... when government grows, our liberty withers.'

The notion of a minimal state also served to strengthen classical liberalism's faith in the dispersal of political power: a state with assorted checks and balances, after all, would be one where bold state action was fraught with difficulty — and therefore infrequent.

Laissez-faire capitalism

Negative liberty and a belief in minimal government eventually led classical liberalism into the realms of economic activity. More specifically, it became linked to the issue of how the state should respond to the emergence of capitalism in the eighteenth century.

The most famous response, that of Adam Smith's *The Wealth of Nations* (1776), became one of the most important expressions of classical liberalism and, arguably, the original economics textbook. Smith duly argued that capitalism, via the 'invisible hand' of market forces, had a limitless capacity to enrich society and the individuals within it. The wealth acquired by individuals would accordingly 'trickle down' to the rest of the population — just as long as the state took a laissez-faire (let-it-happen) approach to the workings of a market economy.

Smith therefore advocated the end of tariffs and duties, which had 'protected' domestic producers, and the spread of 'free trade' between nation-states and their commercial classes. In the UK, these ideas were radical in 1776, but became orthodox in the century that followed.

Key term

Minimal state A feature of classical liberalism, the minimal state was one that reflected the concept of 'negative liberty' by minimising state activities — for example, legislating and taxing as infrequently as possible, while confining its range to areas such as defence and the protection of private property.

John Stuart Mill feared 'the tyranny of the majority'.

Later classical liberalism (early–mid nineteenth century)

By the 1800s, countries like Britain and the USA looked very different to the societies surveyed by Locke and the Founding Fathers. They had become more industrialised; most individuals now worked and lived in an urban environment; individuals had a growing sense of class consciousness; and, as a result, there was growing interest in concepts like democracy and socialism.

In such a changed environment, classical liberals faced a serious challenge if their core ideas were to remain relevant. A response duly came, but it was far from uniform. The ideas of four 'late classical' liberals provide an indication of how variable the response was.

Jeremy Bentham (1748–1832), known as the father of utilitarian philosophy, developed a supposedly scientific alternative to natural rights theory, based on the idea that each individual would seek to maximise their own 'utility' by maximising personal pleasure and minimising personal pain. Yet Bentham also acknowledged that, in an industrialised society, this could produce more clashes between individuals than early classical liberals had envisaged. As a result, he suggested that the liberal state would need to be more proactive, using the algebraic formula of 'the greatest happiness of the greatest number' to inform legislation and government policy. In the process Bentham laid the foundations of 'political science' and provided liberalism with one of its earliest justifications for democracy: as Bentham observed, governments were more likely to follow the 'greatest happiness of the greatest number' if they were elected by and accountable to 'the greatest number' of voters.

Samuel Smiles (1812–1904), fearing that individualism was threatened by the advent of socialism, with its related calls for more state provision, argued in his influential book *Self Help* (1859) that self-reliance was still perfectly feasible for most individuals, including members of the new working class. Smiles acknowledged that industrialised societies made it harder for individuals to be self-reliant: an increasing number were faceless employees in a bulging factory system. Yet Smiles argued that, in seeking to overcome the new obstacles, individuals would merely be challenged more rigorously and, in the process, become more fully developed. If 'self-help were usurped by state help', Smiles argued, 'human beings would remain stunted, their talents unknown, and their liberty squandered'.

Herbert Spencer (1820–1903), a contemporary of Smiles, acknowledged the importance of self-help and echoed Smiles' contempt for more state intervention. However, in *Man Versus the State* (1884), Spencer questioned Smiles' belief that all individuals could rise to the challenge of self-help, noting the presence of 'the feeble, the feckless and the failing' in many Victorian cities. Fearing that this 'feeble' minority could justify the extension of state power, and therefore (what he saw as) an erosion of the majority's freedom, Spencer sought to apply the principles of 'natural selection', recently unveiled to science by Charles Darwin. In what became known as 'social Darwinism', Spencer restated the classical liberal belief in a minimal state and negative freedom, claiming that this would lead to 'the survival of the fittest' and the gradual elimination of those unable to enjoy the benefits of individualism. The eventual outcome would be a society where rational self-reliance was the norm and where individual freedom could thrive.

In terms of long-term importance, however, Bentham, Smiles and Spencer were eclipsed by John Stuart Mill. Mill's contribution to philosophy in general was immense, with some of his ideas summarised in the 'Key thinker 3' box. Indeed, some have suggested that Mill's ideas represent a separate strand of liberalism, known as transitional liberalism or developmental individualism. Mill's contribution to liberalism and political thought was crucial, given that it took place at a time — the mid-nineteenth century — when many liberals were struggling to work out how liberalism (with its stress upon individualism) could harness trends towards universal suffrage (with its capacity for what Mill himself termed 'the tyranny of the majority'). Mill's response to this dilemma would have a profound effect upon the way in which later liberals reconciled themselves to democratic governance.

Anticipating universal suffrage, Mill updated Locke's case for representative government into a case for representative democracy. Under this model, the enlarged electorate would not make policy decisions themselves but elect

Jeremy Bentham: author of utilitarianism

liberally minded representatives to make decisions for them. When making those decisions, such representatives would not simply side with the majority view, they would seek to aggregate the various opinions within society so as to produce the broad consent of all. In putting forward this particular model of democracy, Mill also equipped later liberals to rebut alternative models — such as 'direct' democracy — which he claimed were much more conducive to the 'tyranny of the majority'.

Mill was still concerned, however, that during the mid-nineteenth century most would-be voters were ill-equipped to choose 'intelligent' representatives to act 'rationally' on their behalf. With that in mind, Mill argued that universal suffrage must be preceded by universal education, hoping this would promote **developmental individualism**. By this, Mill meant the advancement of individual potential, so as to produce a liberal consensus in society; this in turn would safeguard tolerance, reason and individualism. Meanwhile, a vote would be withheld from the illiterate and unschooled, while those with a university education (like Mill) would receive more than one vote.

Once widespread education had been secured, Mill argued, democracy could actually further liberal values — promoting, for example, political education and opportunities for enlightening debate. Such a progressive society, Mill argued, could allow a pleasing refinement of Bentham's utilitarianism: 'the greatest happiness of the greatest number' could then be a calculation made by politicians *and* voters, thus encouraging ordinary citizens to consider and aggregate everyone's interests, not just their own, when forming a political judgement.

Despite his commitment to mass education, Mill remained vague about how it would be provided. As someone wedded to the classical liberal ideas of a minimal state and negative freedom, he was reluctant to countenance extensive state provision of schooling. But this key issue was one that his successors, the so-called modern liberals, were prepared to answer with more clarity and boldness — and not just in relation to education.

Key term

Developmental individualism This relates to the liberal philosophy of John Stuart Mill, who wished to focus on what individuals *could* become rather than what they *had* become. It explained Mill's strong emphasis upon the value of formal education within a liberal society.

John Stuart Mill (1806–73)

Regarded by many as one of the greatest English philosophers, John Stuart Mill's contribution to liberal thought is immense. The son of utilitarian philosopher James Mill, John Stuart was not just an intellectual but also, at varying points in his life, a politician and campaigner who served to develop the ideas posited by Locke, Wollstonecraft and others. He would also provide a valuable bridge between classical liberalism and the 'modern' liberalism that proved so important in the twentieth century, which explains why Mill's political ideas are often said to represent 'transitional liberalism' and 'developmental individualism'.

■ Mill's most enduring idea, outlined in his seminal work *On Liberty* (1859), was one which later became known as 'negative freedom'. Put simply, it argued that freedom mainly involved an absence of restraint. This connected to Mill's 'harm principle' — the notion that an individual's actions should always be tolerated, by either the state or other individuals, unless it could be demonstrated that such actions would harm others.

■ With a view to clarifying tolerance, Mill divided human actions into 'self-regarding' and 'other regarding'. The former (involving, for example, religious worship or robust expression of personal views) did not impinge on the freedom of others in society and therefore should be tolerated; the latter (involving, for example, violent or riotous behaviour) clearly did 'harm' the freedom of others in society and therefore should not be tolerated by a liberal state. The tolerance of diverse opinions was

especially important, Mill argued, because it would ensure new ideas emerged while bad ideas were exposed via open, rational debate.

■ Mill's importance lay in the fact that many of his arguments represented something more sophisticated than that provided by early classical liberalism. He saw liberty, for example, not just as a 'natural right' and an end in itself but as the engine of ongoing human development. As such, Mill's human nature was never the 'finished article' (as it had been for earlier liberals); there was always room for improvement.

■ This naturally affected Mill's approach to the core liberal principle of individualism. Mill did not just want to liberate individuals as they were at present; instead, he pondered what individuals could become — a concept he termed 'individuality' and which has since been referred to as developmental individualism. As he famously stated, it was 'better to be Socrates dissatisfied than a pig satisfied', while any support for liberty had to be 'grounded on the permanent interests of man as a progressive being'.

■ Mill's distinction between 'individualism' and 'individuality' would have crucial implications for how he approached the looming issue of democracy. He was particularly concerned that the timeless liberal principle of 'government by consent' would be compromised if the wishes of some individual citizens were overwhelmed by the wishes of most individual citizens. In other words, Mill feared that a democratic state had the potential to create a 'tyranny of the majority'.

Activity

Summarise, in no more than 200 words, why Mill thought democracy carried dangers and how he thought those dangers could be countered.

Liberal democracy: a contradiction in terms?

Yes

- Democracy tends to be guided by majorities. It therefore threatens some individuals with the 'tyranny of the majority'.
- Classical liberals favoured a limited electorate, so as to safeguard property rights.
- John Stuart Mill thought votes should be given only to those with appropriate, formal education.
- Modern liberals flirt with supranational bodies like the European Union, where there is a 'democratic deficit'.
- Liberals seek to mitigate democracy's effects via assorted constitutional devices (e.g. Bill of Rights, Supreme Court).

No

- Democracy complements individualism, allowing individuals to shape their lives via the ballot box.
- Democracy complements 'government by consent'.
- Democracy helps avoid the concentration of political power.
- Democracy is optimistic about human nature: it presupposes an intelligent electorate, capable of rational decisions.
- John Stuart Mill thought democracy would have an 'educative' effect upon voters and thus abet developmental individualism.

Modern liberalism (late nineteenth century–present)

As suggested at the end of the 'Key thinker 3' box, Mill did not just offer solutions to the dilemmas of liberalism in the late nineteenth century; he also raised a number of possibilities that later liberals could develop.

In particular, Mill's notion of individuality began to prompt fresh questions about the precise nature of 'liberty'. In order to liberate an individual's potential, was it really enough just to leave them alone (as supporters of negative freedom would argue)? Was it enough for the state simply to guarantee equal political rights and equality before the law?

The answers to such questions would produce a new and radical interpretation of what liberty involved, one that would lead to a very different form of liberalism. It was one that had a number of distinguishing characteristics.

Positive liberty/social justice

During the late nineteenth and early twentieth centuries, a number of English philosophers — later known as the 'new liberals' — re-examined the core principles of liberalism and reached radical conclusions about liberty, individualism and society.

T.H. Green (1836–82), L.T. Hobhouse (1864–1929) and J.A. Hobson (1854–1940) were prepared to argue that modern, advanced societies made a mockery of the idea that individuals were innately autonomous. The nature of modern economics and society, they argued, meant individuals were increasingly subject to socio-economic forces beyond their control. Such forces would then make it impossible for affected individuals to seek self-determination and self-realisation, even though they might not have caused the socio-economic problems now restricting their liberty. As a result, these new liberals argued that social justice, as well as legal justice, was now required if individuals were to fulfil their potential.

This led Green and others to revise the meaning of liberty, so as to make it a less 'negative' concept. In other words, instead of freedom being seen merely as the absence of restraint, it would now be interpreted as something more cooperative and altruistic, namely some individuals enabling or empowering other individuals. This approach — helping others to help themselves — would then allow certain individuals to act in a way that would have been impossible had they simply been left alone: a concept that became known as **positive freedom**.

The new liberals thus asserted that individuals had to be enabled in order for them to be free from socio-economic problems (such as poor health care, unemployment or a lack of education) and for social justice to be secured. But this raised an obvious question: how might this 'enabling' take place? This leads to the second feature of modern liberalism.

Enlarged and enabling state

As we saw earlier in the chapter, classical liberalism was strongly associated with the idea of minimal government — one that was closely linked to a belief in 'negative' liberty. By contrast, modern liberalism had no qualms about claiming that only a larger state could repel the new, socio-economic threats to freedom and individualism. Consequently, modern liberals like **John Rawls** (1921–2002) (see 'Key thinker 4' box) found themselves justifying a substantial extension of the state in the name of individual liberty: more laws, more state spending, more taxation and more state bureaucracy. In short, this brand of liberalism became strongly linked to *collectivism*, some examples of which are listed in Box 1.3.

Key term

Positive freedom A vital aspect of modern liberalism, this term denotes the belief that individuals left alone are often inhibited rather than 'free'. Such individuals may need enabling so that they are 'free' to exercise their individual talents.

Activity

Examine, in approximately 200 words, the extent to which liberals disagree about freedom.

31

The quest for social justice: examples of modern liberal collectivism

- Liberal government 1906–1910: in the UK, it was a Liberal government, led by Herbert Asquith (1852–1928) and his chancellor David Lloyd-George (1863–1945), that provided one of the earliest instances of modern liberalism in action. The most important illustration of this was the 'people's budget' of 1908, which introduced a state pension, designed to liberate people from the financial problems of old age and funded by increased taxation of property owners.

- The most influential liberal economist of the twentieth century, John Maynard Keynes (1883–1946), was a professed liberal, committed to the maintenance of a capitalist economy. But the economic depression of the 1920s and 1930s convinced him that neither individual freedom nor the survival of capitalist economies and constitutional states was served by the cyclical nature of laissez-faire capitalism. Mass unemployment, he feared, not only deprived millions of their individual freedom; it also paved the way for utterly illiberal doctrines such as fascism and communism.

- In his key work, *The General Theory of Employment, Interest, and Money* (1936), Keynes therefore argued that the state must constantly 'steer' the economy and manage demand so as to secure full employment, without which (according to Keynes) individual liberty would be difficult. Keynes's brand of dirigisme, or state-directed capitalism, duly influenced a series of western governments in the mid-twentieth century, shaping President F.D. Roosevelt's 'New Deal' in the USA in the 1930s and the economic strategy of every UK government between 1945 and 1979.

- The Beveridge Report: William Beveridge (1879–1963) was a liberal social scientist whose 1942 report, 'Social Insurance and Allied Services', proved the bedrock of Britain's post-war 'welfare state'. Developing the ideas first mooted by T.H. Green, Beveridge predicted that individuals in the post-war world faced 'five giants' threatening their freedom and individual potential: poverty, unemployment, poor education, poor housing and poor health care. In a powerful statement of modern liberal thinking, Beveridge argued that these threats could be overcome only through a major extension of state provision (such as a national health service).

Activity

Summarise, in approximately 200 words, the 'modern liberalism' of one presidency in the USA. (Those of F.D. Roosevelt, J.F. Kennedy and Barack Obama might be examples.)

Key term

Enabling state Linked to the notion of positive liberty, an enabling state was one that extended its activities so as to 'liberate' individuals from restrictive social and economic problems, thus 'enabling' them to fulfil their potential.

Having embraced collectivism, modern liberalism faced the charge (from liberal critics like Friedrich von Hayek) that it had betrayed the fundamental principles of classical liberalism and had seriously blurred the distinction between liberalism and socialism. Later modern liberals, notably John Rawls, resisted such a suggestion, arguing that only an enlarged state could guarantee the equality of opportunity necessary to enable individual freedom.

Rawls insisted, however, that while an enlarged state would require some individuals to sacrifice more of their earnings to the state in the form of progressive taxation, those same individuals could still be persuaded that this was a good and necessary thing (see 'Key thinker 4' box). That being so, Rawls argued, the **enabling state** was perfectly consistent with the liberal principle of government by consent.

Rawls also pointed out that, while modern liberalism wished to improve the lot of society's least fortunate (via extensive state intervention), it remained indifferent to inequality of outcome. For modern liberals, this was the inevitable side effect of individual freedom and was the key difference with socialism. The priority, Rawls insisted, was to ameliorate the social and economic condition of society's most deprived members and thus enable them to exploit their individual potential and achieve control of their lives. As long as this occurred, Rawls contested, the gap between society's poorest and most prosperous elements was of secondary concern (a claim most socialists would vigorously refute).

Key thinker 4

John Rawls (1921–2002)

An American philosopher, Rawls is thought to be the most important exponent of modern liberalism in the twentieth century. Rawls' major work, *A Theory of Justice* (1971), remains a key reference for students of liberal thinking. It had two principal objectives:

- First, to restate the idea that the core liberal principle of 'foundational equality' meant individuals required not just formal equality under the law and constitution but also greater social and economic equality. This was necessary, Rawls argued, to ensure the just society, where all lives could be rich and fulfilled. Yet this could be provided, Rawls stated, only by a significant redistribution of wealth via an enabling state, with extensive public spending and progressive taxation.

- Second, *A Theory of Justice* set out to show that such a redistribution of wealth was not (as Friedrich von Hayek had suggested) a 'surrender to socialism' but perfectly consistent with liberal principles. To do this, Rawls constructed a series of philosophical conditions. The first of these was termed 'the original position', whereby individuals would be asked to construct from scratch a society they judged to be superior to the one they lived in currently. Central to such an exercise would be questions about how wealth and power should be distributed. The second condition was one Rawls termed the 'veil of ignorance', whereby individuals would have no preconceptions about the sort of people they themselves might be in this new society. They might, for example, be white or they might be from an ethnic majority; they might be rich or they might be poor.

- Rawls argued that when faced with such conditions, human nature — being rational and empathetic — would lead individuals to choose a society where the poorest members fared significantly better than in present society. From a liberal angle, Rawls argued that the key point here was that this 'fairer' society, where inequalities were reduced, was the one individuals would *choose*. So an enlarged state, with higher taxation and significant wealth redistribution, was indeed consistent with liberalism's historic stress upon government by consent.

- Rawls denied this was simply a fresh justification for socialism and egalitarianism. He noted that though most individuals would indeed choose to improve the lot of the poorest, they would still want considerable scope for individual liberty, self-fulfilment and, therefore, significant inequalities of outcome. So although Rawls argued that the lot of the poor should be improved by the state, he did not argue that the gap between the richest and the poorest should necessarily be narrowed — thus ensuring that his philosophy was still distinct from socialism.

Activity

Summarise, in no more than 200 words, how Rawls reconciled liberal principles to the growth of state intervention.

Constitutional reform/liberal democracy

The third feature of modern liberalism has been a passion for ongoing, constitutional change. Put another way, precisely because it has sought to extend the state, modern liberalism has also been keen to reform it. As Hobhouse observed: 'If the state is to be enlarged, it must also be improved.'

If only to secure the principle of government by consent, modern liberalism has been associated with ongoing constitutional reform, so as to update this key liberal principle. In the UK, such liberal demands for reform have included a written or codified constitution, devolution of power from central government to regional government, electoral reform (especially proportional representation), and a more accountable House of Lords.

Yet the most important facet of modern liberalism's interest in constitutional reform has been its support for liberal democracy — in other words, completing the link between core liberal values and universal adult suffrage. So, in the UK for example, it was a Liberal prime minister who (in 1918) oversaw the enfranchisement of most women and nearly all men, irrespective of property ownership. Likewise, since 1945, UK liberals have tended to champion a lowering of the voting age, first (in 1969) to 18 and more recently to 16.

However, modern liberalism's enthusiasm for democracy is not unqualified. It has shown little interest, for example, in direct democracy, fearing that referendums and initiatives threaten the 'tyranny of the majority', and has seemed willing to dilute even representative democracy in order to protect 'liberal' values. This has been demonstrated by modern liberals' support for the UK's Human Rights Act (which effectively transferred powers from elective representatives to unelected judges) and their widespread enthusiasm for supranational bodies like the European Union. Indeed, 'Eurosceptics' have often depicted the EU as a vehicle for 'liberal bureaucrats' afraid of democracy — allowing them, for example, to advance 'liberal' initiatives (such as tolerance and anti-xenophobia) without being hindered by accountability to voters. Meanwhile, many modern liberals certainly regarded the outcome of the UK's EU referendum of 2016 — in which 48 per cent of voters wished to 'remain' — as a particularly unfortunate example of 'the tyranny of the majority', and a vindication of Mill's argument that such vital decisions were best left to a more liberally minded parliament.

Activity

Explain, in approximately 100 words, the links between social liberalism and classical liberalism.

Debate 2

Has modern liberalism abandoned the principles of classical liberalism?

Yes

- Classical liberalism defined liberty as individuals being left alone (negative freedom). Modern liberals think individuals are not free unless they are actively 'enabled' via interference from others (positive freedom).
- Classical liberalism championed a minimal state. Modern liberals champion an enlarged, enabling state.
- Classical liberalism was inclined to see taxation as 'theft' and sought to restrict it. Modern liberals often see increased taxation as the key method for implementing positive freedom.
- Classical liberalism favoured laissez-faire capitalism from which the state is detached. Modern liberals favour Keynesian capitalism, where the state seeks to 'manage' market forces.
- Classical liberalism had an ambivalent view of democracy, prioritising instead the interests of property owners. Modern liberalism has championed representative democracy.

No

- Both classical and modern liberalism have an optimistic view of human potential.
- Both classical and modern liberalism believe in rationalism and insist upon tolerance of minorities.
- Both classical and modern liberalism see individualism as the goal of politics and society — they differ merely about how to achieve it.
- Both classical and modern liberalism believe in capitalism and oppose state ownership of the economy.
- Both classical and modern liberalism believe in a constitutional ('limited') state and 'government by consent'.

Social liberalism

The final aspect of modern liberalism is its attempt to update classical liberalism's stress on tolerance — especially the tolerance of minorities. This argument has since become known as social liberalism.

From the mid-twentieth century onwards, modern liberalism became strongly linked with calls for greater racial and sexual toleration, with key thinkers like Betty Friedan (see 'Key thinker 5' box) arguing that too many individuals in western society were held back on account of innate factors such as ethnicity, gender, sexual orientation and physical disability. Given their acceptance of positive liberty and an enlarged state, modern liberals like Friedan argued that the solutions to these problems lay in further legislation, further state regulation and, sometimes, 'positive discrimination' (known in the USA as 'affirmative action'). This involved the state and other employers correcting an historical imbalance, by discriminating in favour of individuals from groups that were said to have been discriminated against previously, thus securing greater equality of opportunity.

From the 1960s onwards, modern liberalism thus became associated with initiatives like President Kennedy's Equal

Key term

Social liberalism This represents an updated version of the historic liberal belief in tolerance. It involves legislation that may criminalise actions that discriminate against individuals on the grounds of race, gender, sexual orientation, disability and religious persuasion.

Employment Opportunity Commission (EEOC), which required those managing projects financed by the state to take 'affirmative action' in respect of hiring employees from racial minorities. In the UK, meanwhile, modern liberals gave strong backing to legislation like the Race Relations Act 1976 and the Sex Discrimination Act 1975, which criminalised various forms of negative discrimination against ethnic minorities and women respectively.

Betty Friedan's importance to modern liberalism lay in her insistence that such reforms were perfectly consistent in many ways with the liberal tradition. Citing Mill's 'harm principle', Friedan claimed that laws criminalising sexual discrimination, for example, were designed merely to prevent some female individuals having their freedoms 'harmed' by others. Consistent with modern liberalism's support for an enlarged state, these laws were usually accompanied by interventionist agencies like the EEOC. Yet, as Friedan explained, these agencies were still consistent with the liberal state's original aim, namely the protection and advancement of natural rights.

Activity

Explain, in no more than 100 words, why Friedan's feminist views were consistent with liberalism in general and modern liberalism in particular.

Key thinker 5

Betty Friedan (1921–2006)

Betty Friedan is linked mainly to the development of feminist ideology, via her acclaimed work *The Feminine Mystique* (1963). Yet her ideas have also served to broaden liberalism's interest in equality of opportunity.

- As with all liberals, a concern for individualism lay at the heart of Friedan's philosophy. As such, she insisted that all individuals should be free to seek control over their own lives and the full realisation of their potential. Yet, in *The Feminine Mystique*, she argued — like Mary Wollstonecraft almost two centuries earlier — that gender was a serious hindrance to all those individuals who were female.
- Friedan argued that it was illiberal attitudes in society, rather than human nature, that condemned most women to underachievement. She contested that these attitudes were nurtured and transmitted via society's various 'cultural channels', notably schools, organised religion, the media, and mainstream literature, theatre and cinema.

These channels of 'cultural conditioning' left many women convinced that their lot in life was determined by human nature rather than their own rationality and enterprise. Friedan sought to challenge this 'irrational' assumption.

- Friedan's reputation as a liberal, as well as feminist, thinker was underlined by the fact that she always disdained violence or illegality as a means of pursuing change, arguing that significant progress was possible via legal equality, brought about by the procedures of a liberal state. She thus acknowledged the principles of the US Constitution (widely seen as a document inspired by the philosophy of John Locke) and endorsed its capacity to allow continuous improvement to individuals' lives. Consequently, she rejected the more radical feminist argument — that the state was 'patriarchal' and forever under the control of the dominant gender — in favour of a theory consistent with liberal constitutionalism.

Neo-liberalism: liberalism or conservatism?

By the end of the twentieth century, neo-liberalism was a widely recognised branch of political ideology, and a term often used by commentators to describe political thinking in countries like the UK and the USA. Yet there seems to be some confusion as to whether it is an expression of liberal or conservative thinking.

For neo-liberalism's most distinguished exponent, Austrian philosopher Friedrich von Hayek (1899–1992), there was absolute certainty that neo-liberalism represented the 'third strand' of liberal ideology. In his seminal work *The Road to Serfdom* (1944), Hayek was adamant that he was 'not a conservative', later arguing that he and like-minded philosophers such as Karl Popper, and like-minded economists such as Milton Friedman, favoured radical change, not conservative stability — a choice, Hayek argued, based upon their boundless faith in human potential.

Friedrich von Hayek: doyen of neo-liberals

As a self-proclaimed liberal, Hayek also had little time for conservatism's rigid defence of the constitutional status quo (especially when it involved a defence of hereditary influence), and was as passionate as most other liberals in respect of constitutional reforms that checked executive power. Recent neo-liberals, such as those at the Adam Smith Institute, have also opposed some of the social policies associated with conservatism. The Cameron government's promotion of marriage via the tax system, for instance, has been attacked as an unwelcome example of state intrusion into people's private lives (although neo-liberals would welcome the state's promotion of social liberalism, via the granting of equal status to gay couples).

So what makes neo-liberalism a distinctive branch of liberalism? First, it seeks to update the principles of classical liberalism within a twentieth- and twenty-first-century setting, aiming (for example) to reapply the ideas of Adam Smith and Thomas Jefferson to modern societies and modern, globalised economies. Second, it offers a liberal critique of modern liberalism, accusing it of a betrayal of individualism and a 'sell-out' to both socialism and conservatism. The Beveridge Report, for example, with its talk of the state supporting the people 'from cradle to grave', was criticised by Hayek for fostering a form of 'state paternalism', or 'dependency culture', while legitimising an endless extension of state restraint upon individual initiative.

Spurred on by the crises of the 1970s — when the efficiency of both Keynesian economics and welfare spending were brought into question — neo-liberals have thus re-advertised the merits of negative freedom and a minimal state, calling for politicians to 'roll back the frontiers of the state' and thereby 'set the people free'. Specifically, neo-liberals have demanded a reduction in public spending, often facilitated by the privatisation of public services, and much less state regulation of the economy. This, in turn, would allow lower rates of taxation and a gradual replacement of the 'dependency culture' with a new ethos of enterprising individualism.

Yet, despite their protestations of being 'real' liberals, neo-liberals have routinely been labelled as conservatives. This is partly because their views are thought to be reactionary rather than progressive, seeking to restore the economic arrangements of the nineteenth century as opposed to promoting innovative and novel ideas for the future. It is also undeniable that neo-liberal ideas have played a key role in the development of New Right conservatism, via politicians like Margaret Thatcher and Ronald Reagan. The relationship between neo-liberalism and conservatism will therefore be explored in more detail in Chapter 2.

The key liberals and their themes are summed up below.

Activity

Examine, in approximately 100 words, the links between classical and neo-liberalism.

Summary: key themes and key thinkers

	Human nature	The state	Society	The economy
John Locke	Human beings are rational, guided by the pursuit of self-interest, but mindful of others' concerns.	The state must be representative, based on the consent of the governed.	Society predates the state: there were 'natural' societies with natural laws and natural rights.	State policy should respect the 'natural right' to private property and arbitrate effectively between individuals competing for trade and resources.
Mary Wollstonecraft	Rationalism defines both genders: intellectually, men and women are not very different.	The monarchical state should be replaced by a republic which enshrines women's rights.	Society 'infantilised' women and thus stifled female individualism.	A free-market economy would be energised by the enterprise of liberated women.
John Stuart Mill	Though fundamentally rational, human nature is not fixed: it is forever progressing to a higher level.	The state should proceed cautiously towards representative democracy, mindful of minority rights.	The best society was one where 'individuality' co-existed with tolerance and self-improvement.	Laissez-faire capitalism was vital to progress, individual enterprise and individual initiative.
John Rawls	Mankind is selfish yet empathetic, valuing both individual liberty and the plight of those around them.	The state should enable less fortunate individuals to advance, via public spending and public services.	The society most individuals would choose would be one where the condition of the poorest improved.	Free-market capitalism should be tempered by the state's obligation to advance its poorest citizens.
Betty Friedan	Human nature has evolved in a way that discourages self-advancement among women.	The state should legislate to prevent continued discrimination against female individuals.	Society remained chauvinistic towards women, though women were complicit in their repression.	Free-market capitalism could be an ally of female emancipation, if allied to legislation precluding sexual discrimination.

Tensions within liberalism

- **Human nature:** all liberals believe that individuals are generally rational, intelligent, keen to prioritise their individual happiness and fulfilment, and respectful of other individuals' wish to do the same. However, early classical liberals like Locke, and neo-liberals like Hayek, believe that individuals are innately blessed with such qualities, while Mill and modern liberals like Rawls tend to think that such qualities are *potential* features of human nature, to be developed by enlightened liberal authorities. This is why modern liberals endorse Mill's concept of individuality — one that refers to what individuals could *become*, once 'enabled' to fulfil their potential.

- **Society:** classical liberals believe that human society predates the state, while all liberals see society as a collection of diverse and potentially autonomous individuals, seeking self-determination, self-realisation and self-fulfilment. Modern liberals like Rawls, however, believe that industrialised and urban societies are those where individuals are less autonomous and therefore require state support to be free ('positive liberty'). Neo-liberals often see society as one where individuals have been stymied by 'positive liberty' and that the 'dependency culture' must now be corrected by a radical reduction of the state. Some neo-liberals might see the ideal situation as one where 'there is no such thing' as society, just a collection of atomised individuals pursuing self-interest.

- **The state:** all liberals believe that the state should function according to prearranged rules and procedures, with power fragmented and authority subject to the consent of the governed. However, liberals vary on the extent of state activity. Classical liberals like Mill, in accordance with 'negative' liberty, believe state intervention should be minimal and individuals left unchecked (unless they hamper the freedom of others). Modern liberals like Friedan, in accordance with the concept of 'positive liberty', believe state intervention should be much more extensive so as to 'enable' individuals to reach their potential. Liberals have also varied over how democratic the state should be. Modern liberals are satisfied that representative democracy enhances constitutional government, whereas early classical liberals saw democracy as a threat to property rights.

- **The economy:** following Locke's assertion that property is a 'natural right', all liberals believe that the economy should be based on private property and private enterprise. However, while classical liberals and neo-liberals support Adam Smith's thesis (that the state should adopt a laissez-faire attitude to the economy), modern liberals have more sympathy for the view of John Maynard Keynes (that capitalism requires regular state management to ensure full employment). Modern liberalism's belief in 'managed' capitalism also explains its support for supranational organisations like the European Union, which many neo-liberals see as an obstacle to global free trade.

Do liberals have a coherent view of the state?

Yes

- Liberals are optimistic, believing that human beings are rational. It is therefore coherent that liberals believe in a constitutional state, drawn up as a result of rational discussion.
- Liberals believe in 'government by consent'. It is therefore coherent that their constitutional state should be seen as a 'contract' between government and governed.
- Because of the 'contractual' nature of the liberal state, it is therefore coherent that liberals believe in 'limited government', with politicians restrained by the rules of the constitution.
- Liberal philosophers like Locke speak of a 'natural society' in which all individuals enjoy 'natural rights'. It is therefore coherent for liberals to support a 'limited state' that embodies such natural advantages via mechanisms such as a bill of rights.
- The liberal state was a reaction against the medieval state in which power was concentrated in the monarch. It is therefore coherent that the liberal state should be one in which power is more dispersed.

No

- The liberal state supposedly supports foundational equality, in which all individuals are treated equally. Yet the liberal state was slow to adopt the principles of democracy, sexual equality and universal adult suffrage.
- The liberal state extols the natural right to property. But it fails to recognise that most individuals under the state's jurisdiction have not owned property.
- The liberal state defends 'government by consent', yet its constitution allows the consent of a majority to sometimes be defied via courts and assorted 'checks and balances'.
- The liberal state is supposed to be 'limited', yet modern liberals have advocated a significant extension of state intervention in the name of 'positive liberty'.
- Modern liberals have compromised their belief in 'government by consent' by supporting supranational bodies like the European Union, which arguably erode the authority of elective parliaments and elected representatives.

Conclusion: liberalism today

During the last decade of the twentieth century and the first decade of the twenty-first, liberals had several reasons to be optimistic. The collapse of Soviet communism in 1989, and the emergence of new capitalist states in eastern Europe, strengthened the idea (put forward by US academic Francis Fukuyama) that market economics and liberal democracy represented 'the end of history', the goals to which all states eventually aspire.

This was reinforced by recognition of 'globalisation' — in other words, the worldwide spread of economic liberalism — as hitherto illiberal states like China and Russia eagerly embraced market forces and modern capitalism. And, as many modern liberal economists pointed out (with reference to undemocratic countries like China), once individuals are given economic choices, it is increasingly hard to deny them political and philosophical choices as well.

Meanwhile, in established liberal democracies like the UK and the USA, society seemed to be assuming an even more liberal character. The liberal doctrine of individual choice and self-determination, already fuelled by the expansion of capitalism, was extended by the state-sponsored tolerance of diverse lifestyles (exemplified by the UK's legalisation of same-sex marriage) and by the revolution in communications. Widespread ownership of mobile telephones and personalised computers, for example, and the growing ease with which individuals 'express themselves' (via phenomena such as Facebook and Twitter), all served to make society increasingly orientated towards individualism.

Such developments in society and the economy inevitably affected the tone of political debate. In the UK, for example, 'New Labour' embraced economic liberalism by revising Clause IV of the party's constitution (that which had committed it to 'common ownership'), while David Cameron's Conservative Party embraced social liberalism by, among other things, promoting same-sex marriage. Meanwhile, a concern for improved constitutional government (another constant of modern liberalism) became a recurrent feature of UK governments after 1997, with both the Blair and Cameron governments undertaking various constitutional initiatives designed to bolster 'government by consent'.

However, other developments after 2000 gave liberals serious cause for concern. First, the atrocities witnessed in the USA on 11 September 2001, and in the UK on 7 June 2005, marked the rise and spread of Islamist terrorism, an aggressive and apparently irrational phenomenon, which blatantly challenges the most basic of liberal values. Liberal democracies were naturally forced to respond to such challenges. Yet the nature of that response — increased state security, heightened surveillance of suspected individuals, restrictions on immigration — seemed only to threaten liberal values (such as tolerance) even further. Fears were also expressed that among certain religious communities in western states, there was growing support for radical, faith-based politics that again defied the tolerant principles of the Enlightenment.

Such fears were related to the fact that while globalisation had brought benefits, it had also brought problems — notably that of increased migration. In both Europe and the United States, the changes this brought led to a backlash in many of the communities concerned and the emergence of attitudes which were at odds with the liberal mindset. This duly prompted increased support for parties like the United Kingdom Independence Party and, of course, politicians like Donald Trump — so-called 'populist' political movements that, with growing public support, effectively defied the liberal consensus. Indeed,

Donald Trump: populist assailant of liberalism

growing public concern about the effects of both economic liberalism (such as free movement of labour) and social liberalism (such as the emergence of more culturally plural societies) informed the outcome of both the UK's 2016 referendum on EU membership and, later that year, the USA's presidential election.

Yet there were other reasons why liberalism faced fresh scrutiny in the twenty-first century. The financial crash of 2008, and the economic crises affecting the Eurozone countries after 2013, revived fundamental criticisms about market economics while refreshing support for socialist politicians opposing capitalism. The public enthusiasm aroused by 'anti-austerity' parties in Greece, Spain and Portugal, the election of Jeremy Corbyn as leader of the UK Labour Party, and the surprising impact of Bernie Sanders (in the run-up to the US presidential election of 2016) all indicated that liberal economics were not as securely grounded as many had thought.

The social and economic problems besetting liberal states today should cause us to revisit the father of liberalism. John Locke's political philosophy, outlined more than 300 years ago, rested heavily upon an imagined 'state of nature', which depicted the default position of humanity. Yet the state of nature Locke described was one of peace, prosperity and reason. So when the world seems anything but peaceful, prosperous and reasonable, Locke's view of human nature — and the relevance of liberalism itself — becomes questionable.

Debate 4

Can liberalism be reconciled to conservatism?*

Yes	*No*
■ Liberals and conservatives support private property and capitalism.	■ Liberals have an optimistic view of human nature; conservatives are sceptical.
■ Liberals and conservatives see inequality of outcome as a sign of liberty.	■ Liberals see rationalism as central to human behaviour; conservatives stress habit, emotion, instinct.
■ Liberals and conservatives deny the inevitability of class conflict.	■ Liberals prioritise individual liberation; conservatives stress order and restraint.
■ Modern liberals and conservatives support gradual reform and reject revolution.	■ Liberals see individuals as potentially autonomous; conservatives see individuals as communal.
■ Neo-liberals and New Right conservatives reject Keynesian economics and champion a more laissez-faire economy.	■ Liberals extol free-market capitalism; traditional conservatives are more sceptical and protectionist.

*This debate is best addressed after reading both this chapter and the chapter on conservatism.
A similar debate about liberalism and socialism is to be found in the chapter on socialism.

Further reading

Bloor, K. (2016) Is liberalism compatible with democracy? *Politics Review*, 26,2.
Emmett-Tyrrell, R. (2011) *The Death of Liberalism*, Thomas Nelson.
Graham, P. (2016) Have modern liberals abandoned individualism? *Politics Review*, 26,1.
Gray, J. (1995) *Liberalism*, Oxford University Press.
Kelly, P. (2005) *Liberalism*, Wiley-Blackwell.
Rawls, J. (2005) *Political Liberalism*, Columbia University Press.

Exam-style questions

Short questions

The following questions are similar to those in examinations set by AQA. Each carries 9 marks.

1 Explain and analyse the main features of the 'liberal state'.

2 Explain and analyse liberalism's support for a capitalist economy.

Essay questions

The following questions are similar to those in examinations set by Edexcel (Pearson) and AQA.

Edexcel (24 marks) or AQA (25 marks):

1 To what extent do modern and classical liberals agree over the nature of the state? You must use appropriate thinkers you have studied to support your answer.

2 To what extent can liberalism be reconciled to collectivism? You must use appropriate thinkers you have studied to support your answer.

AQA only (25 marks):

3 'Liberalism and democracy are incompatible.' Analyse and evaluate with reference to the thinkers you have studied.

4 Analyses and evaluate the compatibility of liberalism and equality, with reference to the thinkers you have studied.

Chapter 2

Conservatism

Learning outcomes

This chapter will enable students to:

- understand the contrast between conservatism and the two other 'core' ideologies
- understand that there is more to conservatism than conserving
- understand that conservatism is an ideology that bends according to circumstance
- understand the continuities between 'ancient' and 'modern' conservative thinkers

Introduction: the 'politics of maintenance'

As we shall see in the course of this chapter, conservatism is a durable ideology that has responded to a series of remarkable changes over two centuries. Yet despite this durability, it is widely misunderstood. This may arise from two paradoxes that are worth explaining at the outset of this chapter.

The first paradox is that conservatism is a form of change. In other words, conservatism is not just about conserving, and certainly not about avoiding reform at all costs; instead it is a case of changing to conserve. In this sense, it is useful to distinguish between conservative politics and reactionary politics: whereas the latter seeks to resist all change, to restore what has been lost and 'turn back the clock', conservatism argues that such objectives are at best futile and at worst counter-productive.

So, for conservatives, change is inevitable; what matters is that change occurs in an appropriate manner — namely, one drawing upon all that is good about what has gone before. In fact, conservatives would assert that a certain type of change is the *only* way to conserve that which is worth conserving. As **Edmund Burke** (1729–97) (see 'Key thinker 2' box) put it: 'A state without the means of change...is without the means of its conservation.'

Key term

Change to conserve
This is the fundamental principle of conservatism and one that distinguishes a conservative from a reactionary. It indicates a belief that for something valuable to be preserved, it has to be continuously updated and maintained.

The Church of England and Parliament – two institutions conservatives seek to maintain

To understand this paradox, we need only recall that no living organism can survive by remaining in a state of inertia: it needs constant attention, nurturing and renewal. Similarly, the preservation of an ancient building will not come about through inaction and an absence of interference; it requires ongoing maintenance. In fact, a useful starting point for any understanding of conservatism is to see it as a 'doctrine of maintenance': one that advocates change, but in the form of ongoing repair and development rather than outright demolition and the construction of something entirely new.

The other paradox we should consider is that, within the UK, conservatism is not Conservatism. In other words, conservatism is not synonymous with the ideas of the Conservative Party. But it is useful to understand why this is the case.

The basic reason is that the Conservative Party, like many other centre-right parties in the developed world, does not just uphold the principles of conservatism; the party also reflects many of the liberal principles described in Chapter 1 (such as support for free markets and individual aspiration). In short, the Conservative Party is not just conservative; it is ideologically eclectic (as are most electorally successful political parties).

Conversely, not all conservatives are Conservative; Many of those who fear change, for example, see their greatest enemy as free-market capitalism, with all its iconoclastic side effects (such as globalisation). Yet market-driven change often finds its loudest support in the Conservative Party and its sternest opposition within supposedly progressive parties like Labour. Indeed, in recent years, the policies of the Labour Party have become increasingly defensive (in short, conservative) — for example, in respect of the NHS, the welfare state and (for most Labour MPs) UK membership of the European Union.

Clearly, conservatism is a more subtle doctrine than many might imagine. It therefore makes sense to examine its provenance.

The origins of conservatism

Although conservative politics should not be confused with reactionary politics, it is fair to say that the origins of conservatism were themselves a reaction — or, more specifically, a reaction to the politics of the Enlightenment (as described at the start of Chapter 1).

It will be recalled that at the heart of the Enlightenment was a belief in reason and remorseless progress; the notion that there was an 'ideal' society towards which politicians should strive, underpinned by tolerance, equality and individual rights. Indeed, by the second half of the eighteenth century, and certainly after the American Revolution of 1775–1783 (when American colonists successfully defied British imperial rule), it became difficult for politicians and philosophers to argue against the principles of the Enlightenment without appearing regressive and intolerant.

In England, at least, this was the period historians have termed 'the Whig supremacy'. Early liberal politicians, such as those found in the Whig Party, were confident that the progressive principles embodied by England's Glorious Revolution (1689) and America's Declaration of Independence (1776) were intellectually unquestionable and politically irresistible. By contrast, any critique of the Enlightenment seemed rooted in outdated, theocratic thinking — associated, for example, with a defence of monarchical absolutism and the 'divine right' of kings.

At first, the French Revolution of 1789 seemed to vindicate the optimistic spirit of the Enlightenment. The rapid and dramatic overthrow of the despotic French monarchy, the rejection of the 'irrational' religious assumptions that went with it, and the creation of a new Republic founded on 'liberté, égalité, fraternité' were all greeted with enthusiasm by European intellectuals, thrilled that a huge continental power was embracing the ideas of Rousseau, Voltaire and other Enlightenment philosophers. As the English poet William Wordsworth recalled: 'Bliss was it to be in that dawn...but to be young was very heaven.'

By 1792, however, it was clear that revolutionary change, and the ruthless imposition of 'reason' and other Enlightenment ideals, could have shocking and horrific consequences. The public beheading of King Louis XVI was accompanied by what became known as 'the Terror' — a period when thousands of 'citizens' were persecuted and executed in the name of progress, and when genocidal violence became the means of securing an 'enlightened', revolutionary regime.

The course of the French Revolution, and the threat posed to peace across Europe by the new French regime, proved a watershed in political theory. Events in France now made it possible to assail liberal-Enlightenment principles without seeming reactionary, to criticise 'progress' without denying the spirit of the Enlightenment, and to accept reform while rejecting revolution. In this way, the savagery of the French Revolution paved the way for a new sort of political ideology, one that would respect the case for change while warning of its dangers. The political thinker who epitomised this new approach was Edmund Burke, the so-called 'father of conservatism'. (His arguments will be referred to throughout this chapter and are summarised in the 'Key thinker 2' box.)

The core ideas of conservatism

Human nature

The conservative view of human nature is defined largely by its response — and opposition — to those of rival ideologies, notably liberalism and socialism. Whereas these 'progressive' ideologies take an upbeat view of human nature, asserting that human beings have the capacity for endless achievement and improvement, conservatives are inclined to restrain such optimism by stressing human frailty and fallibility. Indeed, conservatism's view of human nature has led to it being described as 'a philosophy of imperfection'.

Conservatives thus deny any possibility of a perfect, utopian society, comprising flawless and rational individuals; their view of human nature tends to be descriptive, not prescriptive, highlighting humanity 'as it is' rather than as it could or should be. In this sense, conservatism rejects the malleable or 'plastic' view of human nature offered by socialism, and scorns the idea that humanity can be significantly remoulded given the 'correct' environment or society. For conservatives, human nature is pretty much fixed and constant, and the job of politicians is to accommodate, not alter, this reality. Yet conservatism's stress on **human imperfection** is more nuanced than many

Key term

Human imperfection
Drawing upon the Old Testament doctrine of original sin, this refers to the timeless flaws of humanity — flaws which make any quest for the 'perfect' society misguided and potentially disastrous.

imagine and comprises a number of interpretations from various conservative thinkers.

When assessing conservatism's view of humanity, it is certainly useful to reference **Thomas Hobbes** (1588–1679) (see 'Key thinker 1' box), whose view of life in the 'state of nature' was sharply different from that of liberal theorists such as John Locke (see Chapter 1). Regarding human nature as ruthlessly selfish, calculating and competitive, Hobbes argued that without the restraints of formal authority, relations between human beings would be marked by 'envy, hatred and war', leading to a life that was 'nasty, brutish and short'.

However, we should be wary of describing Hobbes as the quintessential conservative. As explained in the 'Key thinker 1' box, Hobbes went on to argue (in his classic work *Leviathan*) that underpinning human nature was a cold rationality; this would eventually lead hitherto warring individuals to forge a contract, which would in turn lead to a formal state. By admitting the possibility of such rational calculations and the concept of mankind achieving satisfactory outcomes, Hobbes thereby placed himself closer to liberalism in terms of explaining human nature — which explains why Hobbes is usually seen as an example, rather than a critic, of Enlightenment thinking.

For this reason, Burke has a much stronger claim than Hobbes to be the real 'father of conservatism'. Burke's historic diatribe on the French Revolution (*Reflections on the Revolution in France*) criticised not just recent events in France but the thrust of Enlightenment thinking — including the view of human nature that inspired it. Burke duly rejected the idea that human nature was guided mainly by reason and dismissed any notion that mankind could plan the near-perfect society. Drawing upon the biblical principle of original sin, Burke highlighted the 'chasm between our desire and our achievement' and thus stressed custom, habit and experience as signposts for how we should behave.

Both Burke and Hobbes exhibited scepticism in their view of human nature — they both ridiculed any idea that human nature was saintly or potentially flawless. Yet their definitions of human imperfection were distinct. First, Burke did not think that human beings were as brutally selfish as Hobbes alleged: fallible yes, terrible no. Second, Burke thought that human beings were capable of kindness and altruism, wisdom even, as long as their actions were rooted in history, tradition and the teachings of the Christian church — a possibility that Hobbes did not countenance. Third, Burke did not share Hobbes's view that human nature was ruthlessly individualistic. Instead, Burke argued that human nature was naturally communal, with individuals gaining comfort and support from the small communities around them (what Burke termed 'little platoons').

Burke's theory of human nature would be updated by various conservative scholars in the twentieth century, many of whom argued that the conservative view of human nature was, in fact, the essence of conservatism itself. **Michael Oakeshott** (1901–90) (see 'Key thinker 3' box) stated that conservatism was 'more psychology than ideology', claiming it articulated 'an instinctive preference for what is known, an innate fear of the uncertain'. Unlike Hobbes, however, Oakeshott believed that life without law would be 'not so much nasty, brutish and short…as noisy, foolish and flawed'. Human nature, Oakeshott conceded, was 'fragile and fallible', yet it was also 'benign and benevolent' when framed by routine, familiarity and religious principles.

Later conservative thinkers, notably those associated with the New Right, offered modifications to this view. **Robert Nozick** (1938–2002) and **Ayn Rand** (1905–82), for example, were keen to highlight human nature's yearning for individual freedom, and its subsequent capacity for enterprise and innovation (see 'Key thinker 4' and 'Key thinker 5' boxes). However, the New Right and traditional conservatives agreed that even the most enterprising individuals were still (in Nozick's words) 'freedom-loving pack animals', who need the periodic restraint of formal authority and deeply rooted communities. Indeed, this recognition provides a key link between New Right politics in the twentieth century and Hobbesian philosophy in the seventeenth century. Both Hobbes and the New Right took the view that human nature was driven by self-interest. Yet both also took the view that human nature must be contained in order to provide some peace and stability in human affairs.

> ### Activity
>
> In approximately 200 words, compare and contrast the views of human nature offered by Thomas Hobbes and Edmund Burke.

Thomas Hobbes (1588–1679)

Thomas Hobbes is considered one of England's most important political thinkers. Although widely seen as a 'conservative' philosopher, he is also linked to the liberal principle of government by consent and the philosophical artefact of a 'state of nature', later used to different effect by the liberal philosopher John Locke.

- In his most famous work, *Leviathan* (1651), Hobbes took a profoundly sceptical view of human nature, arguing that it was needy and vulnerable and therefore likely to commit destructive acts. Hobbes also asserted that, prior to the emergence of a state, there was no cooperation or voluntary arrangements between individuals and therefore none of the 'natural rights' later cited by liberals. Instead, the Hobbesian 'state of nature' was a place of scarce resources where individuals would be governed by ruthless self-interest. Human nature was thus shaped by a restless desire for the acquisition of goods, an immovable distrust of others and a constant fear of violent death. In Hobbes's own words, life in this state of nature would be 'solitary, poor, nasty, brutish and short'.

- For Hobbes, such 'natural chaos' stemmed from the absence of any formal authority, which could enforce an unquestioned code of right and wrong. In its absence, Hobbes noted, mankind in the state of nature was left to form his own version of acceptable and unacceptable conduct. Yet because each man's versions of right and wrong were likely to be different, this would lead only to uncertainty and war.

- Nevertheless, because Hobbes did not consider human nature wholly irrational, he believed that mankind would eventually realise that the state of nature was inimical to self-interest and thus agree to a 'contract'. Under this contract, individuals would render to a 'sovereign' (that is, a state) the right to make laws by which all were restrained and thus allow the sort of order and security absent in the state of nature. This would eventually lead to a 'society', where individuals could enjoy some security and progress.

- But for the state to accomplish its side of the bargain, Hobbes claimed it would have to be autocratic. If power were dispersed, Hobbes argued, then the conflicts within the state of nature would soon be replicated.

- In summary, Hobbes argued that the principal reason for the state was the creation of order and security; that without such a state there could be no civil society; and that for the state to be effective, it would have to be autocratic, intimidating and forbidding.

Explain, in no more than 200 words, Hobbes's view of the state's function.

Society

Conservatism's view of society is defined by a variety of themes, all of which are thought conducive to stability, security and orderly (as opposed to revolutionary) change.

Localism

When assessing conservatism's view of society, it is important to say at the outset that conservatives would certainly acknowledge its existence. Unlike some liberals, who see society as little more than a collection of atomistic individuals, conservatives see it as a collection of localised communities — what Burke described as 'little platoons'. These communities provide their individuals with security, status and inspiration, while acting as a brake upon the sort of selfish individualism extolled by classical liberals. Indeed, one of Burke's objections to the French Revolution was that it seemed to inaugurate a single, monolithic French society that would override local loyalties — a view reinforced by the new French Republic's development of a highly centralised state.

Organicism

For conservatives, society is not something that can be contrived or created but rather something that emerges gradually, organically, and therefore somewhat mysteriously. Here we see another illustration of conservative scepticism — this time in respect of liberal-style rationalism. For whereas liberals believe in the infinite possibility of planning and arrangement, based on a belief that mankind can determine its own fate, conservatives see the 'reality' of an unplanned organic society, proof that human life is subject to complex forces beyond the scope of reason. Consequently, conservatives view society as less like a machine, responsive to whichever levers are pulled by human hands, and more like a plant, growing in a way that can never be wholly predicted.

Empiricism

Because of its organic character, conservatives also look upon society in empirical terms. This means that conservatives will deal with society's issues in a practical, evidential, 'this is how it is' fashion, with no clear view of how society might evolve in the years and decades ahead. This empirical take on society is in sharp contrast to the normative view taken by progressive ideologies like liberalism and socialism, which have principled views of how society 'ought' to be and 'plans' for how to create it. As Oakeshott observed, the conservative society is one that merely aims to 'stay afloat' in uncertain waters, rather than sail steadily towards some specific destination (such as a fairer or more equal society) which may ultimately prove illusory.

Key terms

Empiricism This indicates a preference for 'evidence' over 'theory' and tends to emphasise 'what is' over 'what should be'.

Normative This denotes how arrangements theoretically 'should' be in future — a term conservatives disdain, given their stress upon the uncertainty of our existence.

Progressive Linked to the other ideologies (socialism and liberalism), this denotes a belief that problems invariably have solutions and that the future must always be superior to the past and present — an assumption about which conservatives are sceptical.

Key terms

Hierarchy This concept holds that equality of status and power is undesirable, that human affairs require leadership from a small number of individuals, and that the majority should accept their judgements. Hierarchy's apologists claim that successful structures, social and political, tend to have an unequal distribution of power.

Paternalism/noblesse oblige These terms refer to the 'fatherly' obligations that a ruling class — or 'nobility' — has to society as a whole. It can take the form of hard paternalism or soft paternalism.

In the case of *hard paternalism*, it involves elites deciding what is best for the rest, irrespective of what the rest want.

In the case of *soft paternalism*, power still rests with the elites but elite decisions will usually be preceded by listening carefully to what the non-elites want, with perhaps a degree of consultation involved.

Tradition

The effectiveness of an empirical, conservative society rests heavily upon the store it sets by tradition. Customs and habits are thus used to provide security in an uncertain world, with history and experience shaping whatever changes become necessary. It is here that tradition dovetails with organicism. As Oakeshott observed:

> 'Just as a plant's new leaves are connected to, dependent on and explained by the plant's roots and branches, so a society's present direction stems from its past development.'

As a result, conservatives argue that change and reform — though inevitable — must be slow not drastic; respectful not contemptuous of the past.

Hierarchy

While any liberal society would stress 'foundational' equality, or the notion that all individuals are born equal and are of equal worth, conservatives see society in a much less egalitarian way. For conservatives, the imperfections of humanity lead seamlessly to inequalities within human nature. This, in turn, leads to an unequal society, where (to quote Burke) 'the wiser, stronger and more opulent' establish a **hierarchy** of power and privilege. According to Burke, such hierarchies are so natural that even the smallest of 'little platoon' communities is likely to have a top-down structure, with a minority exercising some authority over the majority.

Conservatives are keen to stress, however, that with the privilege of power and authority comes responsibility. This compromise, known as **paternalism** or **noblesse oblige**, derives from the conservative principle that the relationship between society's stronger elements and its weaker elements is akin to the relationship between a father and his children, with the former having a natural — indeed organic — responsibility for the latter.

Judaeo-Christian morality

Unlike liberalism, which stresses rationality and humanity's capacity to control its own fate, conservatism has a much stronger attachment to religion, particularly Old Testament Christianity, with its belief in original sin. As a result, the conservative society often has an important role for the ethical guidance offered by Judaeo-Christian morality, which includes a strong emphasis upon marriage, self-contained

Activity

In approximately 100 words, cite examples of how Christian teaching supports the conservative view of society.

families, and individuals being held accountable for their own actions (conservatives refute the socialist contention that 'dysfunctional' individuals are merely the products of 'dysfunctional' societies). Consequently, in a typical conservative society, religious principles — such as the spiritual rewards of altruism and compassion — will help bind individuals together and curb the imperfections that both conservatism and Christianity see as inherent to human nature.

Property

Crucial to the conservative view of society, and the basis of the 'little platoons' or mini-societies lauded by Burke, is a respect for property. As we saw in Chapter 1, a stress upon property is not exclusive to conservatism: it is one of the main 'natural rights' espoused by liberalism and the root of liberalism's support for capitalism. For conservatives, however, property has different attributes.

First, the conservative view of property is closely tied to its support for tradition and continuity. Rather than being something acquired by autonomous individuals, property is often something inherited by one generation from another, thus providing a degree of stability in a shaky, imperfect world. Indeed, inherited and bequeathed property is seen as a tangible expression of Burke's belief that the ideal society is a 'partnership between those who are living, those who are dead and those who are yet to be born'.

The ongoing, practical maintenance of property could be seen as a metaphor for conservatism's belief in the ongoing maintenance of society — an illustration of its core belief that we must change to conserve. But there is also a connection between property and the paternalistic society conservatism supports. This is because those with property have a 'stake' in existing society and, if only to discourage revolution, should have some concern for those who are less fortunate (that is, those without property). Property ownership thus provides a platform and an incentive for property owners to exercise 'duty of care' towards others — and thereby maintain existing society.

New Right conservatives are even more zealous about property, wishing not just to preserve but to extend property ownership throughout society, thus creating a 'property-owning democracy'. For New Right thinkers like Rand and Nozick, those who own property are generally better placed to resist state-led incursions upon their liberty and will be emboldened to justify the sort of unequal society conservatives defend.

The New Right's overall analysis of society is somewhat distinctive, in that it places particular emphasis upon individual liberty. However, in line with traditional conservative thinking, it concedes that individualism is best pursued in a society that still values hierarchy and a traditional, Judaeo-Christian culture. In the New Right's view, such 'traditional' societies provide the security and discipline that individuals need to flourish.

The state

Order and authority

The conservative view of the state's purpose immediately provides a sharp distinction from liberalism and socialism. For whereas the two latter ideologies see the state as serving 'progressive' goals (such as the advancement of individualism or the creation of greater equality), conservatism sees the state as having more of a disciplinary function. Put simply, the main goal of the conservative state is to provide order, security and authority.

Like Hobbes, conservatives believe that without order there could be no liberty, and there could be no order until the emergence of clear, undisputed laws backed by firm authority. All this connects to the fundamental conservative belief that *the state precedes society* (and not, as liberals argue, vice versa) and that liberal notions of 'natural rights' are fanciful. Indeed, as Hobbes insisted, the feasibility of individual rights is entirely dependent upon law and order — which only the state can provide.

Organic origins

Although conservatives have a Hobbesian view of the state's function, the link between conservatism and Hobbes can again be overdone. As an early Enlightenment thinker, Hobbes was heavily committed to 'government by consent' and the notion of a state being 'rationally' created by a 'contract' between the government and governed. By contrast, conservatives are sceptical about states that arise momentously, from a formal 'rational' discussion. Such states, conservatives argue, are likely to be normative, not empirical, based on ideals rather than reality, and therefore likely to founder. Instead, conservatives prefer a state that emerges gradually, unpredictably and without fanfare: an 'organic' and pragmatic response to humanity's needs. For this reason, conservatives are less likely than liberals to demand a 'codified' constitution and more tolerant of UK-style arrangements, where unwritten constitutions have evolved organically in response to changing circumstances.

A ruling class

The structure of the state, at least for 'traditional' conservatives (see below), also differs from that advocated by liberalism and socialism. Unlike supporters of progressive ideologies, conservatives have been much more comfortable with a state that is overtly hierarchical, reflecting the elitist society they also endorse. Furthermore, the traditional conservative state is one that implicitly acknowledges the notion of a ruling class, whose power will often be aristocratic and hereditary rather than democratic.

Traditional conservatives, from Burke onwards, were therefore keen to signal the merits of a class that was born and trained to rule the state (mindful of its paternalistic responsibilities to society as a whole). For this reason, the traditional conservative state would again show pragmatic and empirical characteristics, legislating whenever there was evidence to show new laws were necessary and governing so as to ensure order and social cohesion. By such flexible means, the conservative state would avert social upheaval and revolution while maintaining traditional patterns of wealth and power in society.

The nation-state

From the mid-nineteenth century to the mid-twentieth century, conservatives tended to emphasise a state based on nationhood. For all conservatives, the nation became a mega-community, one that enfolded all classes and therefore provided a 'natural' basis for the state. For continental conservatives, such as those in Germany or Italy, there remains a powerful sense that the nation preceded the state, that the two are distinct, and that the latter is distinguishable from the former.

For British and American conservatives, however, nation and state are much more intertwined, with the state serving to define much of the nation itself — hence the importance of constitutions, monarchs and presidents as expressions of British and American identity. This would also explain why British conservatives have had a much greater attachment to the nation-state than their continental counterparts, and much less enthusiasm for European political union. Like American

> **Activity**
>
> Explain, in approximately 100 words, why conservatives might be wary of democracy.

conservatives, British conservatives tend to see any diminution of the nation-state as a diminution of the nation itself.

For New Right conservatives (again found mainly in the USA and the UK), the attitude to the state appears paradoxical: to strengthen the nation-state by 'rolling back its frontiers'. Yet for New Right thinkers like Nozick and Rand, the paradox is easily explained: if the nation-state is burdened by nationalised industries and welfare states, it is then harder for it to focus on its 'true' function of order and security. As Rand observed: 'When the state becomes flabby, it also becomes feeble.' So, for New Right conservatives, the aim is to streamline the nation-state's functions and to make it 'leaner and fitter' in the process.

The economy

Capitalism tends to nurture and widen economic inequalities and to sharpen the distinction between rich and poor. Conservatism, meanwhile, defends inequality and hierarchy. So it is unsurprising that 'conservative economics' have a pro-capitalist flavour. Indeed, Burke was a robust ally of Adam Smith, the father of **laissez-faire** economic theory.

Yet despite this overlap with liberalism, traditional conservatism's support for capitalism is nuanced. This is because conservatism worships order, stability and continuity. Yet free-market capitalism promotes risk, innovation and iconoclasm. The dynamic nature of capitalism might well excite liberals, with their optimistic view of human nature and residual belief that (to quote Voltaire) 'everything is for the best in this, the best of all worlds', but it can be quite frightening for conservatives, given their more sceptical view of human nature and their residual fear that radical change threatens dreadful outcomes.

With this in mind, traditional conservatives have sometimes been dubbed capitalism's 'reluctant supporters'. On the one hand, they recognise that any assault on capitalism is also an assault on property, inequality, hierarchy and the status quo. On the other hand, traditional conservatives are sceptical of the classical or neo-liberal belief that markets are at their most effective when left alone by governments. Supporting laissez-faire capitalism, after all, requires an optimistic view of market forces, and is therefore somewhat inconsistent with conservatism's scepticism and pessimism.

Traditional conservatives have tried to resolve this dilemma by supporting a moderated form of capitalism, in which free markets are tempered by state intervention. Under this conservative model of capitalism — sometimes referred to as protectionism — society and the economy would be insured

Political ideas for A-level

Key term

Laissez-faire This involves the state allowing market forces to operate freely. Though strongly associated with economic liberalism, laissez-faire economics has been supported by both traditional conservatives like Edmund Burke and New Right conservatives like Robert Nozick.

Adam Smith: father of liberal economics

Thatcherism This is essentially a synonym for New Right conservatism in the UK. Between 1979 and 1990, the governments of Margaret Thatcher pursued a controversial mixture of neo-liberal policies (such as privatisation and tax reduction) and neo-conservative policies (such as strengthened police powers, curbs on immigration and tax breaks for 'traditional' family structures).

Explain, in approximately 200 words, how conservatism's attitude to capitalism differs from that of liberalism.

against the vagaries of markets by state-imposed tariffs and duties. This 'protection' of national producers and consumers was also consistent with traditional conservatism's emphasis upon national identity and 'one nation' (see later), offsetting the globalising effects of free-market capitalism. Traditional conservatives in the twentieth century were also drawn to Keynesian capitalism, whereby the state 'managed' market forces in the interests of full employment.

Influenced by neo-liberal economists such as Milton Friedman (1912–2006) and Friedrich von Hayek (1899–1992), New Right conservatives have generally had a more sympathetic view of free-market economies. Indeed, in the USA during the 1980s, free-market capitalism was often referred to as 'Reaganomics', on account of the support it had in the Republican administration of President Ronald Reagan (1980–88). At the same time, the New Right governments of Margaret **Thatcher** (1979–90) aimed to 'free' the UK economy through the privatisation of formerly state-owned industries.

Yet New Right economics still manages to complement traditional conservatism in a number of ways. First, the New Right argues that by disengaging almost completely from the economy, the state could then focus on its true Hobbesian purpose of order and security. Second, the New Right believes that a free-market economy will be a prosperous economy. This might promote 'popular capitalism' and destroy socialism, but it would also fund greater state spending on the police, armed forces and other agencies vital to the defence of a conservative society.

Different types of conservatism

Unlike socialism, with its various tensions and subdivisions, there are just two strands of conservatism: traditional conservatism and New Right conservatism. Yet it would be wrong to conclude that conservatism is therefore a more straightforward ideology. Like classical liberalism, traditional conservatism is a creed that spans over two centuries; it is therefore an amorphous doctrine, evolving in accordance with changing circumstances.

Traditional conservatism (i): aftermath of the French Revolution

As explained in our review of conservatism's origins, the principles of conservatism were grounded in a reaction to the French Revolution of 1789 — an event that, by offering a radical interpretation of Enlightenment values, challenged established notions of state and society across Europe. Although conservatives were primarily concerned about the effects this would have upon their own security, it was the Whig politician Edmund Burke who offered the first philosophically coherent objection to what the French Revolution represented.

Key thinker 2

Edmund Burke (1729–97)

As a Whig MP, Edmund Burke was known as the champion of numerous radical causes during the mid to late eighteenth century. He was a firm supporter of the American Revolution after 1776, defended Irish tenants in their clashes with extortionate landlords, demanded the impeachment of the Governor General of Bengal (Warren Hastings) for alleged cruelty towards Hindustanis, and was a fervent advocate of Adam Smith's call for free trade. Yet despite this radical pedigree, Burke is widely considered the father of conservatism and one of the Enlightenment's most important critics. How did this arise?

- The answer lies in Burke's impassioned opposition to the French Revolution, via his famous text *Reflections on the Revolution in France* (1790). It was in this book that Burke defined various tenets of conservative thought, including human imperfection, empiricism, organicism, tradition, aristocracy and localism.
- In respect of human imperfection, Burke stressed mankind's fallibility and its tendency to fail more than succeed. He therefore denounced the idealistic society that the French Revolution represented, claiming it was based on a utopian — and thus unrealistic — view of human nature.

- Burke argued that while change was necessary to conserve, change should proceed on the basis of fact and experience — in other words, empiricism and tradition — rather than theory and idealism. Burke duly criticised the French Revolution for discarding what was known in favour of an entirely new society based on 'philosophical abstractions'.
- Burke claimed that both society and government were more akin to a plant than a machine. He thus argued that both had a mysterious dynamism that was beyond reason and planning. In the political and social context, Burke therefore insisted that change must be cautious and organic, and denounced the French Revolution for disregarding history and tradition.
- Burke was scathing about the French Revolution's stress on equality, asserting that within all 'organic' societies, a ruling class was inevitable and desirable. However, this class had a clear obligation to govern in the interests of all. For Burke, it was the French aristocracy's failure to do this that led to revolution.
- Burke condemned the new French Republic for its highly centralised structures, praising instead a society of 'little platoons': a multitude of small, diverse and largely autonomous communities, which would 'acknowledge, nurture and prune… the crooked timber of humanity'.

Activity

Explain, in no more than 200 words, Burke's view of how change should occur.

Debate 1

Is conservatism 'ruling-class ideology'?

Yes

- It was a claim regularly made by both fundamentalist socialists such as Beatrice Webb and revisionist socialists like Anthony Crosland.
- Those making such claims cited Burke — the 'father of conservatism' — who attacked the egalitarianism of the French Revolution while defending aristocratic rule.
- Since Burke, conservatives have always defended property, privilege and inequality.
- Conservative paternalism is merely an attempt to make inequality and elitism palatable to the majority.
- The stress on tradition and piecemeal change conspires to prevent *radical* change, which inherently threatens ruling-class interests.

No

- The prime purpose of the conservative state — the maintenance of order — is one with appeal to all sections of society.
- Conservatism's love of habit, custom and familiarity has echoes within all sections of society.
- Traditional conservatism has frequently promoted the interests of the poor in order to ensure the maintenance of 'one nation'.
- The conservative wish to avoid revolution is altruistic — during periods of revolutionary upheaval it is often society's most vulnerable members who suffer most.
- New Right conservatism is meritocratic, not aristocratic, identifying with ambitious and talented individuals from all backgrounds.

Key term

Tory Along with the Whigs, the Tories were one of the two main parties in England from the seventeenth to the early nineteenth centuries. They were linked to themes such as authority, tradition, hierarchy and religion. Following alliances with sections of the Whig Party, the Tories eventually evolved in the 1830s into a broader political grouping known as the Conservative Party.

Conservatism's opponents have since argued that Burke's thesis, as expounded in *Reflections on the Revolution in France* (1790), merely provided a sophisticated justification for existing society — one in which he, like other members of the 'ruling class', had a vested interest. Yet there can be no doubt that Burke's cogent analysis, based upon a web of philosophical principles, shaped not just the origins of conservatism but also its development in Britain during the early nineteenth century.

Tory prime ministers such as William Pitt (1759–1806), George Canning (1770–1827) and Robert Peel (1788–1850) were essentially conservative in their political practice. Like Burke, they displayed a reverence for order and property, showed an antipathy to revolutionary change, extolled tradition, endorsed the notion that society comprised a multitude of small communities, insisted that society and state emerged 'organically', praised experience and 'evidence' over theory and 'abstraction', and defended the principle of paternalistic, aristocratic rule.

Yet among such senior political figures, Burke's influence was most marked in their attitude to change. Once again, it is worth recalling the core conservative belief that we must 'change to conserve'. Within the UK, this principle was duly applied by a series of 'enlightened Tory' governments in the early nineteenth century — governments which sought to avert the spread of revolutionary ideas by embracing moderate reform in the name of continuity.

George Canning, for example, supported Catholic emancipation and, as prime minister, prepared legislation that allowed Roman Catholics to participate in Parliament (claiming that 'though emancipation carries dangers, civil strife carries even greater dangers'). Canning also championed the abolition of slavery, arguing that it brought property ownership into disrepute, while supporting demands from various Latin American countries for independence — all of which echoed Burke's support for the American Revolution of 1776 and his campaigns against corruption inside British colonies.

Within a decade of Canning's premiership, Robert Peel offered another example of changing to conserve, seeking to harness the interests of the new merchant and business classes to Britain's traditional constitution and society. To this end, Peel, along with other newly named 'Conservatives', supported the Great Reform Act of 1832, thus ensuring representation at Westminster for the new industrial towns. Peel's reasoning was that if the interests of the newly enriched were not harnessed to the existing social and political structure, there was a danger that those same interests would be harnessed instead to property-less forces with no vested interest in evolving the status quo (a conservative rationale for reform that was central to Burke's explanation for the French Revolution).

In addition to offering clear examples of 'changing to conserve' while prime minister (1841–46), Peel's political career offers a practical example of conservatism's belief in order and authority. As Home Secretary (1828–30), he established the Metropolitan Police Force in London, a measure which led to the creation of similar forces throughout the country. Peel's assertion that 'without security there can be no liberty' effectively updated Hobbes' justification for the state and strengthened the association between conservatism, order and authority.

Traditional conservatism (ii): the emergence of 'one nation'

Although the governments of Canning and Peel served to stem the effects of the French Revolution, the threat of disorder and insurrection persisted throughout the nineteenth century, fuelled by loud demands for greater democracy (and less aristocracy) within the UK's political system. All this required a further development of conservative thinking.

Of particular importance to this development were politicians like Benjamin Disraeli (1804–81) in Britain and Otto von Bismarck (1815–98) in Germany. Sensing that socialism, with its stress upon class conflict, was a new and grave threat to stability and tradition, conservatives like Disraeli and Bismarck understood that the case for orderly change would have to be refined. Likewise, they were aware that to ensure social cohesion and orderly change, new themes were needed to offset the class-conscious politics encouraged by early socialists like Marx.

It was at this point that the importance of the nation emerged in conservative thinking. This was ironic because, until the nineteenth century, nationalism had been associated with anti-imperialism and anti-monarchism. The French revolutionaries, whom Burke opposed so vehemently, were self-styled 'patriots', while subsequent revolutions across Europe (such as those of 1848) had frequently been hailed as 'patriotic' movements. In short, until the mid–late nineteenth century, 'the nation' was seen as anything but a conservative concept.

Disraeli and Bismarck, however, understood nationalism's conservative potential. Unlike contemporary liberals, whose individualistic outlook led them to deny social class, conservatives like Disraeli embraced class differences — but in a way that fostered unity rather than rupture. Against the rhetorical background of **one-nation conservatism**, Disraeli and Bismarck argued that a society's classes were, in fact, all members of the same national 'family' and that revolutionary politics (including Marxism) represented an attack on the nation itself. For Disraeli, 'the nation' was

Key term

One-nation conservatism
Dating from the 1870s, and linked to British politicians like Benjamin Disraeli, this term denotes a belief that conservatism should prioritise national unity by attending to the condition of society's poorer classes. It has been used by conservative politicians to justify greater state intervention in society and the economy, and thus higher levels of public spending and taxation.

not an alternative to the status quo but the *essence* of the status quo, with the existing nation-state being something that all classes had a vested interest in defending.

Conservatives like Disraeli therefore poured scorn on the supposed links between the workers of one nation and those of another (as suggested by Marx's call for 'workers of the world' to 'unite'). Instead these one-nation conservatives updated Burke's notion of an organic affinity between a nation's richer and poorer classes, arguing that the nation's aristocracy had a paternalistic duty to (in Disraeli's words) 'elevate the condition of the people'. Once this obligation was recognised by all classes, Disraeli and Bismarck asserted, social and political progress could be achieved harmoniously and without the horrors of class war and revolution. As Disraeli remarked: 'The palace is not safe when the cottage is not happy.'

However, in pursuit of this 'one nation' strategy, neither Disraeli nor Bismarck advocated mere philanthropy on the part of society's 'haves'. In a way that would never have occurred to previous generations of conservatives, they endorsed state-sponsored social reform, thereby distinguishing conservatism from the minimal-state principles of classical liberalism. (Indeed, they regarded laissez-faire individualism, like class-based socialism, as the enemy of 'one nation'.) As a result, the one-nation conservatism of the mid–late nineteenth century became associated with legislation that tempered the effects of laissez-faire capitalism, supposedly on behalf of the nation's working classes.

In England, this resulted in legislation such as the Factory Act 1874 and the Artisan Dwellings Act 1875, restricting the freedom of factory owners and landlords respectively, while Bismarck's chancellorship of Germany (1871–90) led to what some historians regard as the first welfare state, providing German workers with state-backed insurance against sickness, accident and destitution in old age. Bismarck's conservatism also led to the imposition of tariffs and import controls, thus confirming traditional conservatism's ambivalent attitude to free-market capitalism.

Activity

Explain, in approximately 200 words, why and how Disraeli promoted 'one-nation conservatism'.

Traditional conservatism (iii): response to egalitarianism and fascism

During the twentieth century, political debate was reshaped by two seismic events: the spread of socialism and communism after the First World War and the emergence of fascism prior to the Second World War. These developments were to have a profound impact upon the evolution of traditional conservatism.

For most of the twentieth century, conservatives regarded the existence of the Soviet Union as the most powerful example of the threat now posed by egalitarianism — an ideology, enfolding socialism and communism, which inherently challenged conservatism's belief in property, hierarchy and modest reform. In the UK, the conservative fear of egalitarianism was underlined by the extension of the franchise in 1918 (which flooded the electorate with working-class voters) and the accelerated growth of a new political party — Labour — committed to wholesale common ownership. Indeed, until the late twentieth century, it was common for conservatives to lament that socialism and communism were inevitable unless stern political action was taken.

With that in mind, traditional conservatism sought to temper the effects of a capitalist economy with a view to sustaining a society based on property ownership and inequality. Prominent inter-war conservatives, such as future Tory prime minister Harold Macmillan (1894–1986), spoke of a 'middle way' between capitalism and socialism, one that would address economic inequalities while respecting property rights, cultural tradition, national identity and other themes close to conservative hearts.

Although Macmillan did not become prime minister until the 1950s, as early as the 1930s it was clear that conservatism was now prepared to sanction a much greater degree of state intervention so as to protect privilege and stifle socialism. Between 1935 and 1937, for example, Conservative politicians supported Public Health, Housing and Factory Acts, all of which checked market forces in the name of social cohesion and 'one nation'.

After 1945, conservatism took further steps towards an acceptance of 'big government'. Across western Europe, conservatives seemed to yield to many of the ideas espoused by rival political ideologies, notably those of democratic socialism and modern liberalism, and thus embraced Keynesian

Key term

Fascism This was a revolutionary ideology which emerged in Europe during the 1920s and 1930s, finding its most devastating expression in the politics of Adolf Hitler's National Socialism in Germany and Benito Mussolini's nationalist politics in Italy. Because of its nationalistic and nostalgic character, it is sometimes seen as a form of 'ultra-conservatism'. Yet its belief in radical and immediate change, its contempt for traditional institutions and local diversity, and its glorification of dictatorship also make it abhorrent to orthodox conservatives.

economics, 'welfare states' and 'mixed economies' involving extensive state ownership of industries and services.

To a large extent, this was opportunistic and pragmatic. After all, to give effect to their views, conservative politicians in the twentieth century needed to win elections, and elections were now dominated by working-class, non-property-owning voters. This encouraged socialist theorists, such as Crosland, to argue that 'conservatives conserve no principles...they simply go along with whatever situation they inherit, in the interests of winning office and stemming the tide of change'.

Yet post-war conservatives denied such taunts and insisted they were evolving, rather than forgetting, their previous ideological positions. In his book *The Case for Conservatism* (1948), Quentin Hogg claimed that 'conservatism, unlike liberalism, has always recognised that unchecked laissez-faire can be destructive as well as creative', while R.A. Butler (in *The Art of the Possible*, 1971) argued that 'our support for state welfare, and the Keynesian principle of an economy based on full employment...were little more than updated expressions of our belief in one-nation and paternalism'.

Christian democracy

Outside the UK, traditional conservatism after 1945 evolved rather differently. The main reason for this was that other western European nations felt the effects of fascism much more acutely. Revolution, violent nationalism, totalitarian government, military defeat and national humiliation all had a huge effect on the psychology of continental conservatives like West Germany's Konrad Adenauer (1876–1967), France's Robert Schuman (1886–1963) and Italy's Luigi Sturzo (1871–1959). After 1945, such European conservatives therefore developed a variant of traditional conservatism known as Christian democracy.

However, this post-war European conservatism is not wholly dissimilar to traditional conservatism in the UK. In fact, there are numerous overlaps:

- There is the same belief in Judaeo-Christian morality as a force for binding society together.
- There is the same belief in authority and hierarchy (underlined, in Christian democracy's case, by its links to the Roman Catholic Church).
- There is the same commitment to social conservatism, the same emphasis upon marriage and family life, and the same scepticism towards socially liberal causes such as abortion and sexual equality.

Activity

Explain, in approximately 200 words, conservatism's contribution to the UK's post-war consensus.

Activity

In approximately 200 words, explain the differences between post-war conservatism in the UK and elsewhere in western Europe.

Key term

Supranationalism This refers to a state whose authority cuts across national boundaries. The Soviet Union was a clear example; the European Union is said to be a developing example. British and American conservatives tend to dislike the concept, seeing it as a threat to 'one nation' and the traditional nation-state. Post-war continental conservatives, such as the Christian democrats, are much more receptive, seeing supranationalism as an antidote to the legacy of fascism's 'ultra-nationalism'.

- There is the same scepticism towards free-market economics. Christian democracy thus stresses the 'social market', a form of capitalism that draws upon Roman Catholic principles of obligation and communal duty, but with echoes of Disraeli's 'paternalistic' conservatism.
- There is the same acceptance of an enlarged state: like post-war conservatism in the UK, Christian democracy was comfortable with Keynesian (state-managed) capitalism, high public spending and an expansive welfare state.

What makes Christian democracy distinct from British (and American) conservatism is its attitude towards the nation-state. In countries like Germany, Italy and Spain, the experience of fascism left conservative politicians explicitly wary of nationalism and traditional notions of patriotism. (In Germany in particular, references to 'one nation' sat uncomfortably alongside its recent history of Nazism.) In other continental democracies too, the experience of invasion, occupation, collaboration and national shame deeply affected conservative attitudes towards national identity and national self-determination.

One crucial effect of this was to make post-war continental conservatives amenable to **supranationalism**, an idea first hinted at by Schuman's plan for limited economic integration in the 1950s and later embodied by the European Economic Community and the European Union. Here again the Roman Catholic influence within Christian democracy was helpful for continental conservatives, given that the Roman Catholic Church itself practises supranational authority.

For many British conservatives, meanwhile, the suspicion has always been that the real aim of Christian democracy's supranationalism is to eliminate 'the nation' as a feature of conservative philosophy and instead make 'the region' the main focus of communal identity (as it is now for many German and Italian conservatives). For this reason, many British conservatives — such as the philosopher Roger Scruton — regard Christian democracy as a form of 'no-nation conservatism' and therefore something for which they feel little affinity.

Michael Oakeshott (1901–90)

Michael Oakeshott is regarded as one of the most important conservative philosophers of the twentieth century, bringing a fresh perspective to the core themes of traditional conservatism. Oakeshott's key text on the subject, *On Being Conservative* (1962), is renowned for its fresh interpretation of how conservatives regarded human imperfection. In particular, it is remembered for its argument that a 'philosophy of imperfection' need not be a 'philosophy of pessimism' or indeed unhappiness.

- First of all, Oakeshott wished to qualify the negative view of human nature associated with Hobbes and, to a lesser extent, Burke. Most men and women, he argued, were 'fallible but not terrible' and 'imperfect but not immoral'. Though incapable of the 'perfect' societies linked to other ideologies, humanity was still able to secure 'both pleasure and improvement through the humdrum business of everyday life'.
- From this perspective, Oakeshott tried to make conservatism seem more optimistic than ideologies such as liberalism and socialism. He argued that such ideologies — with their clear views of how society 'should' be — produced impatience, intolerance and frustration. Oakeshott claimed that conservatives, who are reconciled to human imperfection, have a greater appreciation of the pleasures that already exist in life (from families and friends, for example). Conservatives, he claimed, 'prefer the familiar to the unknown, the actual to the possible, the convenient to the perfect…present laughter to utopian bliss'.

- Being dismissive of 'normative' politics, with its 'simplistic visions that overlook the complexity of reality', Oakeshott also affirmed the merits of an empirical and pragmatic approach to both politics and life generally — what might be termed 'the art of the possible'. He argued that it was through experience, trial and error, rather than abstract philosophy, that wisdom was achieved. In a memorable aside, Oakeshott remarked: 'In a kitchen, cook books are only useful after experience of preparing a meal.'
- These perspectives on human nature informed Oakeshott's views about the state. In his final work, *The Politics of Faith & the Politics of Scepticism*, he argued that the state existed to 'prevent the bad rather than create the good', restating that the best things in life normally emerge from routine, apolitical activity. This also led him to offer his celebrated 'nautical metaphor': that, during our lives, 'we all sail a boundless sea, with no appointed destination' and that the job of government is to reflect this by 'keeping the ship afloat at all costs… using experience to negotiate every storm, stoicism to accept necessary changes of direction…and not fixating on a port that may not exist'.
- Oakeshott's critics, especially conservative critics on the New Right, claim his philosophy is too fatalistic and underestimates our ability to shape circumstances. For New Right philosophers like Nozick, the 'Oakeshott mentality' was 'lazy' and had allowed socialist ideas to advance unchallenged after 1945.

Activity

Explain, in no more than 200 words, how Oakeshott's view of human nature differs from that of Hobbes.

Is conservatism merely the politics of pragmatism?

Yes

- The 'father of conservatism', Edmund Burke, made his attack on the French Revolution an attack on 'abstract philosophy', claiming it ignored human imperfection.
- Traditional conservatives have consistently advocated an 'empirical' approach to politics, one based on 'what is', not 'what should be'.
- Traditional conservatism prides itself on 'flexibility'. This has helped conservatism endure several centuries of dramatic change.
- Conservative pragmatism is shown by the different policies adopted by various conservatives at different times. Robert Peel, for example, supported laissez-faire capitalism, while (a century later) Harold Macmillan backed a more Keynesian (interventionist) approach.
- Michael Oakeshott therefore argued that conservatism is a short-term, 'getting by' approach to politics: unlike liberalism and socialism, it has no long-term objectives concerning society and the economy.

No

- Traditional conservatism, far from being philosophically neutral, is based on philosophically contentious assertions (for example, that slow change is preferable to radical change; that 'vision' and 'principle' are inferior to 'tradition' and 'evidence').
- Traditional conservatism does not reject revolution merely as a method of change; it does so to protect a society based on certain principles, such as hierarchy, inequality and private property.
- As a result, socialists see conservatism as 'ruling-class ideology', a changing set of biased policies, reflecting the evolving tactics of elites determined to preserve their privilege.
- Oakeshott described traditional conservatism as 'a psychology rather than an ideology', drawing upon humanity's 'instinctive love of the familiar'. Conservatives may therefore reject 'pragmatic' change if it conflicts with their instincts and emotions.
- New Right conservatism draws upon the neo-liberal/libertarian doctrines of philosophers like Hayek and Nozick, while New Right politicians, such as Margaret Thatcher, proclaimed themselves 'conviction politicians'.

New Right conservatism

An American export

For much of the twentieth century, conservatism in the UK — and most of western Europe — was defined by a combination of social conservatism and qualified support for economic liberalism. In other words, while conservatives stressed order, authority and traditional communities, their support for private property and capitalism was tempered by a fear that market forces could generate gross inequalities that would outrage the majority of (working-class) voters. As a result, traditional conservatives in Europe and the UK supported interventionist economic policies, such as Keynesianism, and high public spending on state welfare.

In the United States, however, conservatism had a rather different mixture. There, conservatives placed much more emphasis upon individual freedom, laissez-faire capitalism, private property and minimal government, largely because these values squared with different traditions (those of the USA), reflecting the communities that emerged organically after the discovery of the New World.

Many of these traditions were essentially liberal in character, stemming from the individualist values of the USA's Founding Fathers and a Constitution that owed much to the philosophy of John Locke. But it is important to remember that those values were quickly blended with other values that were more obviously conservative, such as traditional Christian morality, a respect for marriage and family life, intense patriotism and a belief in 'strong' (albeit limited) government.

In other words, American conservatism had always involved a synthesis between classical liberalism and social conservatism. From the 1970s onwards, conservatives in Europe were increasingly convinced that this (American) model of conservatism was one that they too should adopt.

The 'crisis' of traditional conservatism

To understand New Right conservatism, it is first necessary to appreciate that it was primarily an analysis of the 'crisis' engulfing states like the UK by the mid-1970s. This crisis was supposedly characterised by spiralling inflation, mounting unemployment, unsustainable welfare spending, increased crime rates, moral laxity and a growing sense that society was becoming ungovernable, largely on account of trade union militancy.

For the New Right, however, this crisis also represented an indictment of traditional conservatism. After 1945, traditional conservatives (like Macmillan, Hogg and Butler) had clearly endorsed a post-war consensus involving Keynesian economics, state welfare and social liberalism. According to the New Right, traditional conservatives were therefore complicit in a rapidly declining economy, a bloated welfare state, a 'permissive society' and an increasingly feeble country — one lacking in both moral and formal authority and struggling to resist both socialism at home and communism abroad. So, as well as new government policies, a new interpretation of conservatism was urgently required.

Harold Macmillan: Tory PM and practitioner of one-nation conservatism

In most of Europe, where conservatives remained faithful to the ideas of Christian democracy, such a reinterpretation was largely resisted. However, conservatives in the UK and the USA proved much more willing to challenge traditional conservative thinking. This was eventually expressed in the UK by the Conservative prime minister Margaret Thatcher (1925–2013) and in the USA by the Republican president Ronald Reagan (1911–2004).

Margaret Thatcher and Ronald Reagan: two leading advocates of New Right ideas

Debate 3

Is conservatism compatible with capitalism?

Yes

- Capitalism is based on private property, which historically conservatives support.
- Capitalism generates inequality, which conservatives defend as 'natural' and 'organic'.
- Capitalism has been at the heart of economic activity for several centuries and therefore squares with conservatism's support for tradition.
- Capitalism provides the ruling class with wealth that can then be used for paternalistic support for the less fortunate.
- New Right conservatism is keen to extend private property and market forces in the name of greater individual freedom.

No

- Capitalism is often described as economic liberalism — it is focused on individuals rather than the communities that conservatism champions.
- Capitalism creates economic and social divisions that threaten 'one nation'.
- Capitalism is dynamic and volatile, threatening the stability and continuity conservatives crave.
- Capitalism tends towards globalisation, undermining the national identity conservatives value.
- Capitalism promotes a meritocracy that challenges hereditary ruling classes.

New Right conservatism: a two-dimensional doctrine

New Right conservatism is best described as a merger between two distinct ideologies: neo-liberalism and neo-conservatism.

Neo-liberalism is principally associated with Austrian philosopher Friedrich von Hayek, whose 1944 thesis, *The Road to Serfdom*, is regarded as the 'bible' of neo-liberal thinking. Hayek's views were subsequently reinforced by American economist Milton Friedman and, in the UK, by think-tanks such as the Adam Smith Institute and the Institute of Economic Affairs. It also chimes with the libertarian philosophy of Robert Nozick and Ayn Rand.

Neo-liberalism's aims can be distilled into the following objective: to extend individual freedom by 'rolling back the frontiers of the state' in order to create a free market economy. According to thinkers like Nozick and Rand, such measures would not just promote freedom, they would also lead to the return of economic growth and a vibrant, prosperous society. In more specific terms, neo-liberals wished to see:

- a drastic reduction in taxation
- a much tighter control of government spending (along the monetarist lines prescribed by Friedman)
- an end to the dependency culture arising from expensive welfare states
- the deregulation and privatisation of services carried out by government
- the neutering of 'obstructive' bodies wedded to 'statist' ideas (such as trade unions and many local councils).

Neo-conservatism, meanwhile, is associated with American scholars like Irving Kristol (1920–2009) and British philosophers like Roger Scruton (1944–). Whereas neo-liberalism's concern was the salvation of individual liberty, neo-conservatism's main objective was the restoration of authority, national identity and a society informed by Judaeo-Christian morality. In more specific terms, neo-conservatives wished to see:

- a tougher approach to law and order, involving more powers for the police and stiffer sentences for offenders
- a more robust approach to national defence, including a less conciliatory approach to the nation's potential enemies (principally, in the context of the 1970s, the Soviet Union)
- a less tolerant approach to immigration (mainly because of its challenge to traditional national identity)
- anti-permissive social policies (in respect of issues like abortion and homosexuality) and the promotion of 'traditional' family structures via the state's tax and benefits system.

Key term

Anti-permissive Linked to the neo-conservative wing of the New Right, such policies seek to reverse much of the social liberalism dating from the 1960s. Neo-conservatism takes a critical view of issues like divorce, abortion and homosexuality.

Key thinker 4

Ayn Rand (1905–82)

The sharp differences between traditional and New Right conservatism were highlighted by the writings of Ayn Rand, one of the USA's most provocative New Right thinkers.

- Rand's defining work, the novel *Atlas Shrugged* (1957), secured her status as one of America's most influential libertarians. Its theme was that talented individuals, rather than ambitious governments, lay at the heart of any successful society. The novel suggested that without the energy of such individuals, a society would quickly wither — no matter how much activity was expended by governments.
- This theme was restated in a non-fictional way through Rand's works of philosophy. *The Virtue of Selfishness* (1964) explained a philosophical system Rand described as 'objectivism', its core belief being that we should all be guided by self-interest and 'rational self-fulfilment'.
- For this reason, Rand became associated with the New Right's **atomism**, the term for a society defined by millions of autonomous individuals, each independently seeking self-fulfilment and self-realisation. Indeed, Rand's work provided a philosophical justification for the idea that society did not exist in any practical form, it was ideally just a loose collection of independent individuals.

- Although Rand's ideas are consistent with both classical and neo-liberalism, they gained political traction on account of New Right politics in the 1970s. Her 'objectivist' philosophy became strongly linked to the New Right's support for a more laissez-faire brand of capitalism and its renewal of negative liberty, thus providing a philosophical justification for 'rolling back the frontiers of the state' and projects such as tax cuts and privatisation.
- Rand was proud to call herself a libertarian, in that she defended not just free markets but also an individual's 'right to choose' in areas like homosexuality or abortion. But she firmly rejected any suggestion of anarchism, claiming that both free markets and cultural laissez-faire needed the parameters of a small state.
- In her later work, Rand strengthened her connection to conservatism by stating that liberty was impossible without order and security, which only a state could provide. Her conservative credentials were further strengthened by her support for the ultra-conservative Republican candidate Barry Goldwater in the 1964 US presidential election, during which she wrote: 'The small state is the strong state.'

Activity

Explain, in no more than 200 words, the connection between New Right conservatism and the philosophy of Ayn Rand.

Key term

Atomism This relates to the view that human beings seek autonomy and 'space', which therefore leads to only a vague sense of society. Conservatives traditionally reject this view, arguing that individuals are closely connected by their communities. However, New Right conservatives are much more atomistic in their view of human nature and society (see below).

Robert Nozick (1938–2002)

During the 1970s, Robert Nozick emerged as one of the key thinkers for New Right conservatism. His key work, *Anarchy, State and Utopia* (1974), remains a vital reference for modern conservative philosophy.

- Nozick developed many of the themes first raised by neo-liberal philosopher Friedrich von Hayek in *The Road to Serfdom* (1944). Like Hayek, Nozick argued that the growth of government was the gravest contemporary threat to individual freedom. More specifically, Nozick thought the growth of welfare states in western Europe fostered a dependency culture.

- Nozick's hostility to the state went beyond that of neo-liberalism. Unlike Hayek, Nozick became closely identified with libertarianism, a creed which argues that the individual should be 'left alone' not just in the economic sphere (as neo-liberals and all New Right conservatives would argue) but in the social and cultural spheres as well (an idea many on the New Right would find at odds with their social conservatism). As a result, libertarianism is tolerant of a liberal, 'permissive society' and takes a relaxed view of issues like abortion, divorce and homosexuality.

- Despite the title of his most famous work, *Anarchy, State and Utopia* (1974), Nozick was not a 'true' anarchist in that he believed in a minarchist state — one that mainly involved outsourcing public services to private companies.

- This minarchist prescription owed much to Nozick's optimistic view of human nature, which seems very different to that of Hobbes and Burke. Indeed, some have suggested that Nozick's philosophy has less in common with conservatism than with strands of anarchism. For example, his claim that 'tax, for the most part, is theft' indicates an upbeat view that individuals have self-ownership — that they are the sole authors of their talents and abilities and should be left alone to realise them, without the intervention of government. However, there are reasons why Nozick is considered a conservative.

- First, although he believed that society predates the state, Nozick's view of human nature was not wholeheartedly positive. He argued that while dishonesty, theft and violence were not the main characteristics of humanity, the preservation of life, liberty and property 'could not be taken for granted' without some formal authority enforcing laws: a vital concession to the legacy of Hobbes.

- Second, the purpose of Nozick's limited state was not simply to facilitate raw individualism and free-market capitalism. For Nozick, the minarchism he prescribed would allow a multitude of self-sufficient communities to emerge alongside the extension of individual freedom. In Nozick's minarchist society, each of these communities would be free to practise its particular moral codes and values, including values which might be seen as socialist or anti-Christian. This arguably represents an updated version of Burke's view that the best form of society is one comprising a variety of 'little platoons'.

Activity

Explain, in no more than 200 words, how Nozick's minarchist society is compatible with traditional conservatism.

New Right conservatism: a contradictory doctrine?

New Right conservatism proved to be one of the most controversial ideologies of the late twentieth century. Yet some of its fiercest critics were themselves conservatives. Some conservative commentators, for example Ian Gilmour in his book *Inside Right* (1977), argued that the New Right marked a 'betrayal' of traditional conservative principles. Other studies of conservatism, such as Anthony Quinton's *The Politics of Imperfection* (1978), contested that because it mixes neo-liberalism and neo-conservatism, the New Right enfolds a series of 'fundamental contradictions'. For example:

- While neo-liberals wish to 'roll back the frontiers of the state' (hence the Thatcher governments' promotion of privatisation), neo-conservatives wish to roll the frontiers of the state forward (hence the Thatcher governments' restrictions upon trade unions and local authorities).
- While neo-liberals wish to advance individual liberty (hence the Thatcher government's commitment to income tax cuts), neo-conservatives are prepared to restrict it (hence the Thatcher government's extension of police stop and search powers).
- While neo-liberals are relaxed about immigration (Rand saw it as a side effect of free markets and individual choice), neo-conservatives are much more wary (hence Thatcher's fear that immigration in the 1960s had 'swamped' traditional communities and Britain's traditional culture).
- While neo-liberals are keen to minimise government spending, in pursuit of what Nozick called the 'minarchist state'), neo-conservatives are prepared to increase it so as to strengthen the nation's profile (hence Thatcher's decision to upgrade the UK's nuclear deterrent, plus her government's ongoing financial commitment to the defence of the Falkland Islands).

Yet despite these tensions, there is reason to argue that New Right conservatism is a blend rather than a mismatch, and that neo-liberalism and neo-conservatism complement, rather than contradict, each other. This can be illustrated in three ways.

First, Irving Kristol famously observed that a New Right conservative was 'a liberal mugged by reality'. By that he meant that neo-liberals, with their optimistic view of human nature, fail to anticipate the tensions arising from a free-market capitalist society, where inequalityß flourishes. So to contain such tensions, they require a strong authoritarian state (of the sort favoured by neo-conservatives) to maintain order and protect private property.

Second, to achieve the low taxation they desire, neo-liberals would have to reduce dramatically levels of state spending on welfare. But for this to be viable, there have to be alternative sources of support for those blamelessly in need. So neo-conservatives provide an answer: the restoration of traditional morality (which neo-conservatism supports) and an end to the 'permissive society' should lead to the restoration of supportive families and altruistic voluntary communities, while reviving a sense of individual responsibility. All this will effectively 'privatise' compassion and social security and thus weaken the state's obligations.

Third, neo-conservatives wish to strengthen the state by reinforcing the police, security services and armed forces. All this requires extra state funding. But neo-liberals claim this will be easier once state spending has been reduced in other areas, following measures like privatisation and welfare reform. So neo-liberalism's wish to 'roll back the frontiers of the state' in economic and welfare policy effectively finances the more statist objectives of neo-conservatism. This arrangement was neatly summarised by the title of Andrew Gamble's study of Thatcherism: *The Free Economy and the Strong State* (1988).

> ### Activity
>
> Highlight, in approximately 200 words, the differences between neo-liberalism and neo-conservatism.

Summary: key themes and key thinkers

	Human nature	The state	Society	The economy
Thomas Hobbes	Cynical: individuals are selfish, driven by a restless and ruthless desire for supremacy and security.	The state arises 'contractually' from individuals who seek order and security. To serve its purpose, the state must be autocratic and awesome.	There can be no 'society' until the creation of a state brings order and authority to human affairs. Life until then is 'nasty, brutish and short'.	Constructive and enduring economic activity is impossible without a state guaranteeing order and security.
Edmund Burke	Sceptical: the 'crooked timber of humanity' is marked by a gap between aspiration and achievement. We may conceive of perfection but we are unable to achieve it.	The state arises organically and should be aristocratic, driven by a hereditary elite, reared to rule in the interests of all.	Society is organic and multi-faceted, comprising a host of small communities and organisations ('little platoons').	Trade should involve 'organic' free markets and laissez-faire capitalism.
Michael Oakeshott	Modest: humanity is at its best when free from grand designs and when focused on the routines of everyday life.	The state should be guided by tradition and practical concerns. Pragmatism, not dogmatism, should be its watchword.	Localised communities are essential to humanity's survival, especially when guided by short-term requirements rather than abstract ideas.	Free markets are volatile and unpredictable, and may require pragmatic moderation by the state.
Ayn Rand	'Objectivist': we are — and ought to be — guided by rational self-interest and the pursuit of self-fulfilment.	The state should confine itself to law, order and national security. Any attempt to promote 'positive liberty', via further state intervention, should be resisted.	In so far as it exists at all, society is atomistic: the mere sum total of its individuals. Any attempt to restrict individuals in the name of society should be challenged.	Free-market capitalism is an expression of 'objectivist' individualism and should not be hindered by the state.
Robert Nozick	Egotistical: individuals are driven by a quest for 'self-ownership', allowing them to realise their full potential.	The minarchist state should merely outsource, renew and reallocate contracts to private companies providing public services.	Society should be geared to individual self-fulfilment. This may lead to a plethora of small, variable communities reflecting their members' diverse tastes and philosophies.	The minarchist state should detach itself from a privatised and deregulated economy, merely arbitrating disputes between private economic organisations.

Tensions within conservatism

- **Human nature:** traditional conservatives, such as Burke and Oakeshott, take a sceptical view of human nature, drawing attention to the gap between aspiration and achievement while warning against the grand, utopian schemes of progressive politicians. For them, the horrors of supposedly idealistic movements — such as the French and Russian Revolutions — are not tragic accidents, they arise from a misreading and overestimation of human potential. By contrast, New Right thinkers take a more optimistic view, emphasising the possibilities of individuals with initiative and liberty. Key thinkers like Nozick and Rand take an especially positive view of what individuals can achieve in the economic sphere, arguing that the key to unlocking human potential lies in fostering a pro-capitalist environment where individual energies are unleashed.

- **Society:** traditional conservatives see society as a collection of small communities (what Burke termed 'little platoons'), overseen by a hierarchical structure in which 'paternalistic' elites exercise their inherited power in the interests of the majority. Such communities are considered organic, in the sense that they emerge in a natural and unplanned way, and place great store upon tradition and continuity. By contrast, New Right conservatives are ambivalent about society's very existence, drawing upon the libertarian belief that society is a mere collection of atomised individuals seeking self-determination. New Right conservatives are more sceptical about paternalistic communities, preferring a society defined by those who have achieved, rather than inherited, power, status and property — in other words, a society that is meritocratic rather than aristocratic.

- **The state:** traditional conservatives like Burke defend a state where political power is wielded by those who are 'born to rule'. As such, traditional conservatives believe the best states have a natural 'ruling class', reared according to the principles of duty and sacrifice, and instilled with a sense of responsibility towards the governed. Traditional conservatives are pragmatic about the extent of the state and are prepared to enlarge it in the name of social stability and 'one nation'. By contrast, New Right conservatives wish to 'roll back the frontiers of the state' (outside areas such as security and defence) so as to advance individual freedom and reverse the dependency culture. New Right conservatives are hostile to the principle of aristocratic rule — they fear that ruling classes have too much stake in the status quo and are therefore reluctant to admit the need for radical change by New Right governments.

- **Economy:** traditional conservatives, while keen to defend an economy based on private ownership, are sceptical about free-market capitalism, fearful that its dynamic effects exacerbate inequality, threaten 'one nation' and fuel support for socialism. As capitalism becomes more globalised, traditional conservatives also fear that market forces promote a more cosmopolitan society that erodes national identity and national culture. As a result, traditional conservatives have been prepared to countenance state intervention via Keynesian economics, higher taxation and high public spending on state welfare. By contrast, New Right conservatives like Nozick zealously advocate free-market economies where state functions are privatised and deregulated, and where levels of taxation and state spending are significantly reduced.

Debate 4

Can conservatism be reconciled with socialism?*

Yes

- Traditional conservatives and socialists play down the importance of individualism.
- Traditional conservatives and socialists stress the importance of communities.
- Traditional conservatives and socialists stress the importance of unity within communities.
- Traditional conservatives and socialists see capitalism as potentially problematic.
- Traditional conservatives and socialists are sceptical of meritocracy, highlighting 'fate' and 'chance'.

No

- Conservatives see inequality as natural, socialists see it as unacceptable.
- Conservatives are sceptical of progress, socialists see it as essential.
- Conservatives defend private property, fundamentalist socialists favour common ownership.
- Conservatives reject revolution, some fundamentalist socialists see it as desirable and inevitable.
- Traditional conservatives advocate noblesse oblige, socialists think paternalism is patronising.

This debate is best addressed after reading both this chapter and Chapter 3. A similar debate about conservatism and liberalism is to be found in Chapter 1.

Conclusion: conservatism today

There is a case for saying that an ideology preaching order, stability, continuity and incremental change will always have some appeal. However, such an ideology is likely to have particular appeal during an era of economic, social and cultural volatility. For this reason, it could be contested that traditional conservative values are more resonant than ever as the twenty-first century progresses.

One illustration of this, in most of the developed states around the world, has been a shift in the focus of the state's responsibilities. During the late twentieth century, it may have seemed that the state's primary concern was the advancement of individual freedom. In the UK, for example, the first New Labour government (1997–2001) devoted much of its energies to devolving political power, establishing a Freedom of Information Act, and passing various laws that illegalised discrimination against individuals from minority backgrounds.

By the second decade of the twenty-first century, however, the growth of terrorism and the problems of mass migration had prompted a change of focus, with the state now giving precedence to order, safety and security. In short, the state's priorities, in both the UK and elsewhere, seemed to have regained an authoritarian character which traditional conservative thinkers — notably Hobbes — would readily understand and wholeheartedly applaud.

Another conservative trend in politics after 2010 was the growing interest in the concept of society and community. According to contemporary conservative theorists, such as Phillip Blond and Jesse Norman, this trend arose largely from a sense that liberal individualism spawned selfish, narcissistic cultures, devoid of collective identity or purpose. Of course, such trends may equally vindicate the case for socialism, given its timeless stress on solidarity and fraternity (see Chapter 3). Sadly for socialists, however, the renewed interest in society was not always accompanied by a resurgent faith in state intervention, akin to that which existed just after the Second World War.

As a result, society and collectivism seemed to become decoupled within political debate. This development helped revive one of the key themes associated with Burke's conservatism — namely, a 'little platoons' society, comprising a vast assortment of local and voluntary communities. In the UK, Conservative prime minister David Cameron tried to advance this Burkean idea with his campaign for a 'big society'. Indeed, Cameron's defence of 'voluntarism', and his claim that 'there is such a thing as society...it's just not the same thing as the state', was a vivid illustration of how traditional conservatism can be both relevant to modern politics and distinct from both liberalism and socialism. In short, the 'big society' idea, and the continued attempts to foster 'a bigger society and a smaller state', provided evidence of a lingering conservative mentality in political life.

Yet it was another feature of that lingering mentality that led to the end of Cameron's political career. In the UK, the diminishing appeal of European, supranational authority (about which British conservatives have never enthused) was confirmed in 2016 by the electorate's decision to withdraw from the European Union. The reasons for this decision remain contentious. But it was hard to deny a yearning among voters for a greater sense of national identity and a

David Cameron (PM 2010–16): a neo-Burkean conservative?

form of government that was national, not continental, in character — yearnings which have been central to British conservatism for almost two centuries. Political trends elsewhere, in both Europe and the USA, show a similar wish to avert the sort of change that promotes cosmopolitan individualism, and the same preference for a different form of change, one that is more attuned to history, tradition and nationhood.

Even though the UK's Conservative Party has tried to reflect some of these changes — latterly by repudiating European supranationalism in order to reclaim national sovereignty and identity — we should remember two points made at the start of this chapter: Conservatism and conservatism are not indivisible (most Conservative MPs backed membership of the EU, for example), while conservatism in the UK is not confined to the Conservative Party.

Many of those concerned with the direction of the modern Labour Party, for instance (notably philosophers like Maurice Glasman), have argued for a new brand of politics dubbed 'Blue Labour', linking left-wing themes like equality and social justice to conservative themes such as 'family, faith and flag'. Similarly, in the USA, President Donald Trump (though fundamentally radical and iconoclastic rather than conservative) effectively exploited a number of themes that echoed the traditional conservative critique of liberalism — notably a wish to protect the US economy by curbing free markets, a desire to prioritise the national interest rather than global capitalism and individual rights, and a conviction that safety and security, rather than individual liberty, were the state's prime responsibilities.

Clearly, conservatism is a persistent and adaptable ideology, rooted in the importance of custom, habit, community and kinship. Change may be constant and inevitable, yet the desire to change in a certain way — one that is respectful, not contemptuous, of tradition and communal identity — will always be present and shows no sign of decaying. Maybe that was the real lesson of the UK's 2016 referendum: a Conservative prime minister was punished, perhaps, for not being sufficiently conservative in an increasingly conservative era.

Brexit: was the UK's 2016 referendum a 'conservative moment'?

Yes

- The UK's participation in a supranational political system was at odds with the UK's traditions.
- The decision to leave the EU was an attempt to restore national self-governance.
- The ability to take back control of immigration would help restore national identity.
- The EU was a contrived system of government, with normative principles (i.e. eventual political union within Europe), at odds with conservatism's preference for organic systems of government.
- The EU represented 'big government' and continental dirigisme, at odds with the 'leaner and fitter' state advocated by the New Right.

No

- Leaving the EU was a 'leap in the dark' — a radical change with highly uncertain consequences.
- Rejecting David Cameron's 'renegotiated membership' offer was a rejection of the case for gradual, incremental change.
- Leaving the EU was a rejection of an arrangement which, though imperfect, had worked for decades (the UK's 43-year membership was proof that its EU partnership had not been wholly ineffective).
- Leaving the EU was tied to a faith in global, laissez-faire capitalism — an historically liberal form of economics that defied traditional conservative scepticism.
- Brexit threatened 'one nation' by allegedly encouraging racism and xenophobia.

Further reading

Blond, P. (2010) *Red Tory*, Faber and Faber.

Grant, M. (2013) 'Conservatism — is it an ideology?', *Politics Review*, 23,1.

Heywood, A. (2015) 'Conservatism — a defence of the privileged and prosperous?', *Politics Review*, 25,1.

Honderich, T. (2005) *Conservatism*, Pluto Press.

Scruton, R. (2001) *The Meaning of Conservatism*, Macmillan.

Scruton, R. (2014) *How to Be a Conservative*, Bloomsbury Continuum.

Exam-style questions

Short questions

The following questions are similar to those in examinations set by AQA. Each carries 9 marks.

1 Explain and analyse how conservatives have justified private property.

2 Explain and analyse the grounds on which conservatives have supported tradition.

Essay questions

The following questions are similar to those in examinations set by Edexcel (Pearson) and AQA.

Edexcel (24 marks) or AQA (25 marks):

1 To what extent is conservatism a philosophy of imperfection? You must use appropriate thinkers you have studied to support your answer.

2 To what extent is conservatism a coherent ideology? You must use appropriate thinkers you have studied to support your answer.

AQA only (25 marks):

3 'The New Right has little in common with traditional conservatism.' Analyse and evaluate with reference to the thinkers you have studied.

4 'Less an ideology than a state of mind.' Analyse and evaluate this view of conservatism with reference to the thinkers you have studied.

Chapter 3

Socialism

Learning outcomes

This chapter will enable students to:
- understand the core values of socialism
- understand how socialism has evolved since the nineteenth century
- understand the various strands of socialism — from the works of Karl Marx to the influences upon Tony Blair
- understand the continuing relevance of socialism today

Introduction

Like liberalism, socialism is an ambiguous ideology, embracing followers with a range of competing views. Indeed, even the most basic knowledge of political history would indicate that socialism attracts an astonishing variety of champions: Karl Marx, Gordon Brown, Joseph Stalin, Harold Wilson, Chairman Mao, François Hollande, Fidel Castro, John Prescott, Che Guevara, Jeremy Corbyn, Pol Pot...these are just some of the people who have described themselves as 'socialist'. The issue of what, if anything, unites such an eclectic group will be an important focus of this chapter.

Just as socialism has some contradictory followers, it has also been linked to contradictory outcomes. On the one hand, it has been tied to what many see as the finest aspects of the human condition, such as fraternity, comradeship, altruism, compassion and a dedication to the interests of the underdog. On the other hand (in places like Russia, eastern Europe, China and Cambodia), 'socialist' reform has led to oppression, genocide and some of the most brutal societies ever witnessed. Far from being a glorious cause on behalf of the underdog, socialism in many parts of the world has become a by-word for tyranny and misery.

Of course, all political ideologies — especially the three 'core' ideologies covered in this book — contain contradictions and ambiguities. Yet those of socialism are particularly stark and controversial. This is why it is especially important for students of politics to understand the essence of socialism and the various ways it has been applied.

The origins of socialism

Like liberalism, socialism is an ideology that grew out of the Enlightenment (see Chapter 1). Indeed, socialism and liberalism have much in common. Both:

- take an optimistic view of human nature
- exalt reason over faith and superstition
- are 'progressive' — they believe in the possibility of reform and are always ready to challenge the status quo
- share a desire to liberate human beings from oppression
- believe in 'foundational' equality — men and women are born equal and deserve equal opportunities in life
- reject the 'traditional' state (defined by monarchical absolutism and the divine right of rulers)
- reject anarchism — in other words, both believe a certain type of state can secure significant progress in terms of freedom and foundational equality.

You will recall from Chapter 1, however, that one of liberalism's core features was support for private property, which liberals consider a natural right. Yet as early as the seventeenth century, there were those who were unsure about whether the principles of the Enlightenment could be reconciled to private ownership. During the English Civil War (1649–60), for example, one radical group of anti-monarchists, the Levellers, argued that God had given the land to all mankind, yet some had exercised greed so as to acquire that land for themselves.

Such ideas were developed by a small number of radical theorists during the eighteenth century. Jean-Jacques Rousseau, in his *Discourse on the Origin of Inequality* (1755), suggested that 'many crimes, wars and murders...many horrors and misfortunes' arose from the concept of private ownership, while during the 1789 French Revolution François-Noel Babeuf (1760–97) led a 'conspiracy of the equals', demanding the abolition of private property.

It was during the early nineteenth century that the term 'socialism' was first applied. The so-called **utopian socialists**, such as Charles Fourier (1772–1837) and Robert Owen (1771–1858), offered a radical response to the emerging problems of capitalism and industry. Fourier duly advocated independent communities based on communal ownership and production, involving the equal distribution of resources and a culture marked by tolerance and permissiveness. Owen, meanwhile, set up model 'cooperative' communities in Scotland and America, designed to promote shared ownership, shared responsibility and altruism.

Yet it was only during the mid-nineteenth century, when the pace of industrialisation began to quicken dramatically, that socialist ideas began to be taken seriously. For many of those otherwise sympathetic to liberal principles, liberalism now offered an inadequate response to the profound changes wrought by the industrial revolution. It was felt that liberalism was in denial about the effects of urban life and blinkered to the fact that in the new industrial areas there was little scope for individual autonomy and individual freedom. As a later socialist thinker, Eric Hobsbawm, wrote (in respect of conditions in mid-nineteenth-century England):

> 'For an individual living in a slum...paying rent to a rapacious landlord, while working in a factory for whatever wages his employer deigned to pay him, any notion of freedom or independence seemed utterly distant.' (*The Age of Capital, 1848–1875*, 1975)

As a result, the early socialists argued for a new approach, one that would make Enlightenment principles (such as self-determination) more achievable in an industrialised society — one where employment was much less individualistic and where individuals seemed to have much less autonomy in their everyday lives.

Key term

Utopian socialism Linked to philanthropists like Robert Owen, this refers to the earliest form of socialism, one based on a vision of the perfect human existence. For Karl Marx, however, its 'utopian' character stemmed from the absence of any clear method for bringing about such 'socialism'.

Activity

Explain, in approximately 200 words, how industrialisation led to socialist ideas.

The core ideas of socialism

As explained earlier, there is considerable overlap between socialism and liberalism. As a result, any explanation of socialism's core themes should take account of the core themes it shares with liberalism (see above). This section of the chapter, however, will largely examine the core themes that distinguish socialism from liberalism — although, as we shall see, there is also an overlap between the core themes of socialism and those of certain strands of anarchism.

Human nature

Like liberalism, socialists have an upbeat, optimistic view of human nature, which helps explain why both liberalism and socialism are seen as 'progressive' ideologies. Yet liberals and socialists differ as to *why* they are optimistic.

Whereas most liberals think individuals are naturally self-reliant and self-sufficient, socialists believe that individuals are naturally cooperative, generous and altruistic. So instead of forever seeking autonomy, independence and supremacy, as liberals claim, human beings (according to socialists) naturally seek solidarity, fraternity and comradeship, reflecting the claim of poet John Donne (1571–1631) that 'no man is an island'.

Socialism concedes, however, that mankind's true nature has been diluted by time and circumstance. So whereas liberalism takes an optimistic view of human nature as it is, socialists are more optimistic about how it could be. This is because socialism, unlike liberalism, sees human nature as malleable, or 'plastic', rather than permanently fixed at birth. Consequently, socialists believe that human nature can be adjusted, thus ensuring that men and women fulfil their true, fraternal potential while contributing to a more cooperative community.

The key issue, of course, is what determines human nature? And by what means can human nature be improved and mankind's potential realised?

Society

According to socialism, any understanding of human nature requires a clear understanding of society. Much more than liberalism, socialism — by definition — focuses upon an individual's social environment: in other words, the individual's society. Whereas liberals tend to see society as the sum of autonomous individuals, socialists see things the other way round — for socialists, individuals are the product of the society into which they were born.

> **Key term**
>
> **Fraternity and cooperation**
> Fraternity denotes socialism's belief that the relationship between human beings should be marked by generosity, warmth and comradeship; that we should regard our fellow humans as 'siblings' rather than opponents, and that cooperation and solidarity, rather than competition and division, should be the norm in human affairs.

Socialists thus see society as an independent construct, formed by impersonal forces (see below) and thereafter shaping the individuals inside it. Key thinkers like **Karl Marx** (1818–83) and **Friedrich Engels** (1820–95) thought these forces were primarily economic, with the 'means of production' — that is, the way a society's resources are determined and distributed — having a crucial impact upon the nature of society and, by implication, human behaviour (see 'Key thinker 1' box).

Socialists are therefore sceptical of the classical liberal claim that individuals can be masters of their own destiny — this will always depend, they claim, on the nature of society. Indeed, society is often cited as the main reason for individuals not fulfilling their potential. Yet for socialists, this is no cause for despair. In keeping with their faith in human potential, socialists argue that if only society can be improved, there will be a corresponding improvement to the prospects of its individuals.

So how can society be improved from a socialist point of view? Socialists argue that in order to prescribe a better society in future, we must first diagnose the society we have today. It is at this point that we see the importance to socialism of social class.

For socialists, the major consequence of the industrial revolution was the emergence of distinct social groupings — classes — based principally upon employment and an individual's source of income. According to socialism, these classes are central to an individual's fate. Rejecting the liberal view — that men and women are autonomous creatures, free to carve out their own identities and destinies — socialists argue that an individual's status, priorities and prospects are shaped by the social class he or she is born into. And as key socialist thinkers like Marx and Engels explained, an individual's social class is determined by their status within society's economy.

Marx and Engels — along with more modern socialist thinkers such as **Anthony Crosland** (1918–77) (see 'Key thinker 4' box): also noted that society's classes tend to be profoundly unequal in terms of power and influence: those in the working class, for example, are seen to earn less and therefore exercise less influence within their society. Put another way, individuals in some sections of society will have more opportunities to exploit their potential than individuals in other sections of society. This in turn leads to socialism's unique perspective on the issue of equality.

You may recall from Chapter 1 that one of liberalism's core themes was foundational equality — or the notion that all men are born equal and are of equal value. This, in turn, relates to liberalism's belief in formal equality, equality of opportunity and therefore justice: in short, the state should treat everyone equally so as to ensure everyone has a level chance to fulfil their potential. Yet socialism, mindful of class differences, insists that such forms of equality are meaningless without another form of equality, namely greater equality of outcome within society — by which socialists mean a greater similarity between people's material resources and material circumstances. It is this additional emphasis, upon what socialists see as social justice, that explains why socialism and equality are more indivisible than liberalism and equality. It also explains why socialism — much more than liberalism — is regarded as an egalitarian doctrine.

In essence, socialists contest that to have equality of opportunity there must first be greater equality of outcome in society. Given that socialism stresses the importance of social class, this means that socialists seek a narrowing of the gap between society's poorer and richer classes. In justifying this position, socialists argue that irrespective of character, ability and intelligence, an individual born into a lower/working/blue collar-class background will have fewer opportunities than a similar individual born into a higher-class background.

As a result, socialists argue that a society which allows inequality of outcome in one generation will be a society that produces inequality of opportunity in the next generation. Socialists therefore argue that until we have a society where there is greater equality of outcome, the noble objectives of liberalism and the Enlightenment — such as self-determination and foundational equality — will never be realised. Unlike both modern liberals, such as John Rawls, and paternalistic conservatives, such as Disraeli, socialists think it is insufficient just to improve the condition of society's poorest — socialists claim that unless there is a narrowing of the gap between social classes, society will continue to lack fraternity, cooperation and solidarity, and instead will foster greed, envy, resentment and division.

Of course, the key question for socialism then becomes: how is greater equality of outcome to be brought about? This leads us to socialism's economic perspectives.

Key term

Social justice For socialists, legal and formal justice (as propounded by liberalism) is not enough to guarantee equality of opportunity. These things must be accompanied by social justice — involving, for example, health care and education accessible to all, or a minimum wage for employees. As such, the case for social justice usually leads to the case for collectivism (see below).

Activity

Explain, in approximately 200 words, the importance of social class to socialism.

The economy

As indicated in the section on 'Society', socialists have always argued that equality of opportunity was precluded by the inequalities existing between social classes. Furthermore, key socialist ers, from Marx and Engels onwards, have argued that social class is determined by the economic system underpinning society. So it has been impossible for socialists to address the fundamental issue of inequality within society without addressing the structure of the economy.

Socialists have always recognised that an economic system based upon private property and capitalism — as opposed to **common ownership** — can be hugely problematic. As explained in this chapter's section on 'Human nature', socialists believe that the 'natural' condition of mankind is one of cooperation and fraternity. Yet these attributes are said to be seriously threatened by both private property and **capitalism**, which are said to encourage competitiveness, ruthless egotism and the callous pursuit of self-interest. Free-market capitalism also generates huge inequalities of outcome, which for socialists, of course, are incompatible with equality of opportunity, self-determination and social justice.

Socialism seeks to rectify the problems caused by capitalism by championing an economy that provides for greater workers' control in employment, and a significant redistribution of wealth and resources within the economy generally. Indeed, socialism is routinely described by its proponents as a 'redistributionist' doctrine, practising what Tony Benn (1925–2014) wryly described as 'the politics of Robin Hood — taking from the rich and then giving to the poor'. For socialists, the 'redistributionist' economy will usually involve two broad principles.

First, there will be an emphatic rejection of the laissez-faire capitalism advocated by classical and neo-liberalism, whereby market forces are given free rein by a state that is disengaged and minimalist in relation to a society's economy. According to socialism, an economy where there is low taxation and little state interference will be one where unfairness and social injustice become exacerbated.

Political ideas for A-level

Key terms

Common ownership This represents an alternative to both private property and a capitalist economy, and a method of ownership seen (by many socialists) as conducive to equality and fraternity. It is synonymous with state ownership and public ownership.

Capitalism Sometimes referred to as economic liberalism, capitalism is an economic system based on private property, private enterprise and competition between individuals and individual organisations. Its tendency to produce unequal outcomes is of concern to most socialists.

Activity

Explain, in approximately 200 words, why many socialists treat private property with suspicion.

Second, and arising from the rejection of laissez-faire, socialists demand greater collectivism. This perspective on the economy claims to focus on the needs of society as a whole rather than on the abilities of a few enterprising individuals, as with economic liberalism. For socialists, economic collectivism can take various forms, for example:

■ Progressive taxation, whereby the state extracts wealth from its citizens but on a 'sliding scale', so that the richer classes contribute much more than the poorer classes.

■ Progressive public spending, whereby the state uses the economic resources it has acquired (via taxation) in a way that enhances the less fortunate elements of society — for example, via state benefits to the unemployed or elderly.

■ Extensive public services, whereby the state uses its yield from taxation to guarantee key public services, such as health care and education. Socialists claim that if left entirely to private enterprise, such services might prove inaccessible to less advantaged sections of society.

■ Extensive state regulation of capitalism, exemplified by various state regulations designed to prevent exploitation by the economy's richer and more powerful elements. A legal minimum wage for employees, equal pay legislation, health and safety directives, and guarantees of maternity leave are examples of such regulation that socialism would applaud.

■ State/common ownership, recommended when private enterprise is seen to fail parts (or all) of the economy, with grievous consequences for society and its more vulnerable citizens. The original Clause IV of the UK Labour Party's constitution — initially championed by socialists like **Beatrice Webb** (1858–1943) (see 'Key thinker 3' box) — was a controversial expression of this belief in a more collectivist economy, while the post-war nationalisation of industries such as coal, iron and steel is an example of it being given effect.

As well as its primary aim, of redistributing a society's wealth and resources, socialism believes that economic collectivism has two other benefits. First, progressive taxation, increased public spending, extensive public services and sometimes public ownership are seen as expressions of a more fraternal, more cooperative society with greater social justice. Second, such collectivist policies are thought to make the economy more efficient. As Marx and Engels were the first to point out, capitalism and market forces are inherently volatile and unpredictable — causing, for instance, periodic mass unemployment. A more collectivist economy, it is argued, will be more stable and manageable, and therefore more likely to provide the material resources society needs.

Activity

Explain, in approximately 100 words, why socialists have favoured collectivism.

The state

It needs to be emphasised that the core socialist values discussed so far — such as equality, fraternity, even collectivism — are not exclusive to socialists: they are also shared by certain anarchists, notably 'collectivist anarchists' like Peter Kropotkin (1842–1921) and Mikhail Bakunin (1814–76). What makes socialism distinctive from collectivist anarchism is that it also advocates a strong state.

Socialists believe that without a strong state, it will be impossible to bring about a fairer and more equal society. In the short to medium term at least, it would certainly be difficult to bring about a redistribution of wealth and greater social justice without a state that was expansive and dirigiste (actively seeking to direct a society's economy).

Some socialists (such as Marxists and orthodox communists — see below) argue that, eventually, the state will 'wither away' — a blissful moment in human evolution, which Marx described as 'the end of history'. However, all socialists agree that for the foreseeable future, a strong state is essential. They also agree it must be a certain type of state, and certainly not the sort that preceded the Enlightenment.

Socialism therefore rejects the monarchical state (one based on the absolute authority of one person), it rejects the theocratic state (one based on religious principles), and it rejects the aristocratic state (one based on a hereditary ruling class). Instead, socialists advocate a state where political power, as well as economic power, has supposedly been redistributed and where decision making reflects the principle of equality and an empowerment of 'the people'. In short, the socialist state will usually pay lip service, at least, to the principle of democracy.

Socialists also agree that the state must be an extensive one; socialists will therefore contest that any reduction of state power is likely to produce increased social and economic inequality. Nevertheless, among socialists, there are still significant differences about the structure of the ideal state, the extent of its activities and how it emerges. These differences, indeed, help explain why socialism has such a large number of variants and subdivisions, some of which will now be examined.

Different types of socialism

Fundamentalist socialism
This represents the earliest form of socialism, which holds that socialist values are fundamentally incompatible with capitalism. Originally asserted by Karl Marx and Friedrich Engels ('classical Marxism'), this form of socialism has since been associated with various strands of socialism such as orthodox communism, neo-Marxism, Euro-communism and democratic socialism.

Marxism and communism
Seen by Marx as the ultimate stage of human development, communism represents (for communists) the perfect society, based on communal ownership, communal living and the principle of 'each according to his needs'. Marxism reflects this prediction and also involves an 'episodic' view of history, a rigorous critique of capitalism and a justification for revolutionary politics.

As explained at the beginning of the chapter, socialism is an ambiguous ideology. So it has produced a wide variety of views about how the core socialist themes (as outlined above) can be achieved. It is possible, however, to divide these views into two broad categories: fundamentalist socialism and revisionist socialism. Each of these categories is defined by the answer to a basic question: are the core themes of socialism compatible with private property and a capitalist economy?

Those socialists who argue that socialism is fundamentally at odds with private ownership and capitalism are described as fundamentalist socialists. Alternatively, those who believe that socialism can be achieved alongside private property, and that socialism and capitalism can co-exist, are usually labelled revisionist socialists.

Fundamentalist socialism

All fundamentalist socialists believe that capitalism, at some stage, must be abolished. However, there are significant differences about how capitalism should be abolished. Does it necessitate revolutionary change, which quickly destroys both the capitalist system and the state that supports it? Or can the elimination of socialism be done gradually, via evolutionary change, and within the confines of the existing state?

This section of the chapter, which examines five strands of fundamentalist socialism, ascertains — among other things — where each strand stands on the issue of 'revolution or evolution?'.

Classical Marxism

Classical Marxism refers to the writings of Karl Marx and his collaborator Friedrich Engels. Although it was not the earliest form of socialism, it was certainly the first form to set out its analysis in detail. Indeed, the term 'utopian socialism', used to describe previous socialist thinkers such as Owen and Fourier, was actually coined by Marx to denote the vagueness and superficiality of their views.

The definitive authors of fundamentalist socialism, Marx and Engels made it plain that capitalism must disappear before socialism — and then communism — could be established. Along with Engels, Marx contested that capitalism promoted 'exploitation', 'alienation' and the 'oppression' of one class by another and was therefore wholly at odds with key socialist principles such as fraternity, solidarity and equality.

Dialectic Associated with the philosopher Hegel, this refers to the clash of ideas and perceptions that will inevitably take place within each 'stage' of history and which eventually leads to the disappearance of existing society.

Historical materialism This refers to the view of Marx and Engels that each 'stage' of history was defined by a clash of economic ideas, relating to how society's resources should be produced and distributed.

Class consciousness According to Marx and Engels, this was a by-product of capitalism that would be especially pronounced among the downtrodden working class, or proletariat. It would eventually be the engine of revolution and capitalism's destruction.

Furthermore, drawing upon the philosophy of Friedrich Hegel (1770–1831), Marx and Engels argued that history was a series of stages, moving towards an inevitable and final destination ('historicism'). Within each historical 'stage' there was — eventually — an intellectual clash, which Hegel had described as **dialectic**. This dialectic occurred when the 'official' narrative about a society's aims and character — as propounded by its ruling classes — no longer corresponded to the perceptions of the majority, who then experienced what Hegel described as 'alienation'. For Hegel, this clash would eventually spawn a new society, a new orthodox mentality and a new stage of history that would survive until the next wave of alienation.

Marx and Engels, however, made a crucial adjustment to Hegel's historicism. For them, the prevailing mentality would always be defined by economics and the way a society's resources were generated and dispersed ('the mode of production'). For them, history was thus a series of economic stages (see Box 3.1), a process they termed **historical materialism**.

For Marx and Engels, the dialectic was not so much a clash of ideas as a clash of economic interests — a process they termed 'dialectical materialism'. Within the Marx–Engels dialectic, one particular class would be economically dominant, while others would be exploited for economic purposes. It was this logic that led Marx and Engels to believe that capitalism was 'historically doomed', given the **class consciousness** it would produce among an economically exploited and therefore 'alienated' workforce (or proletariat).

Box 3.1

Historical materialism and dialectical change (according to Marx and Engels)

1 Primitive societies with no economic organisation.
2 Slave-based societies — slaves are the main mode of production.
3 Feudal societies — land owned by the monarch is leased to lords, tenants and eventually serfs.
4 Emergence of capitalism.
5 Emergence of proletariat and class consciousness.
6 Revolution and destruction of capitalism.
7 Socialism (dictatorship of the proletariat).
8 Withering away of the socialist state.
9 Communism.
10 'End of history'.

Activity

Explain, in approximately 100 words, why Marx believed communism to be 'the end of history'.

The Marx–Engels philosophy was also heavily shaped by a belief in revolution. They argued that when capitalism became unsustainable (on account of its tendency to produce an exploited and 'alienated' workforce that was increasingly class conscious), it was necessary to 'smash' capitalism via revolutionary violence and replace it with an alternative economy and society. For Marx and Engels, such action could not be accomplished peacefully within existing liberal political systems, such as those present in the UK or the USA. According to Marx and Engels, these states were mere 'servants' of the very economic system that socialism must destroy. In short, Marx and Engels emphatically rejected evolutionary or reformist socialism, which they considered an inherent contradiction.

As a result, they insisted that a new economy and a new state, forged by revolution, were essential if socialist values were to be secured. The new state they commended, the 'dictatorship of the proletariat', would supposedly obliterate all traces of liberal-capitalist values and pave the way for a stateless communist society based on common ownership, one that would be so flawless that it would represent the peak of human achievement: what Marx and Engels termed 'the end of history'.

Marxism–Leninism (orthodox communism)

No history of socialism would be complete without reference to Vladimir Ilyich Lenin (1874–1924). Leader of Russia's Bolshevik party prior to the Russian Revolution of 1917, Lenin was a key figure during the revolution itself and the de facto leader of the new, 'socialist' state that emerged in its wake. Yet, in addition to being a major figure in Russian political history, Lenin made a pivotal contribution to the development of revolutionary socialism.

Prior to the revolution, Lenin had accorded great respect to the ideas of Marx. Yet he still sought to refine Marx's prescriptions for how communism should arise. In particular, Lenin was concerned by Marx's insistence that revolution, and a dictatorship of the proletariat, could occur only in societies where capitalism and the proletariat were well developed — a view vigorously disputed not just by Lenin but by German-based socialists such as **Rosa Luxemburg** (1871–1919) (see 'Key thinker 2' box). For both Lenin and Luxemburg, the unacceptable implication was that less developed countries would have to endure many more decades of oppressive rule, plus all the horrors of a developing capitalist economy, before the salvation of socialism could arrive.

Karl Marx (1818–83) and Friedrich Engels (1820–95)

No socialist thinker has had more impact upon both socialism and world history than Karl Marx. Aided by his lifelong collaborator Friedrich Engels, Marx propounded a series of revolutionary ideas that would have a seismic effect on political debate. Indeed, works like *The Communist Manifesto* (1848) and *Das Kapital* (1867) remain essential reading for any serious student of political science.

- Marx and Engels were the first socialist thinkers to offer a fulsome analysis of how humans were social and economic beings. Specifically, they argued that human nature had been contaminated by the prevailing economic system — capitalism — which encouraged selfishness, ruthlessness and greed. They argued further that capitalism had instilled in mankind a 'false consciousness' far removed from mankind's original nature — one that had been cooperative, selfless and fraternal. The task, they argued, was to create a new, non-capitalist economic system that would revive such noble characteristics.
- Marx and Engels were the first socialist thinkers to explain the centrality of social class. They argued that capitalism created two conflicted economic classes: the bourgeoisie (in effect, the ruling class, which owned and managed the economy) and the proletariat (in effect, the ruling class, which sold its labour to the bourgeoisie in return for wages). However, they also argued that class differences were far from harmonious: they involved harsh inequalities of wealth and power, and the exploitation of the proletariat. For this reason, capitalist societies were also unstable and would eventually be overthrown by an 'historically inevitable' proletarian revolution.
- Rejecting the liberal view that capitalism promotes prosperity and individual liberty for all, Marx and Engels explained how capitalism usually sought to be competitive by creating 'surplus value', whereas employers paid employees minimum wages, so as to allow most profits to be used for refining the means of production. Yet surplus value would also, they asserted, implant in capitalism 'the seeds of its own destruction' by nurturing resentful class consciousness among workers, who would eventually overthrow capitalism via revolution.
- Marx and Engels were also the first socialist thinkers to challenge the liberal notion that the state was politically neutral. Instead, they argued that the state would always serve the interests of whichever class controlled the economy. Consequently, the liberal state was 'merely a committee' for the ruling capitalist class and could therefore never provide an evolutionary road to socialism. This argument would inspire later fundamentalist socialists, such as Ralph Miliband (1924–94) and Tariq Ali (1943–), who ridiculed the 'parliamentary socialism' championed by organisations like the Labour Party.
- Marx and Engels thus became the first socialists to explain why revolution was not just inevitable but essential, and to describe what should happen once revolution had occurred. They asserted that, in the wake of revolution, an entirely new state should arise that would govern in the interests of the new, economically dominant class — one they called the dictatorship of the proletariat. Once this alternative state had cemented socialist values, it would 'wither away' and be replaced by communism: a stateless society involving common ownership and the principle of 'from each according to his ability to each according to his needs'. Such a scenario has never been realised, yet Marx and Engels' idea of a dictatorship of the proletariat proved hugely significant, justifying oppressive political systems in post-revolutionary societies such as the Soviet Union and China.

Lenin's vision, therefore, was accelerated revolutionary socialism — designed to ensure that socialism, and ultimately communism, could pre-empt the full development of capitalism. In his key work, *What Is to Be Done?* (1902), Lenin thus argued that revolution in pre-industrial countries should be the cause and not (as Marx argued) the effect of socialist ideas developing. Similarly, Lenin believed that revolution in early capitalist societies would prevent 'the masses' from developing any sympathy for capitalist values (a situation Leninists refer to as 'false consciousness'), which would then be a further obstacle to socialism.

Rosa Luxemburg: Marxist critic of Lenin

Luxemburg endorsed Lenin's argument, but only so far as economically under-developed societies were concerned. Although she admired Lenin's impatience for socialism, Luxemburg was concerned that Lenin's ideas could make revolutionary socialism irrelevant to the already industrialised masses in countries like Germany. Yet it was in respect of how the revolution should arise, and how it should be conducted, that led to the most serious dispute between followers of Lenin and supporters of Luxemburg.

To understand this dispute, it should be recalled that Lenin stressed the importance of a revolutionary elite — or

Key term

Democratic centralism
This was a term and a process developed by Lenin. However, it was not 'democratic' in the way that liberals or democratic socialists (see later) would understand. There would be only one party and only within that party would there be open discussion. Once the party had reached its decision, Lenin argued that the decision would embody the will of the people, making any further debate at best unnecessary and at worst disrespectful of the revolution. This doctrine was later used to justify severe repression in orthodox communist countries such as Russia and China.

vanguard — which would perform four vital tasks. First, it would plot and plan the overthrow of the existing regime (in Lenin's case, Tsarist Russia). Second, it would incite and organise the revolution. Third, prior to and during the revolution, it would start educating the masses into the basic virtues of socialism. Fourth, once the old regime had been toppled, the vanguard would form a new organisation: the Communist Party. This new party would embody Marx's dictatorship of the proletariat and direct all aspects of the new, post-revolutionary society — a doctrine that became known as **democratic centralism**.

Although some of Lenin's ideas, particularly about the dictatorship of the proletariat, were disputed by socialists like Luxemburg, they were aggressively upheld by a series of more important socialist leaders. Joseph Stalin (1879–1953) directed the Soviet Union in the 30 years after Lenin's death and constructed one of the most brutal, totalitarian regimes ever recorded, 'collectivising' agriculture, instituting a Five Year Plan for industrial development, and either relocating or murdering a whole peasant class in the process.

Stalin rejected the 'permanent revolution' theory of his fellow Bolshevik and arch rival Leon Trotsky (1879–1940), who had argued that any new socialist state could only entrench itself by encouraging similar revolutions in neighbouring capitalist countries. Instead, Stalin promoted the idea of 'socialism in one country', whereby the Soviet Union would effectively isolate itself from the outside world and thereafter promote a form of 'socialist nationalism' (a concept Luxemburg abhorred).

Activity

Explain, in no more than 200 words, how Luxemburg's revolutionary socialism differed from that of Marx, Lenin and Stalin.

Mao Tse-tung adapted Marxist-Leninism to peasant society

Having led the Chinese Revolution of 1949, after a prolonged civil war, Mao Tse-tung (1893–1976) applied similar ruthless methods during the first three decades of China's new 'socialist' state. But there were important differences between the Stalinist and Maoist methods. Instead of rejecting Trotsky's notion of a 'permanent revolution', Mao refined it into the notion of an ongoing 'cultural revolution' — one that would destroy the old mode of thinking, in much the same way that the initial revolution would reject the old (capitalist) mode of production.

Conducted mainly between 1966 and 1969, Mao's 'cultural revolution' became a campaign of persecution against any aspect of traditional Chinese culture (such as 'ancestor worship') that was thought to legitimise inequality and 'anti-socialist' values. Religion, deference to the elderly and the subordination of women were duly, and cruelly, discouraged. As with Stalin's Russia, millions died or disappeared in the process.

Despite its notoriety, the Marxist–Leninist method continued to be adopted and practised in the second half of the twentieth century, in countries nowhere near the level of economic development Marx had deemed necessary for revolution. During the 1950s, revolutionary societies in Cuba (under Fidel Castro), North Korea and North Vietnam all invoked the idea of vanguard communist parties, governing on the basis of democratic centralism.

As a result of its widespread application, Marxism–Leninism may now be referred to as 'orthodox communism'. Yet within these states, there has been little evidence of Marx's ultimate objective — communism — being even pursued, let alone attained. Far from withering away, the state in all these regimes became ever more pervasive. As a result, many believe that Luxemburg's critique of Marxist Leninism (offered long before most Marxist–Leninist regimes emerged) has been powerfully and tragically vindicated. For most of today's fundamentalist socialists, Luxemburg's ideas are therefore considered a more compelling brand of revolutionary socialism.

Rosa Luxemburg (1871–1919)

One of those who sought to uphold and develop the ideas of Karl Marx was Rosa Luxemburg. Through her membership of the German Social Democratic Party (SPD), Luxemburg made a distinctive contribution to the development of Marxist socialism.

- In one of her earliest publications, *Reform or Revolution?* (1900), Luxemburg accepted Marx's argument that capitalism promoted exploitation and was at odds with humanity's natural, fraternal instincts. She also agreed that evolutionary socialism was impossible: only revolution could create real change. Like Lenin, she had little sympathy for Marx's 'historicism' and denied that for revolution to occur, capitalism would have to reach an advanced stage of development. However, Luxemburg's analysis of how the revolution should come about would distinguish her from both Marx and Lenin.

- Luxemburg rejected Lenin's claim that revolution could occur only through the planning and leadership of a vanguard elite. Instead, she envisaged revolution arising 'spontaneously', after class consciousness had gradually been brought about through the proletariat's ongoing battle for progress in the workplace. Mass strike action would develop spontaneously from this and eventually ignite a much wider revolutionary movement that would overthrow the capitalist state. Yet Luxemburg rejected the Marxist–Leninist idea of revolution leading to a dictatorship of the proletariat. Instead, she advocated the immediate construction of a new democracy, underpinned by common ownership, open debate and elections.

- In many respects, Luxemburg was more faithful than Lenin to Marxist ideas. For example, she upheld Marx's internationalism by dismissing Lenin's interest in socialist nationalism, claiming Lenin overlooked the transnational character of both capitalism and proletarian interests. Socialist revolution, she contended, should be more than a form of national regime change; it should be a revolt against capitalism and nationalism globally — an argument which continues to be made today by groups like the International Socialist League.

- Luxemburg's concerns about nationalism were brought to a head by the outbreak of the Great War in 1914, which she stoutly opposed. Disgusted by the SPD's support for the German war effort, Luxemburg left the party and began organising anti-war demonstrations, certain that the war provided optimum conditions for revolution, while proclaiming that 'the enemy of socialism remains in our own country'.

- After the war, Luxemburg helped establish the German Communist Party (KPD). Conventional Marxists and Leninists were appalled by Luxemburg's belief that the KPD should contest elections to the post-war German Constituent Assembly, claiming this was a betrayal of Marx's rejection of evolutionary socialism and an heretical compromise with the status quo. Yet Luxemburg argued that having a foothold in the existing political system made it easier for communists to convey the case for revolution to proletarian voters. This argument portended Euro-communism in the late twentieth century and remains popular with modern communist parties in Europe.

Activity

Find out how Rosa Luxemburg died in 1919 and explain (in approximately 100 words) the political circumstances surrounding her death.

Debate 1

Is Marxism redundant?

Yes

- Far from communism marking the 'end of history', recent history has marked the end of communism.
- The collapse of the Soviet Union in 1989–1990 signalled the failure of an attempt (spanning 80 years) to bring Marxist principles to effective fruition.
- The attempts at implementing Marxist principles were not just unsuccessful; in the USSR, China and elsewhere they were catastrophic, leading to repression, torture and genocide.
- Capitalism has not imploded, as Marx forecast. Instead its reach has become ever wider, penetrating states that are either formerly or currently Marxist–Leninist (for example, Russia and China).
- In advanced capitalist states, the working class has not risen to revolution, as Marx predicted. Instead it has taken on the characteristics of the bourgeoisie (for example, acquisition of private property) while enjoying the benefits of market economies.

No

- Just as Marx deduced, capitalism remains unstable and volatile.
- Capitalism continues to leave a legacy of poverty and gross inequality, particularly in developing economies.
- Globalisation has weakened the power of national governments, reinforcing Marx's argument that economic power supersedes political power.
- The 'disappointing' record of socialist governments in capitalist states (such as François Hollande's in France after 2012) vindicates Marx's argument that radical change is impossible without revolution.
- Regimes such as the USSR and China were a distortion of Marxist principles — nowhere in Marx's writings is there explicit justification for the horrors that followed. Just because they were misapplied does not mean that Marx's theories were invalid.

Democratic socialism

In the UK and most other western European societies, the most influential form of fundamentalist socialism has been democratic socialism. It emerged during the late nineteenth century, developed during the twentieth century and (thanks to politicians such as Jeremy Corbyn and parties like Syriza in Greece) remains a feature of western politics in the twenty-first century.

Early democratic socialism

In the UK, democratic socialism was initially associated with the Fabian Society and bourgeois intellectuals like G.B. Shaw, Sidney

Webb and Beatrice Webb. It was also a strand of socialism that proved vital to the development of the Labour Party. Clause IV of Labour's 1918 constitution, heavily influenced by Webb, expressed the fundamentalist-socialist creed by aiming to 'secure for the producers by hand and by brain the full fruits of their industry and the most equitable distribution thereof...upon the basis of the common ownership of the means of production'.

What distinguished Webb's socialism from that of Marx and Lenin, however, was its rejection of 'big bang', revolutionary change. In her book *The Cooperative Movement in Great Britain* (1891), Webb argued that revolutions were 'chaotic, inefficient and counter-productive' and, for that very reason, 'guilty of the same problem besetting capitalism — *unpredictability*'.

Like other early democratic socialists, Webb, despairing of capitalism's volatility, looked forward to a more planned and 'rational' society where 'matters may be resolved sensibly...by rational, educated and civic-minded officials'. So, for Webb and other Fabians, the mayhem associated with revolution did not seem the ideal starting point for a bright and orderly future.

Early democratic socialists believed that the extension of the suffrage, from the late nineteenth century onwards, had facilitated a more orderly, election-based progression towards post-capitalist society. In a scenario Webb and other Fabians dubbed 'the inevitability of gradualism' (see Box 3.2), democratically elected socialist governments would steadily transform society via the existing parliamentary system, gradually replacing a society based on private ownership with one based on common ownership and public control.

Box 3.2

Democratic socialism and 'the inevitability of gradualism'

- Democratic socialist parties would campaign peacefully and gradually win the attention and trust of voters.
- The majority of voters (the working class) would gradually and inevitably realise they had no vested interest in capitalism.
- Voters would inevitably elect socialist governments.
- Democratic socialist governments would inevitably oversee the gradual replacement of private ownership with state ownership.
- Voters would gradually recognise the progress being made and inevitably re-elect democratic socialists to government.
- The continuous effects of democratic socialist governments would gradually and inevitably produce a socialist society.
- The benefits of such a society would inevitably be clear to all, thus making any reversal of socialism unlikely.

Beatrice Webb (1858–1943)

Beatrice Webb made a significant contribution to the development of early democratic socialism and its belief in the inevitability of gradualism (see Box 3.2). Webb's socialism was defined by four principles:

1 Capitalism was the principal cause of 'crippling poverty and demeaning inequality' in society and a 'corrupting force' for humanity, fostering 'unnatural' levels of avarice and selfishness among men and women.
2 Neither paternalism (see Chapter 2) nor philanthropy was a sustainable solution to the problems of poverty and inequality.
3 Poverty and inequality were most likely to be eliminated through vigorous trade unionism and extensive state intervention.
4 Effective reform tends to be gradual rather than revolutionary.

■ Along with her husband Sidney, Webb became active in the Fabian Society, an organisation committed to evolutionary socialism via reforms made at Westminster. She was instrumental in the Fabians' decision to align with the emerging Labour Party and was involved in drafting Clause IV of Labour's 1918 constitution. Although this committed Labour to 'common ownership' of the British economy, Webb helped ensure that Labour would pursue this goal via the existing political system.

■ Between 1905 and 1909, Webb served on a Royal Commission that examined the state's approach to poverty. Her celebrated Minority Report argued that the state should guarantee 'a sufficient nourishment and training when young, a living wage when able-bodied, treatment when sick, and modest but secure livelihood when disabled or aged'. Much of this anticipated the Beveridge Report of 1942, which was implemented by a Labour government after 1945. Webb's views on poverty and inequality therefore pre-dated both the agenda of a democratic socialist government and the emergence of a welfare state in the UK.

Activity

Explain, in no more than 200 words, why Webb rejected revolutionary socialism.

Later democratic socialism

Many regard the UK's post-war Labour government as a prime illustration of democratic socialism in action. After an overwhelming victory at the 1945 general election, Clement Attlee's government duly implemented a series of measures that had been carefully discussed and planned beforehand. The introduction of a welfare state and the transfer of several industries and services from private to public ownership all seemed to promote progress towards a fairer, post-capitalist society — underpinned, of course, by support at the ballot box.

Democratic socialist thinking was further updated by the writings of Tony Benn (1925–2014). In his *Arguments for Socialism* (1980), Benn restated his belief in fundamentalist socialism, arguing that the 'failure' of the Wilson–Callaghan UK governments proved the 'impossibility' of achieving socialism within a mainly capitalist economy. For Benn, the drastic cuts to public spending in 1976, made by a Labour government under pressure from the International Monetary Fund, underlined the danger of a 'socialist government seeking to rescue a flagging capitalist system'. In addition, Benn saw Labour's defeat at the 1979 general election as the inevitable punishment awaiting any socialist government that 'compromised with capitalism's contradictions'.

However, Benn did not accept that this invalidated **evolutionary socialism** — it merely strengthened the case for democratic socialists rethinking their tactics. Benn therefore argued that for fundamentalist socialism to be pursued peacefully, by a Labour government, a number of adjustments were needed. These included:

■ the restoration of parliamentary sovereignty through the UK's withdrawal from the European Economic Community (as the EU then was) — for Benn and many other democratic socialists, the EEC, and then the EU, were simply 'capitalist clubs'

■ parliamentary reform, so as to ensure an easier passage for socialist reforms — Benn therefore advocated the abolition of the unelected House of Lords and the subsequent strengthening of a socialist-dominated House of Commons

■ stronger resistance by socialist governments to pro-capitalist vested interests — this could be achieved if socialist governments mobilised support from their own vested interests, within, for example, the trade unions

■ the internal restructuring of a governing, socialist party — this should happen in a way that gave more power to individual party members outside Parliament, allowing them (for example) to select and de-select party leaders. This would encourage socialist prime ministers to 'stay true' to socialist principles and not be 'diverted' by non-socialist forces once in office.

> ## Key term
>
> **Evolutionary socialism**
> Linked to both democratic socialism and revisionist socialism (see below), evolutionary or parliamentary socialism involves a rejection of revolutionary politics, of the sort associated with Marxism, and a belief that socialism can be achieved peacefully and gradually through the existing constitutional system.

> ## Activity
>
> Explain, in approximately 200 words, why later democratic socialists like Tony Benn retained their faith in parliamentary socialism.

Euro-communism

The belief that capitalism could be gradually decommissioned, via parliamentary methods and evolutionary socialism, was shared from the 1970s by a number of communist parties in western Europe. This gave rise to the phenomenon of Euro-communism.

By the 1970s, many communist parties in western Europe were keen to distance themselves from the excesses of the Soviet Union and wished to establish themselves as radical yet 'respectable' forces in mainstream politics. As a result, groups like the French Communist Party (PCF) and the Italian Communist Party (PCI) rejected the Marxist–Leninist case for revolution. Instead, they contested elections, took up seats won in national parliaments and occupied positions of executive power within the existing constitutional system. George Marchais of the PCF served in France's Socialist–Communist coalition government of the early 1980s, while George Napolitano of the PCI served as Italian president between 2006 and 2015.

In adopting this approach, Euro-communists were much influenced by Italian socialist intellectual Antonio Gramsci (1891–1937), who founded the PCI. Gramsci argued that capitalism could never be overthrown without mass public support. But he argued that such support was hard to achieve given that the ruling economic class had a supreme influence (hegemony) over society's culture. Socialist change, he contested, must therefore be preceded by the emergence of a counter-culture — not just in the workplace, as Marx and Lenin prescribed, but in artistic, literary and recreational life as well. To achieve this, Gramsci argued, socialists needed their own 'cultural vanguard', promoting new ideas from within existing society.

Euro-communists endorsed this idea, claiming that a socialist counter-culture would be more persuasive if parties like the PCF were legitimised by routine election campaigns and responsibility in government. All this meant, of course, that Euro-communism was a significant departure from orthodox communism. To summarise:

- Euro-communists argued that the existing 'liberal-bourgeois' state could accommodate meaningful, socialist change, including the transition from a privately owned to a publicly owned economy.
- As a result, Euro-communists rejected the inevitability and desirability of revolution. The PCF routinely referred to the 'disaster' of both the 1917 revolution in Russia and the 1949 revolution in China.

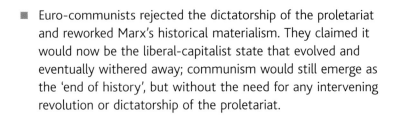

- Euro-communists rejected the dictatorship of the proletariat and reworked Marx's historical materialism. They claimed it would now be the liberal-capitalist state that evolved and eventually withered away; communism would still emerge as the 'end of history', but without the need for any intervening revolution or dictatorship of the proletariat.

Neo-Marxism

During the twentieth century, certain socialist thinkers, though respectful of Marx, nevertheless felt obliged to explain the survival of capitalism in western Europe. One of the most important contributions in this respect came from the so-called Frankfurt School, centred upon philosophers such as Herbert Marcuse (1898–1979) and Max Horkheimer (1895–1973).

Like Gramsci, Marcuse and others embraced the idea of a cultural hegemony when explaining capitalism's durability. As such, like Gramsci, they argued that capitalism's values do not simply infect the economy but also the arts, the media and education. Yet whereas Gramsci argued that this cultural hegemony could be countered if a socialist vanguard infiltrated key parts of society, the Frankfurt School felt that cultural hegemony merely vindicated Marx's belief in revolution. Echoing Marx, they argued that the violent overthrow of the capitalism system was necessary to smash both capitalism and the false consciousness that allowed capitalism to survive. That said, the Frankfurt School was not optimistic that revolution would occur; its spokesmen conceded that capitalism was proving more resilient and adaptable than Marx had envisaged.

Consequently, these neo-Marxists rejected the Euro-communist belief that capitalism could be gradually reformed out of existence. Instead, they asserted that when the next economic slump came, socialists should advocate revolution rather than pursue a long-term project of cultural change. According to Marcuse, a society's economic system would always shape its culture; Gramsci was therefore wrong to suggest that the reverse could ever apply.

During the second half of the twentieth century, there were attempts by other neo-Marxists to update Marx's call for revolution. One of the most important was Ralph Miliband, whose key work, *The State in Capitalist Society* (1973), sought to demolish the idea that socialism could be achieved via gradual, parliamentary reform. Miliband argued that whenever democratic socialist governments had come to power, in the UK and elsewhere, they had been 'blown off course' and forced to dilute their socialist agendas.

Antonio Gramsci: critic of 'capitalism's cultural hegemony'

For Miliband, this was wholly foreseeable — as Marx had predicted, the existing state would always protect the existing, dominant economic class. Examining the record of recent socialist governments in western Europe, Miliband claimed they were confronted and frustrated by a web of state-sponsored, anti-socialist forces, such as the senior civil service, the judiciary, the armed forces and the security services.

All these 'pro-capitalist' forces, Miliband stated, would conspire to divert socialist governments, especially during the economic crises to which capitalism was prone. Miliband thus concluded that a 'parliamentary road' to socialism, on its own, was impossible. It would have to be accompanied, or supplanted, by a revolutionary overthrow of the economic status quo, probably arising from the 'spontaneous' trade union action commended by Rosa Luxemburg several decades earlier.

> ### Activity
>
> With reference to the UK, find an example of a 'socialist' manifesto commitment that was subsequently ignored by a Labour government.

> ### Box 3.3
>
> #### Revolutionary socialism or evolutionary socialism?
>
> Revolutionary:
> - classical Marxism, Marxism–Leninism, neo-Marxism.
>
> Evolutionary:
> - democratic socialism, Euro-communism, all forms of revisionist socialism.

> ### Activity
>
> Explain, in no more than 200 words, why Marx and Engels thought socialism could be achieved only via revolution.

Revisionist socialism

Unlike all strands of fundamentalist socialism, **revisionist socialism** seeks to revise Marx's view that socialism is incompatible with capitalism. Furthermore, like some strands of fundamentalist socialism, revisionist socialism also revises Marx's view that socialism can be achieved only via revolution. Yet despite these two underlying principles, there are three important variations to revisionist thinking.

> ### Key term
>
> **Revisionist socialism**
> This is the belief that socialism can be achieved without the destruction of capitalism and private property, and without the upheaval of a revolution. It is therefore a form of evolutionary socialism. Dating from the late nineteenth century, this view has been associated with Eduard Bernstein, post-war social democracy and the Third Way of the late twentieth century (see below).

Classical revisionism

The earliest form of revisionism came from German socialist Eduard Bernstein, in his book *Evolutionary Socialism* (1898). Bernstein noted that by the end of the nineteenth century, the condition of the working class was steadily improving under capitalism — especially in those states where capitalism was well developed. In short, there was little evidence that history was unfolding in the way Marx had prescribed, or that Marx's 'crisis of capitalism' was about to materialise.

This led Bernstein to argue that, if overseen by socialist governments, capitalist economies could provide an even greater improvement to workers' conditions, with capitalism's worst features forever contained. Furthermore, Bernstein contested that the widening of the franchise, and the advent of a working-class majority among voters, meant that socialist governments were increasingly likely. Such governments could then legally insist, for example, that employers regularly improved conditions for their workers, and that landlords continuously improved conditions for their tenants — all of which would curb the inequalities of a capitalist society, while eliminating the need for revolution.

Bernstein endorsed many of the ideas being promoted by early democratic socialists, such as the Fabians, and supported laws that would extend trade union rights and education for the working classes. He evidently shared the Fabian Society's belief in a gradual, parliamentary road to socialism and was friendly with some of its members. What made Bernstein different was that he did not hold such views alongside an irrevocable contempt for capitalism — in other words, he believed the struggle for socialism could co-exist with an economy based on private property.

Debate 2

Must socialism involve the abolition of private property and capitalism?

Yes

...according to fundamentalist socialists:

- Socialism's core values include equality; private property generates inequality.
- Socialism's core values include fraternity and cooperation. Private property promotes individualism and competition.
- Marx, Engels and disciples like Rosa Luxemburg believed that private property (capitalism) led to exploitation and oppression of working people. Marx and Lenin also believed the collapse of capitalism was historically inevitable.
- Gramsci and the Frankfurt School believed that capitalism's cultural hegemony promoted false consciousness among working people. This made the promotion of socialist values difficult.
- Early democratic socialists like Beatrice Webb believed public ownership to be more rational and efficient than private ownership.
- Later democratic socialists like Tony Benn believed that attempts to achieve socialism alongside Keynesian capitalism had failed.

No

...according to revisionist socialists:

- The debate about private/public ownership merely concerns the means not the ends of socialism — the true ends being equality and fraternity.
- Early revisionists like Bernstein noted that working-class conditions had improved under capitalism, as a result of capitalist economies growing in a way Marx did not envisage. With democratically elected socialist governments (passing laws favourable to trade unions, for example), Bernstein believed this was even more likely to happen.
- Social democratic revisionists, like Crosland, stated that increased public spending, not public ownership, was the key to more socialism. Steady increases in public spending were possible if capitalist economies grew steadily, which would occur if Keynesian economic policies were properly applied.
- Third Way revisionists, like Giddens, argued that a thriving neo-liberal economy could provide the state with a growing tax yield, thus financing the extra public spending socialism required.
- The globalisation of capitalism, and the spread of home ownership in states like the UK, simply forced socialists to reconcile their core values to a society where private property was ubiquitous.

Social democracy

During the late nineteenth and early twentieth centuries, the term 'social democracy' was associated with hostility to capitalism and even a belief in revolution. In the UK, for example, the Social Democratic Federation was formed by Henry Hyndman in 1881 after he was inspired by the works of Marx. By the mid-twentieth century, however, it was regarded as the most important and relevant form of revisionist socialism, far removed from the politics of Marx and Lenin. How did this occur?

The origins of the change lie in developments after 1945 within West Germany's social democratic party (SPD), one of western Europe's most influential socialist groupings. At its Bad Godesberg conference in 1959, SPD revisionists (such as the future West German chancellors Willy Brandt and Helmut Schmidt) persuaded the party to renounce its remaining links with Marxism by embracing both modern capitalism and the post-war West German state. Yet this development also had a British dimension, for Brandt and others had been emboldened to make such arguments by the work of a young British socialist, Anthony Crosland, whose book *The Future of Socialism* (1956) came to be seen as the key work of post-war social democracy.

Crosland argued that the reformed capitalism prescribed by English economist John Maynard Keynes — whereby the state actively sought to 'manage' market forces — had guaranteed full employment and steady economic growth. Crosland

Anthony Crosland redefined British socialism

contested that thanks to **Keynesian economics**, capitalism was no longer vulnerable to 'peaks and troughs' and could now be relied upon to finance a richer, fairer and more classless society. As Crosland noted, the end of capitalism's cyclical character meant a constant expansion of public spending, a constant expansion of state welfare and constant progress towards the ultimate socialist goal of greater equality.

Indeed, Crosland went on to argue that by resolving the problems of capitalism, and by establishing that socialism was not just about 'common ownership', Keynesian economics allowed socialists to look at other methods whereby greater equality could be secured, such as ending the 'unequal' forms of secondary education created by the 11-plus examination.

Despite their personal rapport, there were still serious differences between British social democrats like Crosland and continental social democrats such as those of the SPD, notably over European integration. Whereas the likes of Brandt and Schmidt spoke warmly about the prospect of a federal Europe, Crosland and other Labour politicians like Peter Shore warned that the application of Keynesian economics required national governments to retain autonomy over their economic strategies. As Crosland warned in his final book, *Socialism Now* (1974), a Europe-wide economic policy was more likely to promote austerity than full employment — an argument that would be echoed 40 years later by continental socialist parties such as Syriza (in Greece) and Podemos (in Spain).

Key thinker 4

Anthony Crosland (1918–77)

Anthony Crosland was a senior Labour Party politician, who served as a Cabinet minister during the Labour governments of the 1960s and 1970s. His book *The Future of Socialism* (1956) made a vital contribution to the development of social democracy in Britain.

- Crosland contested that public or common ownership had gone far enough, arguing that public ownership had never been the aim of socialism, merely a method for achieving it. The true objective, Crosland insisted, was equality, which could now be achieved within a managed capitalist economy.
- Crosland asserted that capitalism had been changed for ever as a result of economist John Maynard Keynes, whose belief in state-managed capitalism became orthodox in western Europe after 1945. Thanks to Keynesian principles, Crosland argued, advanced societies could now enjoy permanent economic growth and full employment, without requiring any serious extension of public ownership. Thanks to constant growth, these societies could enjoy a steady expansion of the welfare state which, in turn, would diminish inequality and advance socialism.
- Crosland also noted an important change in society. He argued that owing to economic change, society was less 'binary', less polarised between employers and employees, and 'infinitely more complex than Marx could

ever have imagined'. In particular, Crosland cited 'new classes', such as 'managers' and 'technocrats', whose perspectives were likely to be different to those of traditional workers.

- Crosland argued that socialism now required a 'mixed' economy. This mixed economy would mainly comprise private enterprise and private ownership, alongside key services and a small number of industries owned by the state, a situation which, for Crosland, had largely been achieved following the 1945–1951 Labour governmens. For Crosland, the future task of socialist governments was not more public ownership but more public spending and better public services.
- In his later books, *The Conservative Enemy* (1962) and *Socialism Now* (1974), Crosland focused on other issues affecting society, notably education. He argued for a new form of state education, known as comprehensive education, which would end the segregation of pupils at the age of 11 and create new schools catering for all abilities. Crosland believed these comprehensive schools would break down class divisions far more effectively than any extension of public ownership, while ensuring all pupils had equality of opportunity. Crosland pursued this idea while Secretary of State for Education between 1965 and 1967, initiating a process that made comprehensive education the norm by the time of his death.

Activity

Explain, in no more than 200 words, Crosland's view that capitalism was no longer an obstacle to socialism.

The Third Way

The most recent form of revisionist socialism, sometimes referred to as neo-revisionism, is the Third Way. Associated with the UK governments of Tony Blair and Gordon Brown, and German SPD politicians like Gerhard Schröder, it emerged in the 1990s at a time when the case for fundamentalist socialism was thought to have disappeared once and for all. The Soviet Union had collapsed, market economics were being embraced across Russia and eastern Europe, even surviving communist states such as China were allowing forms of private enterprise. However, this did not simply vindicate post-war social democracy; the globalisation of capitalism was thought to have rendered much of Keynesian economics redundant, while the apparent failure of nationalised industries in the UK — and the extensive privatisation of the 1980s — made support for a mixed economy seem dated. So a new form of revisionist socialism seemed essential for the twenty-first century.

Anthony Giddens (1938–) (see 'Key thinker 5' box) is widely credited as the main author of both third wave revisionism and Third Way socialism. Giddens' political philosophy arose from a desire to 'triangulate' social democracy's wish for more equality with a capitalist economy that was now less Keynesian and more neo-liberal. He also aimed to reconcile the task of socialist parties seeking office (such as Labour in the UK) with an electorate that was increasingly propertied, suburban and individualistic.

Anthomy Giddens: sage of the Third Way

Yet for Giddens these changes merely augured 'the renewal of social democracy' rather than its abandonment. Far from raging against a free-market, neo-liberal economy, Giddens urged modern leftists to 'go with the flow' by encouraging further privatisation and further deregulation. Giddens argued that as this was the modern way to boost economic growth, it was also the best way to boost government tax revenues, and therefore boost government spending in the name of more equality.

However, the most important (and controversial) aspect of Third Way revisionism was its revised attitude to equality of outcome. According to Giddens, greater equality of opportunity probably required more, not less, inequality of outcome. His reasoning was that in a neo-liberal economy, increasingly unequal outcomes often went hand in hand with increasing rates of economic growth, and if outcomes became less unequal, it often indicated slower growth and therefore a smaller tax yield, lower public spending and less opportunity to ameliorate the problems of society's poorest.

These arguments were a long way from both traditional socialism and previous versions of revisionist socialism. Nevertheless, between 1994 and 1995 the case for this Third Way was duly accepted by Tony Blair and Gordon Brown, who persuaded the Labour Party to renounce its Clause IV commitment to common ownership and thus herald the era of New Labour. One of New Labour's architects, Peter Mandelson, later provided a stark illustration of the difference between the Third Way and previous versions of socialism, stating: 'We are intensely relaxed about people getting filthy stinking rich...just as long as they pay their taxes.' To socialist critics of the Third Way, such as Tony Benn, this analysis represented little more than paternalistic conservatism, an effort to make inequality of outcome more palatable while consolidating the position of very wealthy individuals.

Yet it should be stressed that under New Labour governments, the tax burden rose far more than it would have done under an average Conservative government. This, in turn, allowed New Labour to finance a corresponding rise in public spending, from 39% of gross domestic product in 1997 to 47% in 2010. For some, this amounted to brazen economic mismanagement. For Giddens, however, New Labour's stewardship of the economy — involving deregulation of banks and financial services on the one hand, plus steep increases in public spending on the other — was a robust example of Third Way triangulation.

Economic policy was not the only distinction between social democratic and Third Way revisionism. The Third Way also placed much more emphasis upon cultural and political equality, reflecting the fact that society by the 1990s was much more cosmopolitan and diverse than it had been during the 1950s. Giddens also argued that because globalisation made governments less influential in the economic sphere, it was fitting that Third Way governments should address other, 'less economic' examples of inequality within society. As such, governments like Blair's passed various measures promoting greater racial, gender and sexual equality; the legalisation of civil partnerships for gay couples is one example. Blair's government also brought in measures designed to redistribute political influence, such as devolved government and a Human Rights Act. For Giddens and other Third Way exponents, these reforms — with their aim of equalising social and political power — were perfectly appropriate to socialism in a modern setting.

Activity

Explain, in approximately 100 words, the differences between Third Way revisionism and social democracy.

Anthony Giddens (1938–)

Anthony Giddens is known mainly as a sociologist. Yet his work on political theory helped create a new strain of thinking within revisionist socialism: the Third Way.

- In *Beyond Left and Right* (1994), Giddens first established his credentials as a socialist sympathiser, highlighting the 'corrosive' effects of capitalism and individualism upon community and fraternity. Yet he also stressed that capitalism and individualism were irreversible and that any future project towards greater equality would have to take account of this.

- Giddens developed this theme in his next book, *The Third Way: The Renewal of Social Democracy*, written at the time of the 1997 general election and published during the first year of Britain's New Labour government. He argued that the survival of social democracy required recognition that free-market capitalism had an unmatched capacity to empower individuals economically. However, he also argued that capitalism functioned best when there was a strong sense of social cohesion, which neo-liberalism seemed to overlook. So a triangulation — reconciling neo-liberalism's view of economics with social democracy's view of society — was required to make centre-left politics relevant in the twenty-first century.

- Giddens claimed this triangulation was especially important given the emergence of 'post-Fordist' capitalist societies. During the mid-twentieth century, Fordist capitalism, based on huge industrial units of mass production, had spawned tightly knit urban communities, based on a uniformity of income and employment. These communities, Giddens explained, complemented human nature's yearning for solidarity and fellowship by giving their members a strong sense of support and identity, which might then encourage them to challenge both economic and cultural elites (traditional trade unionism being one expression of this). Yet, according to Giddens, the post-Fordist capitalism of the late twentieth and early twenty-first centuries — involving the decline of heavy industry — had fragmented such communities, 'atomised' the modern workforce and left individuals feeling alienated.

- Giddens accepted that, in many respects, this post-Fordist (or neo-liberal) capitalism was liberating for individuals — they were now freer than ever to 'self-actualise' and carve out individual identities. Yet those individuals would also find it harder to develop, precisely because society was becoming increasingly amorphous and ill defined. Stripped of the communities that once gave them confidence, human beings were likely to be less sure-footed and more likely to be influenced by both economic and cultural elites. So, for Giddens, the great irony was that the 'individualisation' of society might actually result in less individualism. Giddens therefore argued that if human nature were to flourish in the twenty-first century, the state — while retreating from economic management — would have to be more proactive, investing heavily in infrastructure (for example, better public transport and community services) and a modernised system of education, designed to prepare citizens for the knowledge economy (one where physical capacity was less important).

- Giddens thus proved a key revisionist socialist in that he revitalised the case for further state action in an era of globalised capitalism. In doing so, he recognised that conventional Keynesian economics (which formed the basis of Crosland-style social democracy)

Continued...

Anthony Giddens (continued)

was obsolete and that socialism needed to reconcile itself to a more free-market brand of capitalism. In the process, however, he was accepting that greater equality of opportunity might have to be accompanied by greater inequality of outcome if the free market were to generate the sort of wealth needed to fund modern public services. His arguments had a profound influence upon the New Labour governments of Tony Blair and Gordon Brown and the German social democratic government led by Gerhard Schröder.

Activity

Explain, in no more than 200 words, how Giddens' Third Way was advanced by Tony Blair's government.

Debate 3

Does socialism require revolutionary change?

Yes

...according to some fundamentalist socialists:

- Marx argued that the pre-socialist state reflected the interests of the dominant economic class — it would not allow the promotion of socialist values. Marx also believed revolution was historically inevitable.
- Lenin believed revolution was necessary to pre-empt the horrors of capitalist development and stifle 'false consciousness' among the masses.
- Rosa Luxemburg believed revolution would inevitably and 'spontaneously' develop from trade union agitation.
- Trotsky believed that 'permanent revolution' was needed until all capitalist states had disappeared.
- Mao believed that to cement socialism, economic revolution would have to be followed by long-term cultural revolution.
- Neo-Marxists such as Ralph Miliband argued that attempts at parliamentary socialism had failed.

No

...according to other fundamentalist socialists:

- Early democratic socialists (such as Webb) believed in the 'inevitability of gradualism' — i.e. slow, steady change within the existing political system.
- Later democratic socialists (for example, Benn) believed that the existing state required reform rather than abolition.
- Euro-communists believed the capitalist state would eventually wither away but could accommodate major socialist reform in the meantime.

No

...according to revisionist socialists:

- Early revisionists like Bernstein believed that, with universal adult suffrage, the existing state could allow socialist governments and steady, socialist change.
- Social democrats like Crosland and Third Way revisionists like Giddens believed that, with the advent of a welfare state, the existing political system could ensure steady increases in public spending and therefore steady progress towards a fairer society.
- Giddens believed the existing state's structures could be reformed (via devolution, for example) so as to produce greater political equality.

Can socialist values be reconciled to liberal values?*

Yes

- Socialism and liberalism are products of the Enlightenment.
- Socialism and liberalism always believe in the possibility of progress.
- Socialism and liberalism stress liberty and equality.
- Socialism and liberalism reject hereditary political power and paternalism.
- Socialism and modern liberalism endorse 'positive liberty' and further state intervention.

No

- Liberals prioritise individual liberty, socialists a fairer society.
- Liberals think individuals shape society, socialists think society shapes individuals.
- Liberals see inequality of outcome as a sign of freedom, socialists think inequality of outcome precludes equality of opportunity.
- Liberals see capitalism as a condition of freedom, fundamentalist socialists see it as a threat to freedom.
- Socialists wish to extend state intervention, classical and neo-liberals wish to reduce it.

This debate is best addressed after reading both this chapter and Chapter 1. A similar debate about socialism and conservatism can be found in Chapter 2.

Summary: key themes and key thinkers

	Human nature	The state	Society	The economy
Karl Marx and Friedrich Engels	Human nature, originally fraternal and altruistic, has been contaminated by capitalism, instilling the 'false consciousness' of bourgeois values. Revolutionary socialism, however, will repair this.	The existing liberal-bourgeois state is a tool of the dominant capitalist class; it must be destroyed by revolution and replaced by a new socialist state: the dictatorship of the proletariat.	Capitalist society is sickeningly, yet fatally, defined by class interests and class conflict. A communist society will be the perfect 'end of history'.	Capitalism is corrupt, inefficient and ultimately self-destructive. It should — and will — be replaced by an economy based on collective ownership.
Rosa Luxemburg	Human nature has not been damaged to the extent Marx alleged. Fraternity and altruism still flourish in working-class communities punished by capitalist economics.	The existing capitalist state must be destroyed by revolution, but one arising from strike action. The replacement state should be a genuine democracy, complete with free speech and free elections.	Capitalist society is class-ridden and morally indefensible, yet alternative societies, or sub-cultures, exist within downtrodden proletarian communities.	Capitalism is more resilient than Marx allowed. Its necessary destruction, and replacement by an economy based on workers' control, will require determination and solidarity among the proletariat.

Continued...

	Human nature	The state	Society	The economy
Beatrice Webb	The damage inflicted by capitalism upon the human psyche will be compounded only by violent revolution. Humanity needs to be guided back, gradually, to its original, cooperative condition.	If harnessed to universal suffrage, the existing state could be used to effect a gradual transition to socialism.	The poverty and inequalities of a capitalist society continue to depress human potential while fostering regressive competition.	A chaotic capitalist economy will gradually be replaced by one which secures for workers the full fruits of their labour, based upon a common ownership of the means of production.
Anthony Crosland	Human nature has a powerful sense of 'fairness' and an innate objection to huge inequalities of outcome.	Democratic socialist governments (for example, Labour 1945–1951) prove that the existing state can be used to effect radical, socialist change.	Society is increasingly complicated, altered by the emergence of new social groups comprising 'meritocratic' managers and 'classless' technocrats.	A mixed economy, underpinned by limited public ownership and Keynesian capitalism, will finance the greater public spending necessary to secure equality.
Anthony Giddens	Human nature has been shaped by changing socio-economic conditions. The pro-fairness instinct is still present, but it now competes with a sharpened sense of individual aspiration.	The existing liberal state should be improved, redistributing and decentralising political power while encouraging greater political participation.	Society has undergone embourgeoisement — egalitarians must harness, rather than deny, these forces.	A neo-liberal economy, propelled by privatisation and deregulation, will provide huge tax yields. This will finance huge increases in public spending, which will secure greater equality of opportunity.

Tensions within socialism

- **Human nature:** all socialists believe that human nature is malleable and improvable, 'plastic' not permanent. Yet some socialists, such as Marx, believe that human nature is especially susceptible to whichever economic system it lives under. Therefore, people are likely to suffer a 'false consciousness' that can be cured only by revolution and authoritarian rule (the dictatorship of the proletariat). Other socialists, including revisionists like Giddens, argue that human nature can prosper under capitalism yet still appreciate the importance of core socialist beliefs such as cooperation, fraternity and collectivism.
- **Society:** by definition, all socialists see our social environment (i.e. society) as the crucial determinant of our personalities. So if society can be improved (i.e. made more equal and fraternal), improvements in our attitude and behaviour will follow. Yet socialists disagree about whether society can be improved gradually. Revolutionary socialists, like Marx and the Frankfurt School, believe existing society is so 'sick' and so inimical to socialist values that only a revolution can provide the necessary 'shock therapy'. Other fundamentalist socialists, like Beatrice Webb, believe society can be 'gradually' improved, and socialist values gradually more entrenched, by a series of reforms that gradually curtail private ownership. Revisionists like Crosland and Giddens also argue that society can be gradually improved and believe such improvements can occur alongside private property and capitalism.

- **The state:** unlike collectivist anarchists, socialists believe a state is vital to the promotion of core socialist values. But they differ dramatically about what kind of state is needed. Marx and orthodox communists believed the existing capitalist state would have to be destroyed by revolution and replaced by a dictatorship of the proletariat, which, in turn, would 'wither away' to produce stateless communism. Democratic socialists like Webb and revisionists like Crosland and Giddens believed that the existing state can be used to steer society towards socialist values and that the traditional state (in capitalist society) requires constitutional reform rather than abolition.
- **The economy:** fundamentalist socialists (like Marx, Luxemburg and Webb) believe socialism is incompatible with a capitalist economy based on private property. Marxists and orthodox communists believe that a new, non-capitalist economy should be created quickly, via revolution, while democratic socialists believe such a non-capitalist economy will be created gradually, via a series of elected socialist governments. By definition, revisionists believe that socialism is possible within a capitalist economy. Social democrat revisionists like Crosland believe that the economy should be mixed (i.e. allowing a degree of public ownership) and run along Keynesian lines by governments. Third Way revisionists like Giddens believe the economy should be neo-liberal, privatised and deregulated, claiming this will produce a greater tax yield and thus more public spending.

Conclusion: socialism today

By the start of the twenty-first century, many commentators believed socialism was a redundant ideology — a 'wasm' rather than an 'ism'. As we saw in Chapter 1, academics like Francis Fukuyama were arguing that contrary to what Marx had predicted, liberalism — not communism — was 'the end of history'.

During the 1990s, there was certainly strong support for this dismissive view of socialism. The collapse of the Soviet Union marked the end of a 70-year experiment in anti-capitalist, and officially socialist, government. Meanwhile, within western states like the UK, parties like Labour formally renounced common ownership — a key feature of democratic socialism — while embracing a Third Way ideology which many saw as indistinguishable from modern liberalism.

At the same time, socialism's support for collectivism seemed ill at ease with an increasingly individualistic society. By the 1990s, the number of UK trade unionists, for example, had been surpassed by the number of UK property owners. Far from seeing an increase in class solidarity, as socialists traditionally recommended, working people in western societies seemed to be undergoing *embourgeoisement*, taking on the characteristics of a propertied class and endorsing the values of a property-based society, which socialism historically opposed. Small wonder, perhaps, that the word 'socialism' was omitted from all four of New Labour's general election manifestos between 1997 and 2010.

However, the apparent dominance of capitalism need not necessarily spell the end of socialism. As we have seen, there is a whole school of socialism — namely, revisionism — that seeks to achieve socialism within a capitalist economy. With that in mind, the notion of a revisionist socialist government (one that pursues core socialist values through public spending rather than public ownership) seems far from fanciful in a modern society. Indeed, this was the message of the French Socialist Party when its leader François Hollande swept to power in 2012.

Furthermore, during the first two decades of the twenty-first century the case for capitalism did not seem as secure as Fukuyama *et al.* had imagined. The economic crash of 2007–2008 forced governments, such as Gordon Brown's in the UK, to increase state regulation of capitalism and, in some cases, extend public ownership. Problems in the Eurozone after 2012, plunging countries like Greece into levels of austerity not seen in Europe since the Second World War, again shook faith in the efficiency of both market economics and 'managed' capitalism.

In view of these traumas, it was unsurprising that in many quarters socialist ideas began to creep back into mainstream debate. Policies once confined to socialism's more extreme supporters, such as the nationalisation of banks, were solemnly implemented by Gordon Brown's government after 2007. In response to the Eurozone crises of 2013–2014, socialist parties — like Syriza in Greece and Podemos in Spain — began to gain electoral traction with a clear anti-capitalist message. Likewise, by the end of 2015, Jeremy Corbyn was leader of the UK's official Opposition, winning two Labour leadership campaigns with a message that restored socialism to the language of front-line politics. Even in the USA, where socialism had been off limits to 'respectable' politicians during the twentieth century, the term began to be used more freely. Socialist politicians were elected to office in states such as Washington and Vermont, riding a tide of hostility to market failure, while the socialist senator Bernie Sanders made a plausible bid for the Democratic Party nomination in the US presidential election of 2016.

This should remind us of two important truths. First, socialism emerged in the nineteenth century as a reaction to the problems caused by capitalism. So as long as capitalism proves problematic, the relevance of socialism will never entirely disappear. Second, even when capitalism seems relatively problem free, it is well to recall that socialism was never fundamentally defined by a desire to get rid of capitalism — such notions were always a means rather than an end. Instead, the essence of socialism has been a belief that society shapes individuals and that the best societies are those that promote fraternity, cooperation and equality. As long as those values appeal to large numbers of people, the relevance of socialism is likely to endure.

Nevertheless, we should always remember that in countries such as Russia, China and Cambodia, socialism in practice has often proved horrific. As recently as late 2016, when many socialists (including Corbyn) were lamenting the death of Fidel Castro, a report from Amnesty International recorded that in Cuba there had been 'more than 8,600 politically motivated detentions of government opponents and activists during the past year'.

We may conclude that socialism's core beliefs have a residual and renewable appeal, one that has clearly outlasted the sort of society attending its birth in the nineteenth century. Yet, judging by the history of the twentieth century, the implementation of socialist ideals can be hazardous and potentially disastrous. For this reason, socialism continues to provoke reactions that are both passionate and polarised.

Further reading

Benn, T. (1980) *Arguments for Socialism*, Penguin.
Cohen, G.A. (2009) *Why Not Socialism?*, Princeton University Press.
Heywood, A. (2016) 'Corbynism — the strange rebirth of UK socialism?', *Politics Review*, 25,4.
Kolko, G. (2006) *After Socialism*, Taylor & Francis.
McLellan, D. (2007) *Marxism After Marx*, Palgrave.
Sassoon, D. (2010) *One Hundred Years of Socialism*, Fontana.

Exam-style questions

Short questions

The following questions are similar to those in examinations set by AQA.
Each carries 9 marks.

1 Explain and analyse the socialist view of human nature.

2 Explain, analyse and exemplify socialism's support for collectivism.

Essay questions

The following questions are similar to those in examinations set by Edexcel (Pearson)
and AQA.

Edexcel (24 marks) or AQA (25 marks):

1 To what extent are socialists committed to equality of outcome? You must use appropriate
thinkers you have studied to support your answer.

2 'Socialists have disagreed over means rather than ends.' To what extent is this true? You
must use appropriate thinkers you have studied to support your answer.

AQA only (25 marks):

3 'Socialism is implacably opposed to an economy based on private property.' Analyse and
evaluate with reference to the thinkers you have studied.

4 Is it possible for socialists to reconcile equality and liberty? Analyse and evaluate with
reference to the thinkers you have studied.

Chapter 4

Feminism

> **Learning outcomes**
>
> This chapter will enable students to:
> - understand how feminist ideas developed in the twentieth century
> - understand the core values of feminism as a political ideology
> - understand the various types of feminism, how they differ from each other and the tensions that exist within the movement
> - understand the ideas of feminism's key thinkers.

Introduction

There is no doubt that feminism is one of the most successful political movements in recent history. Perhaps, even, it is the most successful. Indeed, this claim can be borne out by the fact that many commentators refer to the current age as a post-feminist era. This term implies that the traditional goals of feminism — anti-discrimination, full, equal legal and political rights for women, anti-sexism and equality of opportunity, and so forth — have largely been achieved and therefore are no longer relevant to current discourse on the position of women in society. This is not to say, though, that feminism is an out-of-date philosophy. Far from it. Instead it means that new questions need to be posed and answered with regard to women and relations between the sexes. It is merely the traditional debates about feminist issues that need to be replaced with new ones.

Like many political ideas and ideologies, feminism has often been much misunderstood, misrepresented and distorted by our preconceptions about it. Often it is portrayed as merely an anti-men movement, or as a quest for female dominance of society; in some cases it has even been portrayed as little more than an appeal for the dissemination of lesbianism. While it is true that most feminists do blame male patriarchy for the subjugation of women, that some feminists view a world dominated by female values as superior to one ruled by men, and that there are some feminists who have sought to create a lesbian counter-culture, none of these stereotypes is substantially accurate.

As we shall see, feminism is perhaps best described as two related but different movements. They are liberal feminism and radical feminism (including socialist feminists). The first is a movement for reform, the second can be described as revolutionary in nature. While liberal feminists share very similar values with each other, radical feminism has taken a number of varying and divergent forms. We will explore all of these in this chapter.

The origins of feminism

If we search history for the origins of feminism we will find largely fragmentary evidence of a growing female consciousness and opposition to a male-dominated world. Some, for example, have quoted the example of the Amazons, a semi-mythical tribe of fierce women warriors, as proof that feminist ideas must have flourished in Ancient Greece. Aristophenes' play about Lysistrata is also described as a metaphor for the potential power of women from the same era. Lysistrata was portrayed as a woman who organised the other women of Greece to withhold their sexual favours until the men brought war to an end. Others have pointed to the French Revolution and the Enlightenment period that preceded it as the inspiration for early ideas that women might enjoy equal rights with men. But the first well-known and rigorous work on women's rights was written by the English liberal Mary Wollstonecraft (1759–97). This was *A Vindication of the Rights of Women* (1792).

In this work Wollstonecraft does not go so far as to advocate equality for women, but she does urge that they be offered a good education and that they assert their right to be considered useful members of society, not merely ornaments. Being a good wife and mother, for Wollstonecraft, was a worthy aspiration, but at the same time women should become independent from their husbands and should develop their minds to the fullest extent. As she put it:

> 'To be a good mother — a woman must have sense, and that independence of mind which few women possess who are taught to depend entirely on their husbands. Meek wives are, in general, foolish mothers; wanting their children to love them best, and take their part, in secret, against the father, who is held up as a scarecrow.'

Wollstonecraft was not a feminist in the modern sense of the word, but she was a pioneer of the movement. Much of the attention on the issue of the inferior position of women was to move to the USA in the nineteenth century.

However, these early signs remain merely fragments. Feminism as a serious political and social movement did not emerge until the middle and second half of the nineteenth century. There were, at that time, some concerns about the legal and social position of women. For example, in Britain, the great liberal John Stuart Mill and his wife, Harriet Taylor, campaigned for the passage of the Married Women's Property Act (1882), which allowed women to keep their own property after they married. In the USA, too, **Charlotte Perkins Gilman** (1860–1935) (see 'Key thinker 4' box) was writing extensively about the lack of opportunities for independent women and arguing that the inferior position of women in the home was a model of their subordinate position in wider life. But it was the issue of the franchise — votes for women — that attracted most attention.

In 1890 the National American Woman Suffrage Association was founded, followed later by the National Woman's Party, led by Alice Paul. By 1920 the Nineteenth Amendment to the US Constitution was passed. This guaranteed equal voting rights for women. In Britain, meanwhile, the Women's Social and Political Union (WSPU) was formed in 1903. The WSPU was founded and run by the Pankhurst family and it was they, Emmeline in particular, who led the suffragette movement that was ultimately to secure votes for married women over the age of thirty in 1918 (women were also allowed to stand for parliament in that year) and equal voting rights with men in 1928. It was the suffragettes and their American counterparts who were to form the earliest example of a well-organised women's movement. The suffrage movement thus came to be known as first wave feminism.

The assumption of the suffrage movement was that once women were granted voting rights and could stand for election to representative bodies, two developments would follow. The first was that many women would quickly seek election to office. The second was that, in pursuit of women's votes, parliament and government would pass legislation to improve conditions for women and, in particular, to establish equality in all kinds of economic and social fields. Neither occurred, however. There was little impact at all, save for some improvements in the educational opportunities open to women and the partial opening of the professions to them.

It was not until the 1960s that the movement known today as feminism began to emerge. This second period of advancement for women was known as second wave feminism. The second wave was part of a broader cultural movement spreading at that time which sought to offer a general critique of post-industrial society, especially identifying the alienation of various social groups from a society of growing mass communication and consumerism. These groups included disaffected youth, ethnic minorities, the black population of the USA especially, the gay community, the chronically poor and, of course, women. Feminism had arrived!

The core ideas of feminism

Human nature

Sex and gender

The main issue concerning human nature that feminists address revolves around two concepts: sex and gender. Indeed, the feminist movement developed the distinction between the two. They are crucial to any understanding of feminist ideas.

The term **sex** when discussing the relationships between women, men and society refers to the biological differences between men and women. The most important difference is, of course, the fact that women give birth and play a decisive role in the life of a newborn. It can also refer to the lower levels of physical strength that most women have. For most feminists, sex differences should be irrelevant to the way in which women are treated in society and in relationships between men and women. In other words, the biological status of women should not affect their general status.

Other feminists, however, have seen sex or biological differences as important and some go as far as to say they are the explanation of the inferior status of women. This belief in the importance of biological distinctions is known as **essentialism**. For some feminists, biological (sex) differences are indeed essential to our understanding. In particular, the biological differences have determined the gender roles of women in history and to this day. Other, mostly radical, feminists agree that biology may have determined the inferior status of women in history but they argue that there is no reason for this to continue today.

123

Gender Gender refers to cultural differences between the sexes, leading to feelings of superiority of men and inferiority of women and the assignment of inferior roles in society to women. Feminists view gender differences as the creation of patriarchal society and see them as not natural. Sex and gender stereotypes, such as typical female secretaries or male chief executives, are the result of such distinctions.

Patriarchy This term is used mostly by feminists to describe a society which is dominated by men and where women are seen and treated as inferior.

Gender, meanwhile, has nothing directly to do with biological differences between men and women. This refers to the cultural and economic differences between the lives of men and women. There used to be a dominant attitude in society that sex and gender were linked — that the different roles played by women were biologically determined. Women, for example, would be unable to undertake demanding jobs because of their regular need to give birth and care for young children. Similarly, women would naturally have a more caring and humane attitude to life because of their childrearing role and so would be less suited to the competitive world of business, a characteristic that would become more acute in the competitive world of capitalism. Furthermore, tied to the home as they were by the demands of motherhood, it was perhaps natural that women would become homemakers while men were the breadwinners.

More controversially, pre-feminist, male-dominated cultural perspectives often suggested that women were somehow inferior to men. This was largely because the roles of motherhood and homemaking were seen as less important than those of earning outside the home. In such a world, women were seen as less able to use their judgement and would have little need for more than basic education. Nor would they need to learn highly developed skills or specialised knowledge. The lack of education and occupational opportunities open to women reinforced the general cultural belief that men were superior. Perhaps more seriously, Betty Friedan (1921–2006), often described as the founder of second wave feminism, pointed out that cultural attitudes towards gender differences were so deep rooted that women themselves tended to share them with men. As she wrote famously:

> 'Each suburban wife struggled with it alone. As she made the beds, shopped for groceries, matched slipcover material, ate peanut butter sandwiches with her children, chauffeured Cub Scouts and Brownies, lay beside her husband at night — she was afraid to ask even of herself the silent question — "Is this all?"' (*The Feminine Mystique*, 1963)

Feminists have a number of responses to the issue of sex and gender. They vary a great deal and help to define different strands of feminism:

- Liberal feminists, such as Friedan herself, accept the significance of sex differences but regard gender differences and the superiority of men as an artificial construct, created by male-dominated (**patriarchal**) societies. There is, they say, no reason why biological differences between the sexes should be converted into gender differences. The apparent inferiority of women is learned behaviour by both men and women. It has its roots in the history of civilisations and is reinforced by education and other cultural institutions, including the media. Liberal feminists' response, therefore, has tended to centre on the need for reform, through legislation for equality and through education to combat sexist attitudes. If male superiority and patriarchy are passed down from generation to generation, the cycle must be broken by fundamental changes to the culture.

■ Radical feminists, such as Juliet Mitchell (1940–) and Kate Millett (1934–), see gender differences as all-pervading and more deep rooted than the liberal feminists believe. For Mitchell, male gender exists in all aspects of life — work, home, personal relationships — and in cultural life generally. It must therefore be destroyed in all these places. Mitchell stressed the way in which gender distinctions have been generated within literature and the arts, as well as culture. There needs to be something of a cultural revolution to combat patriarchy.

Perhaps the most radical feminist in this field was Shulamith Firestone (1945–2012). Firestone stressed the importance of sex rather than gender in the oppression of women. She, like Marx, saw history in terms of a dialectic struggle, but not between a ruling class and an oppressed class, rather between men and women. Also like Marx, she believed the oppressed would ultimately triumph. How? By removing the very sex differences that have led to the oppression of women. This, she proposed, can be achieved by removing all sexual functions of women and thus removing all sex differences between men and women. It would be replaced by androgyny — a state where men and women would co-exist without sexual relations.

■ Socialist feminists, the most extreme of whom are also Marxists, see the oppression or inferior status of women as being bound up with the whole operation of capitalism. Women, like workers, have become an oppressed class. For most socialist feminists the link is as follows. Patriarchal societies assign an inferior gender role to women so that they can become a cheap source of labour. In the home they are a largely unpaid workforce, while outside, in the world of paid employment, they make up a large proportion of the low-paid, often part-time working population. Because of their inferior status they have been forced to work for low wages. Furthermore, they are dispensable so that when there is a slump it is largely women who are thrown out of work, while in better times they can be easily re-employed. Thus,

Key term

Androgyny This idea is associated with radical feminism. We all have both female and male characteristics. People should be free to choose their sexual identity and may choose to have no sexual identity at all.

not only are they poorly paid on the whole, but also they lack job security. The solution for socialists is the destruction of capitalism at the most extreme level (commonly advocated by Marxist feminists), or at least its modification. In particular, women should be granted the same protection, working conditions, pay and opportunities as men. In other words, the capitalist world must learn or be forced to end its gender assignment of women as 'second-class labour'.

Debate 1

How relatively important are sex and gender in feminist thinking?

Sex
- It is inevitable that women will take the lead role in child rearing, so men will dominate in the outside world of work.
- Women are physically weaker than men, so will inevitably have an inferior position.
- Women are born with an innate nurturing and unaggressive character, and so are less fitted to the world of competitive capitalism.

Gender
- Men have a vested interest in maintaining their dominant gender role in society.
- The gender role of women is embedded in their consciousness from an early age to such an extent that women themselves do not understand its patriarchal origin.
- In modern society there is no reason why the different biological status of women should affect their role in the economy. Gender differences are therefore an artificial construct designed to perpetuate patriarchy.

The personal is political

The term 'the personal is political' has become something of an emblematic slogan for feminists. It was probably first coined by Firestone, but was popularised by Carol Hanisch in a 1970 essay. It is an important idea which helps us to distinguish between liberal and radical feminists.

Liberal feminists, in common with liberals in general, advocate the separation of the **private sphere** from the **public sphere**. The private sphere concerns those aspects of our lives that are particular to ourselves and perhaps our close family and friends. It concerns those characteristics we possess and modes of behaviour we follow that do not affect others. In a free society the private sphere is no concern of others, and especially not the state. As long as our thoughts and actions do not harm others, say liberals, there is no justification for interference. In the world of liberal feminism, the private sphere relates to how men and women interact and how women themselves choose to live. The public sphere is different.

In the public sphere our actions do affect others and they therefore become the concern of government and the state. Thus, for example, how men treat women, how women are

Political ideas for A-level

126

treated or portrayed in the workplace, in politics, in the media and in society at large, are public concerns. So the position of women in society generally is the concern of all, feminists in particular; it is in the public sphere. This includes such issues as sexist cultural attitudes that demean women, low expectations of women at work, low wages, lack of opportunity, low conviction rates for rape and sexual assault, and discrimination in general.

However, radical feminists, like Hanisch and Firestone, do not recognise the distinction between the private and public spheres. For them, everything is political. By political they mean that they are reflections of the power that men have over women and the nature of patriarchal society. Thus, if women are kept at home engaged in child rearing and homemaking, it is not a private matter because it is an aspect of that wider patriarchy. Furthermore, most women do not understand that the personal is political; their *consciousness* has been distorted by the male-dominated society in which they live.

Germaine Greer (1939–) followed the idea of the personal is political into the field of intimate and sexual relationships between men and women. Such relationships, she asserted, are determined by men who have managed, through history, to make women ashamed of their bodies and their sexuality — their sexuality, in other words, has been manipulated to serve the interests of men. Thus, even such private matters as these relationships become political in nature, expressions of power exercised by men over women.

The state

Feminists do not have a distinctive theory of the state, unlike socialists, liberals and even conservatives. It is true that socialist feminists see the state as the agent of capitalism and, since capitalism naturally exploits women, the state is the ultimate architect of such exploitation. But this criticism is indirect and restricted to socialists.

The main characteristic of the modern state that concerns feminists relates to patriarchy. In short, the modern state is seen as a wider social phenomenon — the oppression and exploitation of women in a male-dominated society. States and governments that run them are accomplices in this exploitation.

Liberals largely point to the reluctance of the state to address the inferior position of women. Why should they when they are, themselves, dominated by men? Nevertheless, if governments are seen as part of the problem, liberals also see them as part of the solution. Indeed, the feminist movement has made huge strides in improving the position of women through legislation and changes in the nature of state-run education. Examples are numerous and include:

- Equality laws and constitutional principles — such developments are designed to impose the principle of gender equality in the public sphere. Most modern states have such principles enshrined (the USA being a notable exception).
- Anti-discrimination legislation — virtually all modern states have outlawed discrimination against women, either in law or in constitutional principles.
- Laws imposing equal pay regulations — this is enshrined in European Union law, for example.
- Laws dealing with domestic violence (both physical and psychological in the UK) and rape in marriage.
- The imposition of various kinds of awareness programmes in school curricula.
- In some cases female quotas have been introduced, notably in politics.

Radical feminists, meanwhile, view such developments as welcome but also superficial. Such reforms do not address the more fundamental problem of the *systemic* nature of discrimination, exploitation and inequality. Patriarchy is more pervasive than these reforms suggest. These problems are deeply rooted in patriarchal culture. This means that the state is powerless to combat them, especially as it is a patriarchal institution itself.

Society

Patriarchy

As we have seen above, many feminists see society as deeply patriarchal in nature. They have developed an analysis of society which has much in common with fundamentalist socialism. For such socialists, capitalism is a complete, integrated economic, social and political system in which workers are an exploited class. For many radical feminists, patriarchy rather than capitalism is the key characteristic of modern society and it is women who are the exploited class rather than workers in general. Therefore, just as extreme socialists see the destruction of capitalism as the solution to workers' exploitation, so radical feminists see the removal of patriarchy as vital to the emancipation of women.

This is no easy task as patriarchy is part of every aspect of society — politics, economy, culture, media, religion, education, sport, etc. It cannot, therefore, be attacked by mere piecemeal reforms, it has to be combatted in one of two ways. The first is a full-scale attack on cultural values in society, possibly involving violent resistance to male dominance. The other is through the

Activity

Explain, in no more than 100 words, what is meant by the term 'patriarchy'.

creation of a female counter-culture, separate altogether from patriarchal society. In particular, this involves women leading completely separate lives from men.

Liberals take a similar view of patriarchy but see the solution in terms of reform rather than revolution. For liberals, patriarchy is a *characteristic* of society, but is not necessarily fundamental. It therefore follows that society can be made less patriarchal gradually, through peaceful political and cultural action.

Equality and difference feminism

The feminist response to patriarchy is echoed in two attitudes towards the position of women in society. These are sometimes described as equality feminism and difference feminism. Equality feminists have limited aspirations. They seek equality for women in all spheres. Most of these feminists describe themselves as liberals. Difference feminism is more complex. From this perspective men and women have fundamental differences and these should be recognised in society.

Most difference feminists do not accept that one gender is superior to another, arguing simply that they are different and that those differences should be embraced but not fought against. For them, the search for equality is fruitless. Furthermore, some difference feminists have claimed, the attributes peculiar to women, such as a caring nature, the ability to nurture the young and non-aggressiveness, are superior to male characteristics. A world dominated by women, therefore, would be a better world. The interests of children would be paramount, there would be less violence and possibly no wars. Some environmentalists have also suggested that women would be better custodians of the environment than men, being more likely to embrace nature than to exploit it.

It is an attitude that has been challenged by many feminists as defeatist. Equality feminists argue that difference automatically leads to inequality and if there is inequality it is inevitable that men will benefit. For them, there must be equality and male superiority must be destroyed. In her great work, *The Second Sex* (1949), **Simone de Beauvoir** (1908–86) (see 'Key thinker 1' box) expressed this idea succinctly:

'Society, being codified by man, decrees that woman is inferior; she can do away with this inferiority only by destroying the male's superiority.'

Simone de Beauvoir, an early French feminist

Simone de Beauvoir (1908–86)

Simone de Beauvoir was known as the first existential feminist. The existentialist philosophical movement, founded by Kirkegaard in the nineteenth century, took hold among French intellectuals in the 1950s, notably Jean-Paul Sartre (de Beauvoir's lover) and Albert Camus. Existentialism set the freedom of the individual against the constrictions placed on him or her by the moral and religious world around them and exhorted them to struggle against such restrictions by imposing their own will upon life. Failing to impose one's own will is known as 'bad faith', but succeeding is known as 'authenticity'. For de Beauvoir, for too long women had lived their lives in bad faith, imposed upon them by men.

■ She also developed the idea of women as the 'Other' (with a capital 'O'). The idea of otherness was that men have characterised women as different, but different in a way of their (men's) choosing, not the choosing of women themselves. De Beauvoir famously declared that 'women are made, not born'. The problem is that they are made by men.

■ In her best known work, *The Second Sex*, de Beauvoir rejects the notion that girls are born with any nurturing instinct; rather, she asserts that they learn it from their parents and from their schooling. In existential terms, therefore, their freedom to choose their own way of life is removed almost from birth. The roles that women play have been determined for them by men. Even in their personal relations, women are inferior, as she writes in *The Second Sex*:

'On the day when it will be possible for woman to love not in her weakness but in her strength, not to escape herself but to find herself, not to abase herself but to assert herself — on that day love will become for her, as for man, a source of life and not of mortal danger.'

■ Her solution to the plight of women was twofold. First, women must be granted the opportunity to make as many choices as men, to be able to escape from the drudgery of housework and their role in marriage as a kind of sex slave. This will be achieved largely through education, economic freedom, state-funded child care, legalised abortion and widespread contraception. But de Beauvoir also asserted that women must liberate themselves. They must seek sexual liberation and freedom from the strictures of the nuclear family.

■ De Beauvoir was an influence on all feminists who came after her, but especially on Friedan. While de Beauvoir used history and philosophy to confirm her theories, Friedan used specific research. However, despite their different methodology both women came to very similar conclusions. This extract from *The Second Sex* perfectly sums up the ideas of the early second wave feminists:

'One is not born, but rather becomes, a woman. No biological, psychological, or economic fate determines the figure that the human female presents in society; it is civilization as a whole that produces this creature, intermediate between male and eunuch, which is described as feminine.'

Activity

Explain, in no more than 100 words, the meaning of the term 'Other' in relation to women.

Intersectionality

In recent times, often described as the era of post-modern feminism, many critics have suggested that feminism has tended to be a largely white, middle-class, one-size-fits-all movement. They point out that women from a variety of social and cultural backgrounds face very different problems. Thus, for example, the oppression faced by black women is different in character from the experience of white women. The same may be true of gay women, women from low-income families and women from minority religions or other ethnic groups. This has led to the idea of a very segmented movement and the philosophy behind it is known as **intersectionality**, a term coined by Kimberlé Crenshaw in 1989. She pointed out that in modern society, we all have multiple identities and gender is only one of them. While gender is important, it is not the only identity we have. Traditional feminism suggests that gender is everything, but this is a false perspective on women.

The black American feminist **bell hooks** (she gives her name lower-case first letters) (1952–) stresses race as a key identity and insists that the battle against racism must go hand in hand with the battle against sexism (see 'Key thinker 2' box). She expresses this clearly in her book *Feminism is for Everybody: Passionate Politics* (2000):

> 'We knew that there could be no real sisterhood between white women and women of colour if white women were not able to divest of white supremacy, if the feminist movement were not fundamentally anti-racist.'

The implication of this is that there needs to be a black feminist movement, a gay women's movement, a working-class feminist movement and so on, recognising the multiple identities women have and therefore the complexity of the oppression they face.

Key term

Intersectionality This contemporary, post-modern idea among feminists suggests that women have multiple identities as well as their female sex and gender. Thus the problems women face are intersectional, involving a combination of their female identity and other identities such as ethnicity, sexual orientation, social class and religion.

Activity

Explain, in no more than 100 words, what is intersectionality in feminism.

bell hooks (1952–)

bell hooks was born Gloria Watkins. She adopted the name of her great-grandmother, Bell Hooks, whom she admired hugely. She does not use upper-case letters for her pen name so she will not be confused with her great-grandmother. hooks is a radical black American feminist. She is best known for her work in intersectionality. In her analysis of the inferior position of women she begins from the starting point that society is completely disfigured by inequality in general. Different groups in society, not just women, suffer from inequality. These include obviously the poor, but also ethnic minorities, gays and religious minorities. It follows from this that seeking to create equality for women is no solution; rather, equality must be fully established in society as a universal principle. In that way women too will become equal.

■ hooks criticises many feminists for not recognising this reality. They have concentrated too much on women, especially white, middle-class women. Using her perspective as a black woman, she asserts that women like her will achieve equality only if black people as a whole also achieve equality. Furthermore, she and all black women face problems that white women do not. The same is true of gay women, the poor and other minority groups. This is the essence of intersectionality. This confluence of multiple forms of discrimination and oppression makes feminist aims more complex than the movement had appreciated. It also means that men have a valid role to play because they can enter the struggle against inequality between all groups.

■ Perhaps the most radical of hooks's ideas, however, is that patriarchy has taught women to hate themselves, to see themselves as inferior. In her influential work *Feminism is for Everybody* (2000) she writes:

'We all knew first hand that we had been socialized as females by patriarchal thinking to see ourselves as inferior to men, to see ourselves as always and only in competition with one another for patriarchal approval, to look upon each other with jealousy, fear, and hatred. Sexist thinking made us judge each other without compassion and punish one another harshly. Feminist thinking helped us unlearn female self-hatred. It enabled us to break free of the hold patriarchal thinking had on our consciousness.'

■ For hooks, the struggle against patriarchy should have two elements. The first is the creation of a more equal society so that the multiple disadvantages that women face can be reduced and then eliminated. The second concerns the direct relationships between men and women. Men must come to understand the patriarchy that they are imposing, while women must break free of the preconceptions about themselves which are the product of men's domination of sexual culture. In her more romantic passages, hooks speaks of the power of love to conquer the current unhealthy relationships, but above all she argues that women need to 'unlearn self-hatred' and 'no longer see ourselves and our bodies as the property of men'.

■ In the history of feminism, bell hooks belongs mainly in the contemporary branch of the movement known as post-modern feminism, as she is attempting to break the movement free of its traditional perspectives and to accept modern realities.

The economy

All feminists are agreed that women are discriminated against in the economic world. The main examples of discrimination and inequality include:

- Women are used as a form of unpaid labour in the home.
- Women are used as a pool of low-paid, often part-time, dispensable labour, employed in times of economic growth but discarded during economic slumps. By working for low wages, women therefore help to keep the general level of incomes down by creating more competition for scarce jobs.
- Women tend to be paid lower wages than men for similar work (the 'pay gap').
- Even in fields where women employees are welcome, the more senior jobs in all forms of organisation tend to be reserved for men (there is a 'glass ceiling'). In other words, women are denied **equality of opportunity**.

Those who describe themselves as socialist feminists, however, go further. They take as their inspiration the ideas of Marx's close collaborator, Friedrich Engels (1820–95), in the late nineteenth century. Engels placed the oppression of women firmly at the door of capitalism. In pre-capitalist society, he claimed, women enjoyed a freer, more prominent place in most societies, but industrial capitalism reduced them to inferior wage-slaves. They also constituted a **reserve army of labour**, available for work at low wages at times when male labour was scarce and there was a danger that wages would rise, reducing capitalist profits, only to be discarded when they were no longer needed to keep wages low.

So, modern socialist feminists also see the exploitation of women and capitalism as bound together in a system of oppression. Just as male workers were exploited in the early days of capitalist development, so women are exploited in modern post-industrial society. British socialist feminist **Sheila Rowbotham** (1943–) (see 'Key thinker 3' box) takes up Engels' theory and proposes an equally revolutionary solution. This is the overthrow of capitalism and its replacement by a new world where equality is paramount. Just as industrial workers need to organise to combat capitalism, she says, so too do women:

Key terms

Equality of opportunity
Feminists demand that women should be offered equality of opportunity with men. This applies mainly to the fields of education and employment.

Reserve army of labour
This idea was developed by Friedrich Engels, suggesting that in industrial capitalist systems, women form such a group to increase output in the short term and also to keep wages low, but the group can be dispensed with when not required.

'It is only when women start to organize in large numbers that we become a political force, and begin to move towards the possibility of a truly democratic society in which every human being can be brave, responsible, thinking and diligent in the struggle to live at once freely and unselfishly. Such a democracy would be communism, and is beyond our present imagining.' (*Women, Resistance and Revolution*, 2014)

Key thinker 3

Sheila Rowbotham (1943–)

Sheila Rowbotham is a leading English socialist feminist who gained a towering reputation among academics, if less so among feminist activists. She came from a Marxist background, but also criticised Marxists for taking a narrow view of the oppression of women by confining themselves to analysing the role of women in industrial capitalism rather than in domestic life and wider society. Her most influential work was probably *Women's Consciousness, Men's World* (1973).

- She wrote one of the best-known statements in feminist literature when she said famously, 'Men will often admit other women are oppressed, but not you.' This implied that men cannot really understand the nature of the oppression they are imposing upon women. In other words, they can recognise it in theory but not in practice.
- For Rowbotham, the best hope for the liberation of women lies in a socialist future; under capitalism there is little hope that women will ever be able to escape from patriarchal society. She points out that the greatest advances for women have taken place after socialist revolutions. While the neo-liberal revolution in capitalist society in the 1980s appeared to offer widening opportunities for women, it did not offer ultimate liberation

and little progress was actually made. Women remain a cheap source of labour and are still denied the same opportunities as men. Only in a society where complete equality is imposed will women achieve equal status with men. This, for Rowbotham, means socialism.

- Paradoxically, Rowbotham is both a Marxist and a critic of Marxism. The inferior, oppressed position of women is seen by Marxists as economically determined, with which she agrees, but she adds that this is too narrow a view. Women are oppressed in the home and in the wider culture too. This means that a socialist revolution will not automatically liberate women; they must also be freed from oppression in home life, in personal relationships and in the wider culture. Firestone and Hanisch's assertion that 'the personal is political' is echoed in Rowbotham's work.
- This leads to one particularly interesting aspect of Rowbotham's feminism. Because she sees the roots of oppression as lying in personal relationships between men and women, it is as much the task of men as women to end patriarchy. Women cannot do it on their own, she believes; men must also become willing to relinquish their dominant position by seeing patriarchy for what it really is.

Activity

Explain, in no more than 100 words, why Rowbotham links feminism to socialism.

Different types of feminism

Liberal feminism

There is no doubt that the early origins of the women's movement and first wave feminism were largely liberal in nature. This was not surprising in view of the fact that they were mainly confined to upper- and middle-class women, among whom such an ideology flourished. The liberal content of early feminism included these principles:

- Liberty — women should be free to choose the nature of their own lives. This would include their roles as wives and mothers as well as their position in the labour force.
- Women should enjoy equality of opportunity with men — this meant they should have full access to education and to entry into any career and any profession.
- Women should enjoy the same civil rights as men — in other words, the rule of law should extend fully to them; the law must never discriminate against women.
- Women should also enjoy equal private rights — in particular, this concerned their relationship with property.
- Women should enjoy the same democratic rights as men — mainly relating to the right to vote and to stand for elected office.

The key figures in this kind of feminism were all liberals. They included Mary Wollstonecraft from the eighteenth century, John Stuart Mill and Charlotte Perkins Gilman from the nineteenth, and the suffragette movement in the twentieth.

As many of these objectives were realised, it became apparent that they were far from enough, that women remained an inferior gender and continued to suffer discrimination and lack of opportunity. By the 1960s it was apparent that there was something else preventing the liberation of women. It was the American Betty Friedan (1921–2006) who supplied the answer: the existence of patriarchy. Friedan discovered in her research into the lives of women that the problem was actually cultural in nature. She called it 'the problem with no name', implying that it was largely undiscovered. In particular, she pointed out that women themselves did not recognise the nature of their oppression. Patriarchy involved not only the dominance of men but also the self-assigned inferiority of women. She also pointed out that men themselves are the victims of patriarchy because they have been socially conditioned to think of themselves as superior. She expressed the hidden nature of women's plight thus:

Charlotte Perkins Gilman (1860–1935)

Charlotte Perkins Gilman expressed her version of early feminism in both fictional works and scholarly writings. Writing at a time when Darwinism was highly popular and being adapted to suit several political philosophies, not least the defence of free market capitalism, Gilman set up an attack on those who suggested that Darwin's theories could be used to justify male domination of society.

- Darwinist theory, mainly the 'survival of the fittest', suggested that it was biologically inevitable that men should be the dominant sex because they were more suited to compete in nature, being stronger and not tied down by the need to rear children. This was no longer the case, Gilman argued, largely because the nature of economic activity had changed so much. There were no reasons why women could not play an equal part alongside men in modern economies. So the biological differences between men and woman had become irrelevant. She asserted that women had equal brain power to men and this justified their equality in modern society.

- The way in which women should be liberated from such male domination lay in equality of opportunity and therefore a full place in the world of employment. Gilman was ahead of her time in this respect as she understood that girls are socialised from an early age, at home and in school, to take on the role of motherhood and homemaking rather than thinking of a wider role and career in the economic world outside the home. In other words, their confinement to roles in the home is culturally, not biologically determined. This notion of 'socialisation' into a male-dominated culture did not reach widespread consciousness until the 1960s.

- Gilman's perspective on the position of women in the modern economy was expressed succinctly and bluntly when she wrote in her book *Women and Economics* (1897): 'The labor of women in the house, certainly, enables men to produce more wealth than they otherwise could; and in this way women are economic factors in society. But so are horses.'

- However, it is probably in the field of family reform that Gilman is best remembered today. Concerned as she was by her belief that child rearing and housework amounted to domestic slavery, she campaigned for the destruction of the traditional nuclear family and its replacement by forms of communal living whereby child rearing and housework would be shared both among women and between men and women, thus freeing women for a wider role in society.

Activity

Explain, in no more than 100 words, what Gilman tells us about the difference between sex and gender.

'The problem lay buried, unspoken for many years in the minds of American women. It was a strange stirring, a sense of dissatisfaction, a yearning that women suffered in the middle of the twentieth century in the United States. Each suburban housewife struggled with it alone.' (*The Feminine Mystique*, 1963)

Both de Beauvoir and Friedan also stressed the concept of **otherness** in their discussion of women's place in modern society. The theory of otherness places certain groups as somehow 'other' or outside society. They are also considered to be inferior. Feminists, including the early liberals, applied otherness to women. In the world of men, they are outsiders, treated like an inferior minority. De Beauvoir called men the 'first sex' and women the 'second sex'.

Activity

Explain, in no more than 200 words, why Friedan and de Beauvoir are known as feminist pioneers.

Once the true nature of patriarchy was revealed by writers like Friedan, women were able to take up the cause for themselves. However, liberals refuse to insist that all women should seek to compete with men for superior roles in society. As liberals they accept that women should be free to choose whether they take up traditional domestic roles, to which they are usually best suited, or whether they should enter the world historically dominated by men. Liberal feminists proposed three main forms of action to combat patriarchy:

- First, the opportunities for women to be able to make their own choices had to be opened up by ending **discrimination** and inequality. This aspiration is often described as **gender equality**.
- Second, cultural attitudes which demeaned and reinforced women's sense of inferiority had to be combatted. This was to be achieved through education, propaganda and all-out opposition to sexist attitudes and language.
- Third, women would have to achieve formal equality in all fields. This largely involved legislation. As first wave feminists had also insisted, there must be **political equality and legal equality**.

Liberal feminism continued to flourish from the 1960s, but it was soon to experience a challenge to its pre-eminence. This came from a growing group of feminists who believed that the liberal agenda was limited in its aspirations and oversimplistic in its analysis of patriarchy. This was radical feminism, sometimes also described as the women's liberation movement. It appeared in the late 1960s.

Key terms

Otherness In feminist theory, otherness refers to the position of women in patriarchal society, treated as separate to society, an inferior minority, subordinate to men.

Discrimination In the feminist discourse, discrimination refers to those aspects of a patriarchal society that limit women's life choices, economic prospects and career options, as well as resulting in lower pay and poor job security.

Gender equality This is an aspiration of liberal, socialist and some radical feminists. It refers to the aim of achieving complete legal and cultural equality for women. All attitudes that suggest men are superior to women are to be outlawed or opposed in education and the media.

Political equality and legal equality These are key demands of early and second wave feminists. Political equality mainly consists of the equal right to vote and stand for office, while legal equality means that the law, in all its aspects, should treat women in the same way as it treats men; there should be no distinction between the sexes.

137

Does liberal feminism fail to understand the true nature of patriarchy?

Yes

- It has been a mainly white, middle-class movement and so does not understand the position of working-class and ethnic minority women who face multiple forms of oppression. This is often described as intersectionality.
- Liberal feminists, in supporting capitalist society, do not understand the ways in which market capitalism inevitably oppresses and discriminates against women.
- Liberal feminists underestimate the importance of 'the personal is political'. They do not understand that personal and sexual relations between men and women are power relationships and therefore are political in nature.

No

- Liberal feminists understand that formal inequality is not the only problem but they claim that the cultural nature of patriarchy is key. Therefore they have made sexism a key target in their struggle for women's liberation.
- By achieving legal or formal equality for women on the whole, liberal feminists believe that patriarchy will decline as men will no longer hold dominant positions in society.
- Liberal feminists claim that women now have a more developed understanding of patriarchy and are steadily achieving sufficient power to be able to combat it.

Reformist A term often used to describe moderate, liberal feminists who wish to reform society rather than transform it. Radical feminists use the term pejoratively of liberals.

Difference and equality feminism These are opposing perspectives on women's place in society. Difference feminists see women as different but equal or even superior to men. Difference should be accepted and even celebrated. Equality feminists seek to eliminate cultural differences between the sexes in the pursuit of equality.

Radical feminism

Radical feminism is not really one movement but a series of different perspectives on the problems posed by patriarchy. They do, however, all have some characteristics in common:

- They propose the destruction of patriarchal society and its transformation into a completely new form.
- While liberal feminists are **reformists**, radical feminists are revolutionary in their outlook, though not normally favouring violent revolution.
- Radical feminists stress the importance of female consciousness in both their critique of patriarchy and their proposals for a new social order.
- They are mostly known as **difference feminists** rather than **equality feminists**. Instead of attempting to ignore the biological and cultural differences between men and women, as liberal feminists do in their pursuit of equality, radical feminists normally stress and celebrate the differences between men and women.

Two types of difference exist within radical feminism. The first lies in how they analyse patriarchal society and the second concerns the way in which they seek to defeat it. Each is explored below.

Radical perspectives on patriarchy

Kate Millett (1934–) (see 'Key thinker 5' box) looked first to the family to aid understanding of patriarchy. In marriage, she argued, women are exploited both sexually and economically. This became a common theme among radical feminists. Her great work *Sexual Politics*, published in 1969, sent shockwaves through the feminist movement. It was a root-and-branch criticism of the role of men in patriarchal society. Men oppress women in all fields: in the home, in the economy and in life in general. Their domination is political in nature because it involves the exercise of power. Millett had much to do with the popularisation of the idea of male chauvinism, the tendency for men to exercise and celebrate their power over women.

Almost as dramatic as the publication of Millett's *Sexual Politics*, Germaine Greer's *The Female Eunuch*, also appearing in 1970 — a key year for radical feminism — brought a new perspective to the radical movement. It helped Greer that she was unashamedly heterosexual, so it could not be claimed that hers was merely a lesbian rant. At the centre of her contention, she asserted that men actually hate women and that is why they oppress them. Furthermore, women have been taught to hate themselves and so willingly subject themselves to an inferior position. In *The Female Eunuch* she asserted that women must understand and then throw off the stigma of inferiority imposed on them by man: 'Until women themselves reject stigma and refuse to feel shame for the way others treat them, they have no hope of achieving full human stature.'

Germaine Greer (born 1939), a controversial and challenging feminist

Another 1970 publication was Firestone's *The Dialectic of Sex*. Firestone saw the history of civilisation as a dialectic struggle between men and women, in the same way that Marx had seen history in terms of a dialectic class struggle. The origins of the gender struggle lay in the biological differences between men and women and the traditional bondage which women faced by being confined to life in the home. Patriarchy exists, for Firestone, because it has always existed and it has always existed because women are constrained by childbirth and housework, destined for ever to be enslaved by men.

The most controversial of all modern radical feminists was perhaps Andrea Dworkin (1946–2005). She campaigned against the sexual oppression of women, and in particular saw pornography as symptomatic of men's view of women as little more than sex objects. The only way this could be combatted would be for women to form themselves into lesbian communities. As long as women allow themselves to be sex objects for men, they will never achieve true liberation.

Such feminists as Millett, Greer and Firestone all have in common their stress on the importance of specifically female consciousness of patriarchy. Women's consciousness of their

Political ideas for A-level

Key thinker 5

Kate Millett (1934–)

American Kate Millett is perhaps the most influential of all the radical feminists. Her best-known book, *Sexual Politics*, published in 1969 at the height of the new interest in feminism, was both controversial and provocative, but it sparked off a new direction in the movement. At first she was active in the National Organization for Women, but she quickly moved towards a more radical form of politics.

- Millett's perception of patriarchy is a dual one. She sees the dominance of men in terms of both sexism — an entrenched belief in male superiority — and heterosexualism — the idea that heterosexual relationships are superior to gay relationships. She herself is bisexual (though predominantly lesbian), which has placed her in a good position to be able to view sexism in a more complete way.

- Her main contention in *Sexual Politics* was that it is necessary for women to find sexual liberation first if they are to achieve liberation in general life. All heterosexual relationships are effectively political in a patriarchal society because they involve men exercising power over women. It follows from this that women who are able to accept their lesbianism or are able to convert to that form of sexuality place themselves on the road to personal liberation. Needless to say, these were highly controversial views, which attracted a huge following but also a cascade of criticism.

- It would be wrong, however, to characterise Millett as nothing more than a 'lesbian feminist'. She also analysed women's place in the society and in the economy. For her, as for many radical thinkers of the time, the word 'politics' had acquired a new, broader connotation. This was the idea that wherever one group oppresses another, the result is political in nature and the solution must be the liberation of the oppressed group (hence the wider term 'liberation politics'). So it is with men oppressing women, Millett argued. Patriarchy is therefore intensely political in nature.

- Millett is not normally classed as a socialist feminist, but some of her ideas chime with socialist ideas. In particular, she described the plight of working-class women thus:

  'The toil of working class women is more readily accepted as "need", if not always by the working class itself, at least by the middle class. And, to be sure, it serves the purpose of making cheap labour in factory and low grade service and clerical positions. Its wages and tasks are so unremunerative that, unlike more prestigious employment for women, it fails to threaten patriarchy financially or psychologically.' (*Sexual Politics*, 1969)

- It is also implied in the above quotations that Millett criticised parts of the feminist movement for being concerned largely with problems relating to middle-class women.

Activity

Explain, in no more than 200 words, why Kate Millett is described as a radical rather than a liberal feminist.

own inferiority stems partly from their biological role, which appears to be subordinate to that of men, and partly from the view of themselves imposed on them by men. Furthermore, patriarchy consciously destroys any ideas of potential liberation among women. In a major criticism of the limited horizons of liberal feminists and the self-delusion that women have the potential to liberate themselves, Zillah Eisenstein wrote:

> 'Patriarchy, as a system of oppression, recognizes the potential power of women and the actual power of men. Its purpose is to destroy female consciousness about her potential power, which derives from the necessity of society to reproduce itself.' (*The Radical Future of Liberal Feminism*, 1981)

Radical responses to patriarchy

Radical feminists have a number of proposals to combat patriarchy and to liberate women from its clutches. On the whole these solutions are based on their perspectives on the nature of patriarchy. Their proposals include the following:

- The abolition of the nuclear family and its replacement by communal forms of child rearing and living in general. This will naturally remove the male domination of the family. Millett was able to combine this vision with her support for the ideals of socialism.
- Sexual liberation is critical for many radicals, notably Greer. By escaping from the limitations of traditional male–female relationships, women can free themselves from male domination and, in Greer's terms, cease to hate themselves.
- The elimination of biological roles is perhaps the most radical solution of all. Firestone, in particular, celebrates the potential of modern bio-technology to free women from their biological enslavement. Recommending androgyny — the removal of sex differences between men and women — she envisaged a world where women no longer need men to reproduce the species. This will result in liberation of a fundamental kind.

Cultural feminism

Cultural feminism is a branch of the radical movement that has persisted from its early days in the nineteenth century and is still well supported. It presents a very different perspective on society to most feminists. Cultural feminists accept that there are natural gender differences between men and women, unlike most radical feminists who see gender roles as an

Key term

Cultural feminism This type of feminism accepts that women are born with different cultural characteristics to men as well as biological differences. These characteristics are seen as both useful to society and, in some cases, superior to male characteristics.

illusion perpetrated on women by men. Some modern cultural feminists have also suggested that female characteristics are actually superior to those that are common in men. Thus, such differences are to be embraced and used rather than opposed.

This form of feminism explores the essence of women and finds that it is more caring and nurturing than the essence of men, which tends to be competitive and aggressive. It therefore follows that a world dominated by the female essence would be more peaceful and just, and would protect the environment more effectively. So-called eco-feminists have adopted this perspective. Cultural feminists accept that women are more likely to take up domestic roles but value them as highly, or even more highly, than roles traditionally played by men.

Socialist feminism

Marxist feminists look back to the ideas of Friedrich Engels, Marx's close colleague, for their inspiration. Engels understood that women were becoming a key element in the future of capitalism. Women, he pointed out, had always been deprived of private property. This resulted in them being oppressed by property owners throughout history, just as property-less peasants and workers always had been. As capitalism developed and needed increasing quantities of workers, women became a vital source of available, low-paid labour. Their lack of property increasingly forced them into paid employment.

Modern Marxist feminists take a similar view but criticise Engels for over-stressing the importance of property. In modern society, as women increasingly have come to own property independently, their oppression has not ceased; they remain an exploited part of the workforce. Needless to say, therefore, Marxist feminists see the destruction of capitalism as a precondition for the liberation of women.

Somewhat less extreme socialists have rejected the idea that class is the only schism in society that has any meaning. They argue that both class and patriarchy are sources of oppression. Not surprisingly, therefore, socialist feminists tend to concentrate on the plight of working-class women. While liberal feminists concentrate on such issues as equal opportunities and equal pay for women, socialist feminists argue that only the extreme modification of capitalism will liberate women from their inferior economic position. Thus, for example, the state ownership of industry will eliminate the need for women to compete against men for employment.

Sheila Rowbotham (born 1943), a leading socialist feminist

British feminist Sheila Rowbotham is described as a socialist rather than a Marxist as she rejects the rigid economic determinism of Marx. For her, female oppression certainly does have economic roots, but it also stems from the traditional nature of the nuclear family and the cultural dominance of male sexuality. While the economic liberation and equality of women is a precondition for the sexual revolution, it is not sufficient to raise the consciousness of women or to ensure their ability to define their own future.

Above all, socialists seek the liberation of women from their economic dependence upon men. This dependence begins in the home but extends to the economic world in general. The Chicago Women's Liberation Union, which was founded in 1969, led the socialist feminist movement in the USA. It was committed to a two-pronged attack upon patriarchy. First, power had to be distributed more evenly in society, so that even working-class women would benefit, and second, there was to be a change in the culture, notably in the education of women.

Activity

Explain, in no more than 200 words, in what ways some feminists believe women are economically oppressed.

Debate 3

Are women inevitably oppressed and discriminated against under capitalism?

Yes

- As long as men dominate positions of economic power, they will discriminate against women.
- The predominance of women playing domestic roles means that men are bound to dominate economic life.
- Women's innate lack of aggressiveness and competitiveness makes them ill-suited to the world of capitalism.

No

- Women are making progress (albeit slow) in achieving senior positions in economic life. Once a critical mass is achieved, male domination will cease.
- It is no longer inevitable that women must concentrate on domestic roles — women can play a full part in economic life outside the home.
- There is no such thing as the 'innate non-aggressive' nature of women — they are able to deal with the competitive world as well as men. In addition, even if women are naturally more caring, this will make for a more humane and just form of capitalism.

Post-modern feminism

Post-modernism is a general term that refers to a modern tendency to reject forms of thinking which have become limited by their confinement to traditional ways of viewing the world. In terms of feminism this means rejecting the fixed ideas of various theorists, such as radicals and socialists, and seeing the position of women as a complex problem with many competing explanations and therefore solutions. Post-modernists also stress the importance of language in carrying forward patriarchal attitudes and sexism. This has given rise to criticisms of 'political correctness', but such feminists continue to insist that gender stereotypes are perpetuated by vocabulary.

In practice, post-modern feminism proposes that women must be given the freedom to make choices for themselves. For some this may entail choosing a traditional female role in the family, for others it may mean competing with men on an equal basis. The same is true of sexuality. Women must choose the nature of their relationships with men or other women without resorting to traditional feminist attitudes. In other words, each woman has her own unique experience of life and must therefore liberate herself in her own way. Of course, the search for legal, political, economic and cultural equality goes on as women cannot make such free choices if patriarchy and male superiority continue to dominate in society.

This is sometimes referred to as third wave feminism. This has a number of themes. It includes intersectionality, as we have seen above, wherein the problems of women are seen in terms of more than one single identity — being a woman — but rather include being a black woman or a gay woman or a working-class woman, etc. This idea is also sometimes described as post-structuralism, suggesting the traditional structures of society have broken down and so cannot be used to explain the problem of women. Post-feminism has also emerged. Post-feminists reject the traditional discourse used by radical feminists, suggesting instead that it is for each woman to choose her own lifestyle and to find her own liberation. The fact that many feminist battles have been won makes such widening of choice for women more possible.

Summary: key themes and key thinkers

	Human nature	The state	Society	The economy
Simone de Beauvoir	Gender differences are created by men in society. They are not natural.	The state reinforces a culture that prevents women from expressing their true freedom and identity.	De Beauvoir's existentialism dominated her feminism. Social constraints prevent individuals, not just women, from attaining self-realisation and true freedom.	Men's domination of economic life restricts the life choices open to women.
bell hooks	Women, in common with men, have multiple identities and therefore experience multiple forms of oppression.	The state is dominated by white males and therefore reflects and reinforces their dominant position in society.	Society is full of complex relationships between different minorities. In order to resolve social conflict, love between different minority cultures must be established.	Women living in poverty have problems that middle-class women do not face. The liberation of the poor is an economic as well as a social issue.
Sheila Rowbotham	Women's consciousness of the world is created by men.	The state is the servant of capitalism.	The nature of society is economically determined. Society reflects the dominant position of both capitalists and men in general.	Rowbotham has a Marxist perspective. Women are a low-paid reserve army of labour.
Charlotte Perkins Gilman	The biological differences between men and women are irrelevant. Women can compete equally with men.	Gilman had no especially distinctive views on the state.	Society has always assigned inferior roles to women. In modern society this no longer has any justification.	The domestic servitude of women allowed men to dominate the outside economic world.
Kate Millett	Women are all capable of freeing themselves from male oppression by engaging in lesbian relationships.	The state is merely the agent of patriarchy. It is part of the problem but not the solution.	Modern society is completely characterised by patriarchy, which is all-pervasive and infests both the private and public spheres.	Millett is a quasi-socialist but this is not fundamental to her feminism.

Tensions within feminism

As in most political movements there are significant divisions within feminism (see Table 4.1). Indeed, all the main feminist thinkers are unique; it is a political ideology rich in its variety and in its analysis of patriarchy. It is therefore difficult to identify the most important tensions within feminism. A few such differences can be emphasised, however:

Continued

1 Radical feminists reject the liberal feminist agenda on the grounds that it fails to understand the true nature of patriarchy. Liberal feminists see patriarchy in terms of the historical dominance of men in society. This, say the liberals, explains the oppression of women; it is merely a characteristic of society rather than a fundamental explanation of how society works for women. Radical feminists provide a number of explanations of patriarchy, all of which suggest that it lies deep in human consciousness, so deep that there is a need for a dramatic and revolutionary change in such patriarchal consciousness. Mere legal, political and cultural reform will not make a significant difference therefore.

2 Liberals counter this by arguing that radical feminists are imposing their own views on female consciousness which seek to restrict their freedom of choice. As long as there is a framework of legal and political equality, women should be free to adopt their own aspirations, say liberals. In particular, liberals criticise radicals on the grounds that they do not recognise that there is a private sphere where women should be free to choose their own status and consciousness. Radicals, say the liberals, are imposing forms of consciousness on women by breaking down the barrier between the public and private spheres.

3 Socialist feminists argue that liberals and radicals have de-emphasised the importance of economic factors in the oppression of women. For them, the inferior, exploited status of women in economic life is the true source of their oppression. Patriarchy has economic origins, they insist, and under modern capitalism this has intensified.

4 Radical feminists take issue with socialists, especially Marxists, for stressing economic factors excessively. The patriarchal domination of society may have economic elements, but the truth is much more complex. Patriarchy is cultural and psychological, not just economic. By over-stressing economics, radical feminists argue, socialists fail to recognise that there is still a great deal of patriarchy in socialist societies.

5 There is tension between difference feminists and equality feminists. The difference feminists say that seeking equality is a recognition that male characteristics are superior. The feminism of difference denies male superiority and seeks a different road to liberated consciousness by stressing sex differences and celebrating the superior qualities of women.

Table 4.1 Key distinctions within feminism

Liberal	Radical	Socialist
This is a reform movement.	This is revolutionary, seeking a social and cultural revolution.	This is often revolutionary but proposes an economic transformation of society towards socialism.
Patriarchy is a modern phenomenon which can be combatted through legal and cultural reform.	Patriarchy has long and deep historical roots. It has penetrated deep into male and female consciousness.	Patriarchy is largely economically based. Men dominate women generally because they dominate them economically.
If legal and economic equality can be achieved for women, they will achieve general liberation.	Male and female consciousness must change if liberation is to be achieved.	Patterns of employment and the economic structure of the family have to be transformed to achieve the economic liberation of women.
Women should be free to choose how they conduct their lives and their relationships with men.	It is not sufficient to create freedom for women — men's domination must be destroyed and their consciousness of superiority reversed.	Women cannot be genuinely free until they achieve economic freedom.

Conclusion: feminism today

Although we live in what some liberal feminists have claimed is 'post-feminist society', most feminists disagree, so feminism remains relevant and vibrant both as an ideology and as a social movement. Many of its objectives have been achieved in terms of legal equality and the outlawing of discrimination, but feminists remain active and numerous. There are five main areas of action:

1 Liberal feminists, having won most of their legal battles in western democratic societies, still campaign against sexist attitudes and language and seek to establish equality in terms of opportunities. They point to the persistence of the apparent discrimination against women in business, politics and the professions. Equal pay also remains an aspiration. Although equal pay for equal work is enshrined in law in most western countries, women still typically earn less than men and populate low-paid employment. The Fawcett Society in the UK, for example, has become extremely active in campaigning to close the pay gap between men and women and to encourage the elevation of more women to company boardrooms.

2 A concern for all feminists, liberal and radical, is the plight of women in many traditional societies. An emblematic issue is female circumcision (female genital mutilation — FGM) but there are several other issues in this field, including forced marriage, the practice of men having more than one wife (polygamy), the denial of educational opportunity for girls and dress restrictions, that have attracted their attention. This does create a problem for liberals who are instinctively reluctant to interfere in alternative cultures, but some of the more extreme anti-female practices are still unconditionally opposed by such liberal thinkers.

3 Socialist feminists, especially Marxists, still insist that women are an exploited class within modern capitalism. They see the liberation of women as synonymous with the destruction of free-market capitalism. In this regard feminists remain active within anti-capitalist movements, in anarchist groups, in radical environmental campaigns and in left-wing political parties in general.

4 Radical feminists continue to argue that liberals are deluding themselves if they believe that women can escape oppression through reform. They see patriarchy as still deeply rooted in modern society. Some radicals continue to urge women to raise their female consciousness by forming their own communes, while others urge resistance to cultural dominance of men in such areas as politics, education, the arts and the media.

5 There are specific campaigns being run by feminist groups in relation to specific groups and issues in society. This includes black and Muslim feminists where issues specific to them have become prominent.

Further reading

Five classic works of feminist thinkers are these:
Simone de Beauvoir. *The Second Sex.*
Shulamith Firestone. *The Dialectic of Sex.*
Betty Friedan. *The Feminine Mystique.*
Germaine Greer. *The Female Eunuch.*
Kate Millett. *Sexual Politics.*
Important works about feminism include:
Gay, R. (2014) *Bad Feminist*, Harper Perennial.
Mackay, F. (2015) *Radical Feminism*, Palgrave.
Randall, V. (1987) *Women and Politics*, Palgrave.
Squires, J. (2007) *The New Politics of Gender Equality*, Palgrave.
Walters, M. (2005) *Feminism: A Very Short Introduction*, Oxford University Press.

Exam-style questions

Essay questions

The following questions are similar to those in examinations set by Edexcel (Pearson) and AQA.

Edexcel (24 marks) or AQA (25 marks):

1 To what extent do radical feminists criticise liberal feminism? You must use appropriate thinkers you have studied to support your answer.

2 To what extent do feminists believe that patriarchy is essentially an economically based issue? You must use appropriate thinkers you have studied to support your answer.

AQA only (25 marks):

3 'The personal is the political.' With reference to the thinkers you have studied, analyse and evaluate why and to what extent this statement is important to feminists.

4 'The issue for feminists should not be equality, but the recognition of difference.' Analyse and evaluate with reference to the thinkers you have studied.

Chapter 5

Anarchism

Learning outcomes

This chapter will enable students to:

- be aware of the early development of anarchism
- understand the core values of anarchism as a political ideology
- understand the various types of anarchism and how they differ
- be aware of the main tensions between the various anarchist traditions
- know how and to what extent anarchism still flourishes
- understand the ideas of anarchism's key thinkers

Introduction

When we hear the word 'anarchism' or 'anarchist' it can tend to conjure up a variety of vivid images in our minds. These may range from the masked, black-clad bomber seeking to assassinate a national leader or wreak havoc in public buildings, to small groups of hippies setting up a commune in a squatted house or perhaps living a natural life of self-sufficiency in the countryside. In truth, these images do have some origin in reality — throughout the history of anarchism, there

149

have indeed been violent revolutionaries as well as peaceful communities who have decided to withdraw from society to lead a 'perfect' existence. They also accurately reflect the immense number of variations that anarchism has thrown up throughout its history. But our images can also be misleading. They underestimate the rigour that many anarchist thinkers and activists have adopted when developing their critiques of society and their proposals for alternatives.

So, one immediate problem when discussing anarchism is the need to separate reality from our preconceptions. A second problem, as we have seen above, is that anarchism is a richly varied tradition, so much so that many commentators have argued that it is not a single movement but rather a series of different traditions which share just one common theme — opposition to the existence of a political state. Finally, a third difficulty is that there has never existed a genuine anarchist order in any society. There have been small, temporary, 'micro' examples in natural, small-scale communes or in hippy-style communities, but nothing on a large scale. There are some kibbutzim in Israel which could be described as anarchist in nature. These are self-governing communities which are, as far as possible, self-supporting and usually operate a form of internal democracy where every member has an equal say in the running of the kibbutz. This is not pure anarchism, though, because the kibbutzim rely to some extent on the existence of the state and maintain relations with central authorities.

The origins of anarchism

It is customary, when considering anarchism, to remind ourselves of the origins of the word itself. This is not out of idle interest but is important for understanding what it is that binds all anarchists together. The Greek and Latin origins of the word suggest mainly 'an absence of government' or 'without a state'. This does not indicate a state of chaos, though the term is often carelessly used in that way today.

We can identify four main origins of the anarchist tradition (Table 5.1). These are very different from each other and reflect the varied nature of anarchism as introduced above and explored fully below. The four developments we should study are these:

■ Philosophical anarchism originated in the period known as the Enlightenment, coinciding with the eighteenth century. This movement looked at the first principles of society and the human condition, without proposing any specific new social order. Two key figures here were Jean-Jacques Rousseau (1712–78) and William Godwin (1756–1836). Rousseau, who influenced anarchism without being an anarchist himself, argued that mankind is 'born free but is everywhere in chains' and so established the principle that we are born with a right to liberty but are constrained by society and government. Godwin's optimistic view of human nature suggested that a more perfect society without a state was feasible if every individual could achieve moral perfection, largely through education. He argued that morally perfect human beings could be trusted to use their private judgement for good ends and so would need no guidance from the law.

Key term

Private judgement This ideal associated with William Godwin refers to the way in which people will be able to make moral, rational and non-selfish judgements about how they should act when society ceases to be corrupt. Such private judgement becomes ever more possible as moral education spreads among the population.

■ Communism emerged in the nineteenth century. This general movement was a reaction both to the remnants of feudalism in central and eastern Europe and to increased industrialisation that was exploiting and brutalising the growing industrial working class. Its best known manifestation is Marxism, but there was also an anarchist communist movement which came to different conclusions from Marx. The anarcho-communists insisted on the immediate abolition of the state, while the Marxists envisaged a workers' state replacing capitalism. Both the anarchists and Marxists, however, saw a stateless, self-governing communist society as the ultimate destination of human history. The key figure in this movement was **Peter Kropotkin** (1842–1921) (see 'Key thinker 2' box).

■ Collectivist anarchism was a form of anarchism based on industrial development and the plight of the working class rather than the peasantry. It appeared in various forms, some of which have characteristics common with socialism. Some described such anarchist movements as decentralised socialism, or 'socialism without a state'. Collectivist anarchism flourished in the second half of the nineteenth century and into the first few decades of the twentieth century. **Mikhail Bakunin** (1814–76) (see 'Key thinker 3' box) was a leading member of this movement.

■ Individualist anarchism appeared both in the USA, where it was a largely peaceful and naturalistic tendency, and in Europe, where it was more violent and intensely egotistical. In this tradition the individual is urged either to revolt against the state and destroy it or to withdraw from the state altogether and become a free, self-supporting individual. Henry Thoreau (1817–62) is perhaps the best example of the former and **Max Stirner** (1806–56) (see 'Key thinker 1' box) of the latter. Its modern manifestation has had two forms. The first was to be seen in the hippy, counter-culture movement of the 1960s and 1970s, and the second in an extreme form of libertarianism, known as anarcho-capitalism. Murray Rothbard (1926–95) was a typical anarcho-capitalist. He and many others, mainly in the USA, proposed a stateless society where free-market capitalism is allowed completely free rein without taxation or regulation.

This brief description of how anarchism has grown and developed over two centuries demonstrates how varied an ideology it is. The deeper exploration of these ideas, below, further demonstrates this reality.

Activity

Explain, in no more than 100 words, the main differences between individualist anarchism and collectivist or communist forms of anarchism.

Table 5.1 Main strands in the development of anarchism

Form	Description
Philosophical	Based on fundamental ideas about human nature and the human condition. Early anarchist philosophy stressed the sovereignty of the individual and their ability to exercise that sovereignty rationally and with sympathy for others.
Communist	Anarcho-communists stress mankind's innate sense of social order, seeing people as social animals who prefer to cooperate than to compete with each other. This branch of anarchism proposes small, independent voluntary communities known as communes.
Collectivist	More associated with the industrial working class, collectivists propose the creation of various forms of associations of workers who cooperate and trade with each other to their mutual benefit.
Individualist	Stresses the egoistical side of mankind. All social and political restraints are opposed so that the individual can give full rein to the pursuit of their own interests. Some forms stress cooperation between individuals, others stress competition.

The core ideas of anarchism

The great Russian–American anarchist **Emma Goldman** (1869–1940) (see 'Key thinker 5' box), in her book *Anarchism and Other Essays*, summed up anarchism thus:

> 'Anarchism stands for the liberation of the human mind from the dominion of religion and liberation of the human body from the coercion of property; liberation from the shackles and restraint of government. It stands for a social order based on the free grouping of individuals.'

Goldman's summation of anarchist thought tells us much about the nature of this philosophy and political movement. We can now dissect this description to understand anarchism better.

Human nature

The philosophers of the eighteenth-century Enlightenment period invariably started their analysis of society and mankind with assertions about human nature. Indeed, many, such as John Locke (see Chapter 1) and Rousseau (see the previous section of this chapter) envisaged what they called a 'state of nature'. This was a real or imaginary world that existed before human society was formed, when people were autonomous individuals seeking to secure the means of their survival. The questions such philosophers asked was: What was the nature of mankind in such an age? What motivates human beings? How did their instincts tell them to behave? The purpose of such speculation was to construct a vision of society that would accord with the natural state of mankind. Many anarchists asked these same questions.

These are especially important questions for anarchists because all of them believe that people through history have had their character corrupted by the nature of society, the state and government in particular. They argue that if the state can be removed along with its corrupting effects, the true form of human nature will be restored. There is, though, a problem we face in studying the anarchist response. This is that different anarchist thinkers have come to very different conclusions about what fundamental human nature actually is.

On the whole anarchists have come to three different conclusions about human nature:

1 That people are basically self-interested or egoistical and will cooperate with other people only if they believe it to be in their own interests.

2 That people are born without any basic nature. We are, in fact, a *tabula rasa*, a blank surface on which society, with all its faults, writes our character. Put another, more contemporary way, human nature is environmentally determined.

3 That people are born 'good' in that they are sociable and rational and that we take into account the interests of others when making decisions — that we prefer **altruism** to selfishness. This also implies that we are naturally social, that we prefer to live and work cooperatively in natural groups rather than to compete with each other as individuals.

Perhaps the most striking advocate of the idea that human nature is self-interested or egoistical was Max Stirner. For Stirner, the **ego** was part of the essence of every individual. Mankind's ego tells him that he is entitled to everything on the earth. So, if people are to be true to themselves, they should pursue that aim. This is not to say that people are naturally irrational.

Key terms

Altruism This is an aspect of human nature where people take into account the needs and feelings of others when making decisions. It also suggests that we will naturally help other people, perhaps even putting the needs of others above our own. Some anarchists see human nature as being imbued with such altruism, though others disagree.

Ego The ego is that part of a person's character that is interested exclusively in itself. In anarchist terms ego implies that people will follow their self-interest, even if this clashes with the interests of others. It is associated with individualist anarchism.

153

On the contrary, it is possible that an individual will take into consideration the interest of others if it is in their own interest to do so. How does this idea impact on social order? Stirner envisaged a world where increasing numbers of people would become egoists and eventually would form themselves into 'unions of egoism' — that is, groups of people united in the common purpose of pursuing their joint interests.

The second view — that we are born without any innate characteristics — was also common among anarchists. This belief led to the assertion that it is the state and society that corrupt individuals. It follows that if a perfect, moral society can be established, individuals will themselves become moral and altruistic. This is extremely important as it suggests that anarchist ideas of order are natural and are not artificial constructions.

Bakunin, in particular, took this view. For him, the only impulse we have when we are born is towards some kind of natural justice. We do understand the difference between good and evil, but there is nothing that compels us to act in any particular way. It depends on our experience of life whether we follow the rules of natural justice.

A third view, which anarchists share with liberals, is that we are naturally good when we are born. This outlook is important because it suggests that anarchist ideas of a 'perfect' order and society are feasible. Associated with this is the belief that we are naturally sociable and prefer to live in social groups. Godwin was an early advocate of the idea that we are capable of moral perfection.

It is fundamental to all anarchists that each individual is sovereign and is entitled to their own liberty. We should ask here: how does this differ from classical liberalism, which also stresses such freedom? The answer is that liberals argue that the state and its laws are necessary to establish and protect liberty by protecting people from each other. Anarchists reject this view and say it is no freedom at all. True freedom consists of individual liberty without any resort to laws and the use of force. They all therefore seek to reconcile the absence of artificial, human laws with the protection of freedom. Different anarchists make this reconciliation in different ways. Godwin, for example, argued that if people are allowed to use private judgement, they will not infringe on the freedom of others, so laws are unnecessary. Peter Kropotkin and his communist colleagues said that mankind is naturally sociable, so people will find freedom within voluntary social groups. 'Are bees in a hive free?' Kropotkin would ask. 'Yes' was his answer because they voluntarily and naturally live collectively without any external force.

Max Stirner (1806–56)

Max Stirner was a German philosopher who became a political activist and revolutionary. He was a major influence upon individualist anarchism, modern existentialism, the radical philosophy of Friedrich Nietzsche (1844–1900) and the extreme form of anarchism known as **nihilism**, which proposes the abolition of both state and society. He developed the concept of the self-interested ego, a fundamental aspect of mankind's character. His best known work was *The Ego and His Own* (1845).

Stirner was opposed not only to the state but also to religion and ideology. He saw ideologies — even socialism and Marxism — as a denial of individual conscience. He called all these threats to the exercise of egoism 'spooks' and 'ghosts'. What he meant was that they were shadowy illusions which appeared to promote individual liberty but which in practice were suppressing it. In place of ideology and organised revolution, Stirner advocated that each individual should develop their sense of ego. As egoism spread it would begin to challenge the authority of the state, religion and ideology in general. This would not, though, be a state of permanent conflict between individuals. Instead, egoists would form themselves into 'unions of egoism', cooperative groups that saw their self-interest in terms of mutual interest. These unions would gradually replace the state.

Stirner believed that the individual was entitled to anything they could find in the world. Furthermore, it was the right of one's ego to use other people for one's own purposes. He put it this way in *The Ego and His Own*:

> 'Where the world comes in my way — and it comes in my way everywhere — I consume it to quiet the hunger of my egoism. For me you are nothing but my food, even as I too am fed upon and turned to use by you. We have only one relation to each other, that of usableness, of utility, of use.'

Stirner acquired a reputation as one of the most radical and revolutionary of the nineteenth-century anarchists, determined to bring down the state by force. His view of human nature was also perhaps the most pessimistic in the movement. He did, however, defend himself against attack by asserting that there was another side to man's nature than mere egoism. People are capable of altruism, he claimed, of fellow feeling, but this would show itself only if a person's ego saw altruism as being in their own interests.

Finally, Stirner can also be seen as a champion of unrestrained individual liberty. Not only must the state and private property be abolished to establish the widest possible freedom, he insisted, but so must any moral restraints that might inhibit the individual. So, morality, religion, ideology and philosophy are all to be resisted by the free individual. Stirner shared this determination to resist morality with the syndicalist Georges Sorel, who believed that committing acts that outraged public morality was a positive step on the road to genuine liberty of the mind.

Activity

Explain, in no more than 100 words, the nature and importance of the ego for Stirner.

Key term

Nihilism This term is used to describe the most extreme examples of individualist anarchism ('nihil' meaning 'nothing'). Nihilists oppose all forms of social organisation, including government, proposing instead a society of free individuals. Most nihilists are also known for their violent methods.

Along with Mikhail Bakunin (1814–76), Kropotkin is seen as a key figure in the development of collectivist or communist anarchism. His belief in self-sufficiency and equality in small communities made him popular within the commune movement which arose in the 1960s among young, so-called hippies. His ideas for promoting self-sufficiency have also endeared him to contemporary 'anarcho-environmentalists' who combine ideas of communal living with the preservation of scarce resources and opposition to further industrialisation. His implacable opposition to the idea of the state, meanwhile, sets him apart from socialists who base their ideas on the importance of the creation of a 'workers' state'. Above all, however, Kropotkin is known for his assertion that anarchy represents order and that the kind of utopia he envisaged is capable of becoming a reality. He was, perhaps, the most scientific of all anarchist thinkers.

Activity

Explain, in no more than 100 words, why Kropotkin is seen as a communist but not a socialist.

Mikhail Bakunin also professed to be a lover of freedom but insisted that the natural state of mankind is to live in communities and to be mutually supportive. Indeed, he argued that we are free only if we live in such groups. He wrote in 1972, 'To be free means every man living in a social milieu not to surrender his thought or will to any authority but his own reason and his own understanding of justice.' He and Kropotkin were arguing that we can be free only if we live in natural communities and that there is no contradiction between close-knit society and individual liberty. This is because all will share the same sense of justice and natural law, so artificial enforcement of laws is unnecessary.

Of course, we must pay attention to the fact that some modern individualist anarchists do not agree with the likes of Kropotkin, arguing that true individual freedom can flourish only if every person is not subject to social constraints of any kind. We will also see below that modern 'anarcho-capitalists' such as Murray Rothbard (1905–82) and David Friedman (1945–) insist on complete economic freedom for individuals with no regulation by the state at all.

In summary, then, anarchists do differ in their view of human nature, but all agree on one principle — that individual freedom

Key thinker 2

Peter Kropotkin (1842–1921)

Ironically Peter Kropotkin was born into the Russian aristocracy, but he became disillusioned by the behaviour of his own class at an early age and by the 1870s he had been converted to anarchism. His conversion was mainly the result of his visit to the Jura Federation in Switzerland where he observed an experiment in cooperative production and living among a community of watch-makers who pooled their resources and the profits of their work.

Kropotkin became interested in the theory of social Darwinism which flourished in the 1860s and 1870s. This theory drew inspiration from the animal kingdom. According to Darwin's theories, animals were engaged in a struggle based on the survival of the fittest. This promoted competition for scarce food resources, with only those able to adapt to a changing environment able to prevail in this struggle. Under capitalism, it was argued, humans were engaged in a similar struggle, in which some would succeed and prosper while others would fail and remain poor. Thus, inequality was natural, said the supporters of social Darwinism. Kropotkin challenged this belief. In most of the animal world, he argued, creatures are cooperative and not competitive. Most animals live in natural social groups and engage in mutual aid. This, he concluded, was the natural state of mankind, too. One of his works was entitled *Mutual Aid: A Factor of Evolution* (1902) to reflect his interest in the human condition.

As the nineteenth century wore on he became increasingly radical in his views and began to involve himself in revolutionary movements. He travelled extensively in Switzerland, France and England, becoming a subject of interest for the Russian secret service.

Kropotkin's brand of anarcho-communism proposed the creation of natural communities. His argument was that if people were free to join whichever community they wished, they would not be subjected to any force. He looked forward to a time when these communities would be self-sufficient and prosperous. Without scarcity, he argued, there would be no competition, and without competition there would be no inequality. His plans were mainly described in *Fields, Factories and Workshops* (1898).

When revolution broke out in Russia in 1917, Kropotkin returned home after years in exile. He saw this as an opportunity to see some of his plans put into practice. Despite his aspiration to see the development of peaceful, natural communities, Kropotkin was a revolutionary who envisaged the overthrow of the state, by violent means if necessary. However, when the Bolsheviks took over in Russia under Lenin, Kropotkin became disappointed, fearing the development of a new state to replace the old one. Perhaps naively, he had hoped that there would be a popular uprising that would destroy the state altogether and begin to build the small natural communities that he supported. By the time he died in 1921 Kropotkin was disillusioned by what he saw in Russia under the Communist Party. He had envisaged a very different kind of **communism** from that of Lenin and the Russian Bolsheviks.

Key term

Communism This term describes various movements which proposed a transition, often by revolutionary means, to a society where people form themselves into natural communities, without government, based on natural cooperation, common ownership of the means of production and the equal distribution of goods.

is the natural state of mankind and that such freedom can never be sacrificed to any kind of external authority if a natural state of society is to be maintained.

Activity

Explain, in no more than 200 words, the relationship between the anarchist view of human nature and the principle of individual liberty.

Key terms

State This refers to the authority, set up over people, which is able to exercise power over them in order to maintain order, to enforce the laws and to protect people both from each other and from external threats. All anarchists oppose the existence of the state, seeing it as an instrument of class rule and a denial of individual sovereignty.

Power Anarchists argue that the exercise of power by one person over another is unacceptable. Instead, they believe that individuals can exercise power over themselves only. Thus the exercise of power by the state must be resisted.

The state

All anarchists insist that the **state** must be abolished. This is for two reasons: either the state is unnecessary or it is evil and corrupting, or both.

The state is unnecessary

It is mostly the anarcho-communists and some philosophical anarchists like Godwin who argue that the state is not necessary — it can be replaced by voluntary associations of one kind or another. These may be small communes (suggested by Kropotkin) or large workers' federations (one of Bakunin's ideas). This is a key idea because voluntary organisations, where people choose freely to come together in cooperative units, preserve the freedom of individuals. By contrast, the state forces people into artificial political units and then subjects them to its laws that run counter to individual sovereignty. So, there are alternatives to the state that can protect liberty.

The state is evil

Others, like the syndicalist Sorel, the collectivist Bakunin, the mutualist Proudhon and individualist anarchists like Thoreau, see the state, and the **power** it wields, as evil, corrupting and oppressive. It is, therefore, to be resisted and ultimately destroyed, whether by violent or peaceful means. Bakunin, in particular, added that the state is the agent of the capitalist ruling class (echoing Marxism), so it must be destroyed and replaced if economic justice is to be established. Bakunin went further still, claiming that those who command the state will themselves be corrupted. In his 1970 work *State and Revolution*, he says:

> 'Nothing is as dangerous for man's personal morality as the habit of commanding. The best of men, the most intelligent, unselfish, generous and pure, will always and inevitably be corrupted in this pursuit.'

Proudhon went even further in his vehement hatred of the state. This passage from *What is Property?* (1840) leaves no doubt about how he felt:

> 'To be governed is to be watched, inspected, spied upon, directed, law-driven, numbered, regulated, enrolled, indoctrinated, preached at, controlled, checked, estimated, valued, censured, commanded, by creatures who have neither the right nor the wisdom nor the virtue to do so.'

Echoing Proudhon, Italian anarchist Enrico Malatesta (1853–1932) insisted that all states are fundamentally the same. In his aptly titled work *Anarchy* (1906), he stressed the dangers of the forces of oppression that all states use:

> 'The basic function of government everywhere, in all times, whatever title it adopts and whatever its origin and organisation may be, is always that of oppressing and exploiting the masses, of defending the oppressors and exploiters; and its principal, characteristic and indispensable instruments are the police agent, the tax collector, the soldier and the gaoler.'

Anti-clericalism

An additional element to the anarchist rejection of the state is its determined anti-religious stance, also known as anti-clericalism. Most, though not all, anarchists have been atheists (Godwin and Tolstoy were notable exceptions), so they saw religions as an artificial construct of mankind, an additional way in which individuals are oppressed and in which their individualism is suppressed. The state and the religious authorities were seen as part of the same nexus of authoritarianism. This was especially true of Russia, home to many of the nineteenth-century anarchists, where the Orthodox Church was seen as the ally of the Czar's totalitarian regime. Like Marx, anarchists viewed religion as the 'opium of the people', a device for deflecting attention away from the true nature of the earthly state by promising the people a better afterlife if they remained obedient to authority during their lifetime. Bakunin, the revolutionary opponent of all aspects of the Russian state, put his objection cleverly thus: 'If God existed, it would be necessary to abolish him.' This was a deliberate distortion of Voltaire's assertion in the eighteenth century: 'If God did not exist, it would be necessary to invent him.' For Bakunin, the very idea of an almighty God was, in itself, oppressive.

Key term

Authority This term is related to government and the state. Authority is the right to exercise power granted to the state and government to carry out its duties. Authority may be granted by the people in a democracy, or by tradition, as with monarchy, or by fear, as with dictatorships. For anarchists, all these forms of authority are illusions — people must be allowed to exercise authority over themselves only.

The anarchist opposition to the liberal state

We may ask, at this stage, what about two liberal defences of the existence of the state — if it is formed with the consent of the people or if it is democratic in nature? The anarchist objection to the first circumstance — government by consent — is that individuals cannot, by nature, give up their sovereignty to a higher authority even if they believe they are doing it freely — it is a denial of basic human nature to do so. Furthermore, even if one generation submits itself to government, there is no reason why succeeding generations should do the same. In other words, the actions of one generation cannot bind future generations. At one stroke this eliminates for anarchists the claims made by states such as the USA of the various French republics to be 'government by consent of the people'.

But what about the highly democratic state which was gradually coming into existence in the nineteenth century? Surely anarchists would approve of democracy? Not so. Goldman warned us about the illusion of democracy when she claimed wittily, 'If voting changed anything, they'd abolish it' (sometimes attributed to Mark Twain and used by British socialist Ken Livingstone in his 1987 book). But the anarchist objection to so-called liberal democracy is not such a simple one. Rousseau had rejected the notion that a democratic system could promote liberty in a fuller sense. He asserted in *The Social Contract*:

> 'If there were a nation of Gods, it would govern itself democratically. A government so perfect is not suited to men.'

What he meant was that democracy is suitable only for exceptionally well-informed people who understand the interests of everyone and not just themselves. He even rejected direct democracy on the basis that people would vote out of self-interest rather than in the collective interests of the community. For Rousseau, the only justification for such direct democracy would be in small communities where all individuals would understand what would be in the interests of all. This was an idea adopted by Kropotkin in his vision of a world of small, independent, self-governing communities.

Other anarchists, such as the revolutionary Bakunin, saw democracy as an illusion, just as the Marxists did. Like religion, democracy was a device used to hide the authoritarian nature of the state. Mankind might imagine itself free if it is granted democratic rights and political equality, he commented, but unless there is economic equality there can be no political

Key term

Direct democracy This is a system of government in which the people themselves make key decisions on behalf of the community. Anarchists reject direct democracy organised by the state, although some collectivist anarchists and communists did support direct democracy in small-scale communities.

equality. In a democracy, those with economic power will also ultimately wield political power.

The state is also an unnatural construction, herding people into a territory where they can fall under the power of a government. The same is true of nations. Anarchists are invariably (though not universally) internationalists who reject the division of the world into artificial units known as nations and countries. This is not to say they oppose the division of the world into different national identities and cultures; what they do oppose is the division of the world into states based on these nations.

Anarchism and the capitalist state

Finally, most anarchists have rejected the state on the grounds that it is based on capitalism. Although modern anarcho-capitalists (see pages 178–81) deny this connection, proposing a capitalist economic system without a state, most anarchists are also opposed to capitalism and see the modern state as the agent of capitalism. Indeed, they believe that the state is the creation of modern capitalism. They share this world view with Marxists and other fundamentalist socialists. Capitalism oppresses workers and promotes inequality. Furthermore, private property is part of the system that denies the freedom of individuals. In other words, those who hold property deny the freedom of those who do not. States, say anarchists, always defend the right of private property.

We can now summarise the reasons why anarchists have opposed the existence of a state:

- It is an artificial way of grouping people into political communities and should be replaced by natural, self-governing communities.
- It is an agent of capitalism which oppresses workers and promotes inequality.
- It exercises power over people and so is a denial of individual liberty.
- It uses violence and force, either overtly or by implication.
- The state corrupts individuals, society in general and even those who exercise power.
- It has used religion as a way of deceiving people into becoming obedient.
- It defends private property and so oppresses those without property.
- The so-called democratic, limited state is an illusion; ultimately it is oppressive.

Activity

Explain, in no more than 200 words, why anarchists see the state as 'unnecessary' and 'undesirable'.

Society

It may seem immediately strange to see order as an anarchist aspiration. After all, the word 'anarchy' is often used as a substitute for 'disorder'. But this is an error. Virtually all anarchists seek to create an ordered society or await its spontaneous emergence. The modern capitalist state, by contrast, threatens order because it creates a revolutionary class that is bound to rise up against it. While it is true that different anarchists have different conceptions of social order, all of them support the idea of order. Similarly, the oppressive state, controlled by a ruling class, will always promote disorder as the oppressed classes seek to overthrow it.

Order promotes freedom and security. It is best achieved by creating equality, argue anarchists, so that different sections of a society will not come into conflict with each other. Even individualist anarchists wish to promote order as they envisage free individuals cooperating in a mutually beneficial way. The idea of the 'natural' community stems from the belief that order cannot be created artificially; it must flow naturally from the nature of the community and the peaceful sentiments of the people who make up the community.

Anarchists largely oppose the ownership of private property

Private property is a threat to social order, most, but not all, anarchists agree. It promotes inequality and inequality causes social conflict. This is one of the reasons why anarchists have generally supported common ownership of property and the equal distribution of the output of that commonly owned property. Perhaps the clearest exponent of an anarchist vision of order is Bakunin.

Key thinker 3

Mikhail Bakunin (1814–76)

Like his anarchist colleagues Kropotkin and Tolstoy, Mikhail (often known as Michael) Bakunin was born into a minor aristocratic family in Russia. He became radicalised after reading philosophical works as a young man and then became a revolutionary activist. In his early life his ideas were close to those of Marx. He opposed capitalism and the existence of private property, seeing both as oppressive. Furthermore, he agreed with the Marxists that the state was the agent of capitalism. Therefore both capitalism and the state had to be abolished.

In 1872, up to which point Bakunin had made common cause with Marx, he split with the fundamental socialists (he was either expelled from the Socialist International or left, depending on which version of events one reads). His objection to their movement was that they were proposing to replace the capitalist state with a workers' state. Though this new state was to be temporary — ultimately to wither away as socialism established itself in the consciousness of the people — Bakunin would not accept it. It was at this point, therefore, that he established the key distinction between socialism and anarchism. Anarchists, he insisted, must oppose any state, even if it claims to operate in the interests in the working class. Bakunin opposed the state on the grounds that power corrupts people, both government and the governed. So however well meaning socialists were in proposing the proletarian state, it would end in disaster. With the value of hindsight we can see that Bakunin seemed to be correct, given the corrupted version of Marxism presented by the Soviet Union under Stalin.

Bakunin was strongly influenced by the experience of the Paris Commune in 1871 — the year before he split from the Marxists. The Commune, which was a spontaneous uprising against the French state on the point of its military defeat by Prussia, seemed to show the way forward for revolutionaries. Bakunin believed it was an anarchist revolt rather than an example of socialist consciousness. It was the replacement of the oppressive state with a commune where there was to be common ownership of property, economic equality and direct democracy in place of political rule. He strongly believed in the power of propaganda and the Paris Commune was the perfect example of 'propaganda by deed'. It served as an example for others to follow even though it was destroyed after a few weeks.

Order and a just society could, for Bakunin, be achieved without a coercive state. For him there was no contradiction between an ordered society and individual liberty. In his book *God and the State* (1871), he wrote: 'The liberty of man consists solely in this, that he obeys the laws of nature because he has himself recognized them as such, and not because they have been imposed upon him externally by any foreign will whatsoever, human or divine, collective or individual.' Bakunin meant by this that it is natural for people to obey the laws of nature and they do not need to be forced to do so, therefore they retain their freedom. The laws of nature include such ideas as the sociability of mankind, natural empathy for each other, equality and respect for each other's freedom.

Bakunin's visions of an ordered society, based on the laws of nature, was known as **federalism**. He saw groups of workers or peasants joining together in voluntary communities of any size. As long as people group themselves in such communes, with common ownership of property and equal distribution of rewards on a voluntary basis, there is no coercion. The relationships between these communes or federations were to be conducted on the basis of mutual benefit. There was to be no capitalist market system, which would promote inequality, but rather a system of free negotiation and exchange on the basis of the true value of goods and services.

Activity

Explain, in no more than 100 words, why Bakunin was originally close to the Marxists but then split from them.

Malatesta and Kropotkin developed similar ideas on an anarchist social order to those of Bakunin. However, they stressed the need for smaller-scale communities. It was difficult to see Bakunin's larger-scale federations working without some kind of system of rule being adopted. Instead they were inspired by the example of the watchmakers' commune in the Swiss Jura mountains. Indeed, Kropotkin claimed it was the Jura watchmakers who converted him from socialism to anarchism. These communities, obviously based on a single occupation, were self-governing cooperatives where the workers operated without any government and shared the fruits of their production equally.

One other anarchist vision of order is important. This has been developed by modern anarcho-capitalists, such as Murray Rothbard and David Friedman. They have proposed the retention of capitalism but the virtual abolition of the state. For them, capitalism can operate in an ordered way without regulation by a state. Indeed, the functions of the state — law and order, the enforcement of contracts, consumer protection, etc. — could be carried out by private-enterprise organisations. As long as there is a demand for something, they insist, the free market will supply it. Thus, an ordered society will ensue because the competing forces of capitalism will balance each other out. The ideas of anarcho-capitalists are explored further in the section on the economy below.

Debate 1

Can we reconcile individualist and collectivist forms of anarchism?

Yes

- Both forms claim to be restoring freedom.
- Both forms believe that human nature can be positive and order can therefore be maintained without a state or artificial laws.
- Both forms envisage mutual cooperation between people. This is on a voluntary basis, so no force is needed. Communities are formed freely and independently.
- Whether in an individualist world or a collective one, liberty is created as coercion is abolished.

No

- Many individualist anarchists suggest that any form of social order restricts liberty.
- Individualist anarchists claim that social organisation is a denial of the ego.
- Individualist anarchists suggest that collectivist forms of society will inevitably lead to the return of some exercising power over others.
- There is a fundamental disagreement over human nature between individualists and collectivists.

The economy

Anarchist conceptions of economic systems fall into two broad categories:

1 Communist and collectivist forms of anarchism that seek to abolish capitalism.
2 Modern anarcho-capitalist ideas that wish to free capitalism from regulation by the state.

Communism/collectivism and economic freedom

Most 'traditional', collectivist anarchists argue that a fundamental cause of conflict in society is economic inequality. The problem for them is, though, that capitalism does create some kind of order of its own. Free markets are self-regulating and though there may be booms and slumps in a capitalist world, it is a system that has endured and promoted wealth. However, anarchists stress the inequality created within capitalism as unacceptable. Any new economic order, therefore, cannot be based on free-market values for goods and labour. Most anarchists (other than modern anarcho-capitalists) wish to see labour being paid its true value, not its market value, and goods exchanged according to how much work has gone into making them, again instead of their market-determined value.

Perhaps the most celebrated example of an anarchist who proposed such an economic structure was **Pierre-Joseph Proudhon** (1809–65) (see 'Key thinker 4' box). His theory of mutualism, also known as 'contractualism', proposed the replacement of capitalism with a system of exchange based on contracts entered into on a free, mutually beneficial basis. Proudhon was concerned that workers and peasants should receive the true value of what their labour produced instead of its market value, which was determined by capitalist forces beyond the worker's control. He proposed a voucher system to indicate the real value of goods, based on labour input, and a national bank to supply funds to independent workers and peasants. These funds were to replace the need to make profits.

Proudhon's idea of mutualism was influential among nineteenth-century anarchists, most of whom proposed variations on his theme to replace capitalism. Kropotkin, for example, wrote *Mutual Aid* in 1902 in which he insisted that the competitive economic world was not inevitable. With cooperation and communal living, mankind could free itself from the strictures of being forced into competition for scarce resources. Bakunin, too, saw no contradiction between economic freedom and collective ownership.

Key term

Mutualism This term was first associated with Pierre-Joseph Proudhon. It refers to an economic system where independent associations of workers cooperate and trade with each other on mutually beneficial terms. Mutualism was to replace the market system of capitalism.

Pierre-Joseph Proudhon (1809–65)

Famous for his assertion that 'property is theft' in his seminal anarchist work *What Is Property?* (1840), Pierre-Joseph Proudhon is credited with first using the term 'anarchist' and is therefore a key figure in the development of the movement in the nineteenth century. In fact, Proudhon did not totally oppose private property, merely property that was used to oppress workers or to promote inequality. Workers and peasants, he accepted, might own what they needed to manage their own production. These he called 'possessions' to distinguish them from 'property'. He was unusual among anarchists of his day in that he proposed the peaceful abolition of the state, even becoming a member of the French parliament after 1848.

Proudhon was something of a bridge between anarchism and socialism, often being described as a 'libertarian socialist'. He agreed with the socialist ideal of the means of production being owned in common and the abolition of the capitalist system of exchange, but also advocated the abolition of any kind of government. Socialists saw the state as a vital part of the creation and maintenance of workers' rights, but Proudhon rejected it on the grounds that it would become oppressive. His brand of socialism was to be decentralised and made up of communities of workers who had come together freely to form cooperative working groups. He was also a bridge between individualist and collectivist anarchism.

Proudhon was collectivist in that he proposed a federal system of communes, very like those envisaged by Kropotkin, and backed by a 'People's bank' which could recycle surplus funds to these productive units. However, he was also individualist as he saw workers and groups of workers freely entering into contracts with each other for the exchange of labour and goods. His hopes for a reconciliation between individualism and collectivism are summed up in these words:

> 'When politics and home life have become one and the same, when economic problems have been solved in such a way that individual and collective interests are identical — all constraints having disappeared — it is evident that we will be in a state of total liberty or anarchy.' (*What Is Property?,* 1840)

Proudhon is still regarded as the 'ultimate' anarchist and the most important example of one whose ideas continue to resonate today. Aspects of his mutualism can be seen in the twentieth-century cooperative movements (of consumers in Britain and of peasants and workers on the continent of Europe), in the commune movement of the 1960s and 1970s, and even in the current 'fair trade' movement which seeks to ensure that producers in developing countries receive the just reward for their goods. Similarly, his ideas of decentralisation can still be seen in the aim of some non-government organisations to promote subsistence production in developing countries to prevent producers being forced to produce for world commodity markets at prices that discriminate against them and force them into large, artificial productive units.

Activity

Explain, in no more than 100 words, how Proudhon saw mutualism working.

Individualism, anarcho-capitalism and economic freedom

The Russian/American anarchist Emma Goldman (1869–1940) campaigned for the abolition of capitalism without expressing any particular preference for what would replace it. All she was concerned with was that no one could be free within capitalism. In this sense she placed herself in the tradition of nineteenth-century individualist anarchists. Henry Thoreau and Josiah Warren (1798–1874) in the USA both advocated a withdrawal of the individual from the capitalist world. Rather than selling their labour to capitalist employers, people could obtain their freedom both from the state and from the economic system. Warren, in particular, devised a scheme whereby all goods could be sold at a price which reflected the amount of labour that had gone into them. As his ideas spread, he hoped, more and more people would free themselves from capitalism and trade freely and fairly among themselves.

Warren's ideas did not take hold, though there remained in the USA a tradition of self-sufficiency, following Thoreau's example. Individuals withdrew from society and lived a simple life of subsistence, and they are still doing so in remote parts of the country. Only by not having to interact with capitalism would true economic freedom be possible. The religiously inspired Amish people, who also reject modern technology, live such an existence to this day in parts of America. But the principal anarchist answer to the problems of capitalism lies with a modern movement which does not oppose capitalism but embraces it to the full. Its advocates are often known as anarcho-capitalists and two of its most prominent have been Murray Rothbard and David Friedman (1945–).

Rothbard and Friedman both envisage a world in which free-market capitalism can flourish without any regulation by the state. In fact, both oppose the existence of any state at all. Economic freedom can exist only in the context of free competition without any external interference. They accept that inequality is natural and suppressing it is therefore unacceptable in a free society. The theory of entitlement asserts that human beings are entitled to retain for themselves anything they earn as the fruits of their labour. Private property which is legally gained can therefore be justified. Rothbard summed up his beliefs thus:

> 'Capitalism is the fullest expression of anarchism, and anarchism is the fullest expression of capitalism. Not only are they compatible, but you can't really have one without the other. True anarchism will be capitalism, and true capitalism will be anarchism.'

Anarcho-capitalism is discussed further below.

Anarchism and utopianism

The general idea of **utopianism** is that it is theoretically feasible to create a society which can accord with true human nature and which can bring traditional conflicts to an end. In a 'utopia' there is no alienation and social harmony reigns. However, utopianism is usually viewed either positively or negatively. The positive perspectives see utopia as feasible, while negative views believe that adherents are deluding themselves and others by mistaking what is desirable for what is possible.

A positive view of anarchist utopia

Adopting the positive sense of utopia, we can say that all anarchists have a vision of what they consider to be an ideal society. While conservatives typically wish to see society develop naturally, socialists have a more scientific analysis of the future direction of society and liberals concentrate largely on the preservation of freedom, anarchists have clear views about what kind of future society they desire.

Of course, as we have seen, different branches of anarchism have different visions, but they have in common a belief that an ideal society can be brought about as long as the state is abolished, to be replaced by a more natural form of social order, a new utopia, as it might be called. We have seen that for individualist anarchists this entails the abolition of the state and any kind of economic and social organisation; however, the anarcho-communists and collectivist anarchists propose a new social system to replace both capitalism and the state itself. In contrast to individualists, they have proposed a new social order based on mutual aid, common ownership of property, economic equality and, above all, natural communities which people are free to form with whatever structure they wish.

Anarcho-capitalists also have a vision of utopia. Their utopia is also a society without a state but one where there is a balance between individuals' competing interests. They see economic competition as natural, so the maximisation of unregulated economic competition is also natural. They also see the accumulation of property as a natural activity so, in their utopian version of capitalism, everyone will receive what they are entitled to as long as it is honestly obtained through their own labour, be it physical or mental labour.

We can leave this section with two defences of the anarchist utopia by American naturalist Edward Abbey (1927–89) and

Emma Goldman (1869–1940)

Emma Goldman was Russian-born but spent much of her life in the USA where she found herself frequently in prison on various charges, including planning assassinations and inciting workers to riot. Most famously she was implicated in the assassination of US President William McKinley in 1901, though she was never convicted and was probably not responsible. Nevertheless, Goldman did preach assassination as a valid tactic for anarchists.

She was also involved in a number of social causes, not least of which was the emancipation of women and the tolerance of homosexuality, and she championed the idea of free love. Some modern feminists have claimed that Goldman was a founder of their philosophy. She certainly did synthesise anarchist ideas with the cause of women's rights. Some have claimed that she was the first anarcho-feminist.

Goldman spent 1936–1937 participating in the Spanish civil war, attempting to form anarchist communes, possibly the most important example of the genuine realisation of anarchist ideals, though the experiment was short-lived. She coined the term 'propaganda of the deed', the idea that the best way to inspire others to join the anarchist cause was to engage in acts of violence against state and capitalist institutions. However, despite this ill-fated attempt to prove that practical anarchism was realistic, Goldman's work was mainly directed at exposing the exploitative nature of capitalism, the oppressive nature of the state, and the need for violent revolution to bring both of them down. She rejected the idea of political reform, arguing, like Bakunin, one of her mentors, as well as Lord Acton, that the exercise of power corrupts people, so any system involving such power must be abolished. In other words, her philosophy was more negative than positive. This passage from *Living My Life*, published in 1931, summarises this negativity:

> 'Men and women...do you not realize that the State is the worst enemy you have? It is a machine that crushes you in order to sustain the ruling class, your masters. Like naïve children you put your trust in your political leaders. You make it possible for them to creep into your confidence, only to have them betray you to the first bidder. But even where there is no direct betrayal, the labour politicians make common cause with your enemies to keep you in leash, to prevent your direct action. The State is the pillar of capitalism, and it is ridiculous to expect any redress from it.'

Goldman's main contribution to anarchism was probably her ability to popularise its main ideas, by connecting its ideals to the emancipation of the individual and the replacement of exploitation by the idea of mutual love. Once freed from oppression, she preached to sizeable crowds in the USA, the true nature of our loving feeling for each other can be released. She raged against virtually every enemy of individual liberty — the modern state, religion, nationalism, Marxism, capitalism, patriarchy and bigotry of any kind. In modern parlance, she might be described as a 'populist of the left'.

Rather incongruously, Goldman loved dancing and saw it as almost as important as politics in her own life. As she famously said, 'If I can't dance to it, it's not my revolution.'

Activity

Explain, in no more than 100 words, why Goldman opposed the modern state.

German anarchist philosopher Rudolf Rocker (1873–1958). Abbey said:

> 'Anarchism is not a romantic fable but the hardheaded realization, based on five thousand years of experience, that we cannot entrust the management of our lives to kings, priests, politicians, generals, and county commissioners.' (*Down the River*, 1982)

Rocker agrees, claiming that anarchism is not just an empty philosophy but is based on realistic aspirations:

> 'For the anarchist, freedom is not an abstract philosophical concept, but the vital concrete possibility of every human being to bring to full development all the powers, capacities and talents with which nature has endowed them, and turn them to social account.' (*Anarcho-Syndicalism*, 1938)

Negative views of anarchist utopia

Opponents of anarchism of all political backgrounds criticise the movement in its various forms on a number of grounds. Among these criticisms are these:

- Conservatives in particular argue that anarchists are over-optimistic about human nature. We are, say conservatives, born to be self-interested and are not capable of being made perfect. Roman Catholics refer to 'original sin' as the reason why attempts to create a perfect society are futile. We are the victims of our own faults of character. We need to be governed effectively, conservatives insist, because we cannot be trusted to act responsibly and with the interests of others at heart.
- Liberals and conservatives alike see private property as a natural aspect of human society. In other words, the drive to obtain and retain our own property is natural, a part of human nature. Furthermore, claim liberals, it is a fundamental right. The liberal slogan, enshrined in the American Declaration of Independence, states: 'We hold these truths to be self-evident, that all men are created equal and that they are endowed by their Creator with certain inalienable rights, that among these are life, liberty and the pursuit of happiness.' This appears to hold no problems for anarchists, but, for liberals, the idea of the 'pursuit of happiness' includes the accumulation of property, so the contradiction suddenly becomes insurmountable. However, this objection certainly does not apply to anarcho-capitalists, who share a belief in the natural pursuit of property.

- Socialists have two main objections to the anarchist utopia. First, they believe the abolition of the state to be incompatible with the aims they hold in common — equality and common ownership of property. Such objectives can be achieved only by the state, say the socialists. Without a state, mankind will simply resort to pursuing private property and an unequal share of rewards.

- Second, they see anarchism as unscientific, being based on a series of generalisations and unsubstantiated assumptions about the nature of man. The Marxists added that anarchism has no theory of history, no explanation of how society has developed and will evolve in the future. Similarly, while anarchists oppose capitalism simply because it is oppressive and unjust, socialists understand its true nature through scientific study. It is more than oppressive, say the socialists, it has control over both consciousness and the progress of history.

- Finally, there is a general criticism of anarchism, which is that it has no vision of society at all, that anarchists know what they are against but cannot agree on what they are for. In other words, there is no single anarchist utopia at all.

Debate 2

Is anarchism merely unscientific utopianism?

Yes	*No*
■ Anarchists share neither a theory of history nor a scientific analysis of human society. ■ Anarchists have an over-optimistic view of the perfectibility of human nature. ■ Anarchists have no clear vision of what kind of society should replace the contemporary state. ■ There has never been a successful, established form of anarchist society.	■ Much anarchism is based on a quasi-scientific analysis of the natural world. ■ Anarchists argue that their aims are attainable as long as the corrupt reality of the modern state is abolished. ■ Anarchists argue that it is conventional ideological beliefs that are unscientific, based on forms of false consciousness such as religion, nationalism, liberal ideology and democracy.

Different types of anarchism

Here we examine five main types of anarchism, divided into two broad categories, collectivist and individualist anarchism. In each case we explore how the tradition has viewed human nature, the state, society in general and the nature of the economic structure.

Collectivist anarchism

Anarcho-communism and mutualism

The two traditions of communism and mutualism are so closely related that they are treated together here.

Man is a social animal, say the communist anarchists. They do not agree with the individualist anarchists who stressed mankind's individuality and ego. Rather than believing people to be self-seeking and competitive, the communists see mankind as naturally empathetic and sociable. Kropotkin, in particular, likened human society to that of the animal kingdom, stressing that most species live in social groups. He rejected the social Darwinist view that people are competitive.

Communist anarchists believe that people are capable of self-government; they do not need to set anyone above themselves as a ruler in order to live in peace and harmony. In his book *Mutual Aid* (1902), Kropotkin wrote:

> 'Therefore combine — practise mutual aid! That is the surest means for giving to each and to all the greatest safety, the best guarantee of existence and progress, bodily, intellectual and moral. That is what Nature teaches us; and that is what all those animals which have attained the highest position of their respective classes have done.'

Mutualism and mutual aid were, for the communists, a key aspect of human nature. People, they insisted, will naturally seek to help each other and not compete. French anarchist Elisée Reclus (1830–1905) insisted that whatever kind of social organisation might be adopted, mutual aid will ensure solidarity and progress:

> 'But whether it is a question of small or large groups of the human species, it is always through solidarity, through the association of spontaneous, coordinated forces that all progress is made...they will owe it to their coming together more and more intimately, to incessant collaboration, to this mutual aid from which brotherhood grows little by little.' (*Evolution and Revolution*, 1891)

Enrico Malatesta, a close colleague of Kropotkin and Reclus, saw such solidarity and mutual aid as best served by people being grouped together on the basis of their occupation. By undertaking similar work, he believed, people would have a greater sense of collective consciousness.

Based very much on the notion of social **solidarity**, the communist branch of anarchism sees the state as unnecessary. If free individuals are allowed to form their own communities, they will naturally tend towards creating communes that are

Key term

Solidarity This is an idea common to most anarchists. It suggests that social solidarity — the tendency for people to group together in mutually beneficial communities and to have empathy for each other — is the natural state of man.

self-governing and well ordered. In other words, mutual aid can replace the need for a state. There is no need for law or coercion in such communities. Furthermore, the rewards of labour will be equally divided because, again, this is natural to mankind.

Anarcho-communism shares the idea of democracy with more conventional ideologies, but it is a very different kind of democracy. Within the communes, decisions could be reached collectively through a natural democratic process. Other ideologies preferred either representative systems or national direct democracy, both of which are flawed according to the communists, either because they represent the tyranny of the majority or because elected representatives do not necessarily reflect the will of the people.

A communist society, as described by anarchists, is very distinctive. Proudhon's theory of mutualism is perhaps the best known version of a communist society. He and other anarchists insisted that society must be based upon the ties that people have as a result of economic cooperation. Capitalist society is oppressive, they argue, because it pits people against each other in a competitive struggle. It is inevitable in such a social Darwinist world that the strong will oppress the weak and that this will result in inequality. The kind of mutually beneficial society that they envisage ensures that all people are equal and that the economic outcomes will ensure equality. Furthermore, it is mankind's natural state, while capitalism is unnatural, a construct of the ruling class.

Goldman summed up the ideas about society of many of her fellow anarchists thus:

Pierre-Joseph Proudhon, who declared that 'property is theft'

'Anarchism, then, really stands for the liberation of the human mind from the dominion of religion; the liberation of the human body from the dominion of property; liberation from the shackles and restraint of government. Anarchism stands for a social order based on the free grouping of individuals for the purpose of producing real social wealth; an order that will guarantee to every human being free access to the earth and full enjoyment of the necessities of life, according to individual desires, tastes, and inclinations.' (*Anarchism and Other Essays*, 1910)

Anarchists share with fundamentalist socialists like Marx a belief that capitalism places a false value upon labour and therefore the goods that are produced by labour. This is especially exploitive because a person's labour is seen as a fundamental aspect of our lives, perhaps *the* fundamental aspect. The value assigned by capitalism to labour and goods can be called 'exchange value'. This means that labour is paid wages according to its place in the market. Where labour is scarce it will be highly paid, but when it is not scarce — the normal situation in capitalism — it will be low paid. In other words, capitalism ignores the true or intrinsic value of a person's labour. The same is true of goods and services. Since the capitalist class (who own the means of production) control the market system, they can ensure that they will earn high returns from economic activity while workers are economically exploited because they are rarely scarce.

Like socialists, most anarchists propose the destruction of capitalism and its replacement by some form of common ownership of the means of production, including the land, the factories and mines, and the financial system. However, this would not be organised by the state, as proposed by socialists and which anarchists would abolish, but would be placed in the hands of smaller, natural communities. They would trade goods with each other based on the true value of the labour that has gone into making them, not the exchange value. Furthermore, the trade that takes place between the communities would be to their mutual benefit, hence the terms mutualism and mutual aid. Under capitalism, economic exchange takes place to the advantage of the capitalist class only. Anarcho-communism does not propose the kind of **collectivisation** which Marxist-inspired regimes promoted in the twentieth century. Collectivisation involved the enforced movement of peasants onto large, state-controlled agricultural units. For anarchists, this is unacceptable — the commune must be voluntary and free from the control of any higher authority.

Kropotkin made his point forcefully in his well-known plea, 'Don't compete! — Competition is always injurious to the species, and you have plenty of resources to avoid it!'

Anarcho-syndicalism

This branch of anarchism, which lies close to socialism, is based on what is seen by its followers as a natural tendency for workers who have a similar occupation to group themselves together in an act of solidarity to resist the oppression caused by capitalism. The most common way in which this happens is through the creation of trade unions. Its most important champion was Georges Sorel (1847–1922). **Syndicalism** was a socialist movement in the nineteenth and early twentieth centuries, but it was the anarcho-syndicalists who combined a stress on trade union organisation with a desire to abolish the state.

For Sorel, the main attribute of the working class was its solidarity, and that solidarity could be used to destroy both capitalism and the state. In particular, by the weapon of the

> ### Key terms
>
> **Collectivisation** This involves the organisation of peasants into large production units where there is no private property and where peasants are treated like industrial workers, in that they produce goods collectively and receive equal rewards for their labour.
>
> **Syndicalism** This term is used for revolutionary movements based on trade union organisation (the French word for trade union is *syndicat*). Syndicalists and anarcho-syndicalists propose a stateless society where workers are grouped into syndicates based on industrial occupations which will cooperate freely with each other for mutual benefit.

general, all-out strike, the workers could bring down the established order simply by refusing to work. Sorel referred to the 'myth of the general strike', meaning that it was a symbolic gesture to demonstrate the rage of the working class against their oppressors. Add the strike weapon to mass demonstrations and acts of violence, he and his associates believed, and the state's will to power, its survival instinct, would be destroyed. Anarcho-syndicalism is, therefore, often known as a philosophy of direct action, insurrection and violence.

After the revolution and destruction of the state, the new social order would be based on trade union (also known as syndicate) organisation. It would be natural for people with similar occupations to form themselves into self-governing federations of workers. The various federations would then exchange labour and goods to their mutual benefit. To some extent the anarcho-syndicalists were inspired by the traditional guild system of the Middle Ages, when each craft was partially independent and self-governing.

American philosopher Noam Chomsky (1928–) has professed himself to be an anarcho-syndicalist. This is in a more general sense than the beliefs of Sorel, however. Chomsky sees syndicalism more as an aspiration for workers to regain control of their own labour. This can be done in a number of ways, but what is important for Chomsky is that workers should free themselves from external control and take charge of their own workplaces. He shares the anarchist view that workers' councils could be formed and be intensely democratic in nature.

Rudolf Rocker (1873–1958) led the anarchist reaction against the march of Marxist-inspired socialism in the first half of the twentieth century, exemplified by the development of the Soviet Union. The emancipation of workers, he argued, could not be realised through the powerful workers' state but can be achieved only if the state is abolished and replaced by independent workers' communes.

Anarcho-syndicalists share a similar view of human nature to that of the other collectivist anarchists. In particular, though, they lay even greater stress on mankind's potential capacity for social solidarity. The reliance they have placed on trade unions demonstrates that they see labour and creativity as fundamental to the human condition. Workers who are engaged in a similar occupation have a natural tendency to form themselves into associations. Work, they say, should be an expression of mankind's creativity, but it can be so only if the oppression of the state is removed.

The syndicalists, whether socialist or anarchist (syndicalism could be both), shared a belief that the state and capitalism are

Key terms

Direct action For most anarchists, direct action is the only way in which the state and capitalism can be effectively destroyed. Direct action includes such methods as demonstrations, strikes, civil disobedience, attacks on the organs of the state, assassinations and, ultimately, full-scale revolution.

Insurrection This implies a full-scale attack upon the organs of the state or upon the structure of capitalism.

inevitably tied together in the same web of exploitation. The anarcho-syndicalists asserted that capitalism can be abolished only if the state is removed, preferably by revolutionary means. In contrast, the socialists aspired to replace the capitalist state with the workers' state. The anarcho-capitalist replacement for the state was to be a cooperative arrangement of independent, self-governing workers' federations, or syndicates. The close relationship between syndicalism and socialism is demonstrated by the fact that anarcho-syndicalism is sometimes described as a form of decentralised socialism.

Like all collectivist anarchists, syndicalists saw people as social animals, so society is a natural phenomenon. The question was, 'What should form the basis of a voluntary community?' The answer was that a community should be based upon occupation. The solidarity of such groups as miners, factory workers or construction workers made them natural bases for a coherent society. The common circumstances of members of such syndicates would grant them sufficient social solidarity for the creation of a stateless but ordered society.

How would a stateless, anarcho-capitalist economy work? The answer generally proposed is that the workers' trade unions or syndicates would become the owners of their own means of production — miners would collectively own their mines, factory workers their factories and so on. Trade between the syndicates would take place, not on a competitive, free-market basis but on mutually beneficial terms whereby the price of goods and services would be determined by the real value of the labour that went into making them.

Ultimately, however, the anarcho-anarchists suffer from the same criticism that is levelled against the anarchist movement in general — that it has no specific idea of what kind of society and economy will follow the abolition of the state. Rocker himself seemed to accept this observation, seeing the vagueness of their vision almost as a virtue. As he wrote:

> 'Anarchism is no patent solution for all human problems, no Utopia of a perfect social order, as it has often been called, since on principle it rejects all absolute schemes and concepts. It does not believe in any absolute truth, or in definite final goals for human development, but in an unlimited perfectibility of social arrangements and human conditions which are always straining after higher forms of expression, and to which for this reason one can assign no definite terminus nor set any fixed goal.' (*Anarcho-Syndicalism*, 1938)

Debate 3

Is anarchism merely socialism without a state?

Yes

- Both anarchism and socialism are critiques of the capitalist state.
- The two ideologies share an optimistic view of human nature — that mankind is capable of cooperation without coercion.
- Most anarchists propose economic equality and common ownership of property.

No

- Socialism is a doctrine of social solidarity while anarchists mainly wish to restore individual liberty.
- While communists and collectivist anarchists propose collective ownership, anarcho-individualists accept the existence of private property.
- While socialism is a class-based ideology, anarchists are concerned less with class and more with the restoration of individual sovereignty.

Individualist anarchism

The two main traditions of anarcho-individualism emerged in nineteenth-century America and Europe. The more peaceful, scientific form was found in the USA. We have seen above that Thoreau wrote of the need to escape the clutches of the state and restore one's individual liberty by withdrawing completely from society and becoming self-reliant. Lysander Spooner (1808–87) observed that it was the necessity of mankind to sell its labour that was the main reason for oppression. He therefore recommended self-employment as a way of removing such exploitation. Generally, Spooner campaigned against the interference of the state in free markets, as did his close associate Josiah Warren. Warren had flirted with communism but ultimately rejected it in favour of the idea of the worker as an individual economic unit, free to negotiate with other workers in cooperative ventures and in mutual trade. The modern form of American nineteenth-century individualism eventually evolved into anarcho-capitalism.

Meanwhile, in Europe a more violent, radical form of individualism was developing. This is sometimes described as egoism. It is mostly associated with Max Stirner. It takes a view of human nature which is abhorrent to collectivist anarchists and liberals alike. This is that the ego — the desire for our own self-realisation even at the expense of others — is the main driving force of the individual's life aspiration. We are, Stirner insisted, rational creatures who understand our self-interest, but we are also without morality. Social morality restrains us and prevents us from being truly liberated. The only way in which people would cooperate with each other would be for selfish reasons — when they saw it as in their self-interest to do so.

When such communities formed they were to be described as unions of egoists.

The so-called egoists developed a reputation for extreme violence and opposing any form of organised society. Their most notorious exponent was Sergei Nechaev (1847–82). He summed up the idea that the revolutionary can have no morality thus:

> 'The revolutionary enters the world of the State, of the privileged classes, of the so-called civilization, and he lives in this world only for the purpose of bringing about its speedy and total destruction. He is not a revolutionary if he has any sympathy for this world. He should not hesitate to destroy any position, any place, or any man in this world. He must hate everyone and everything in it with an equal hatred. All the worse for him if he has any relations with parents, friends, or lovers; he is no longer a revolutionary if he is swayed by these relationships.' (*The Revolutionary Catechism*, 1869)

The ideas of the egoists were intensely pessimistic about human nature and the possibility of the creation of an anarchist community. They shared the general anarchist hatred of the state, but had few positive ideas about what should replace it. Nor did they develop coherent economic ideas, save for the notion that free individuals would find a way to trade with each other on the basis of their pursuit of their rational self-interest. Some of the more extreme individual anarchists have been so vehement in their opposition to all social and political organisation that they have been described as nihilists. The term 'nihilism' suggests a belief that individual liberty is a more powerful force than society and morality.

Here we will concentrate on two of the main individualist traditions: anarcho-capitalism and egoism.

Anarcho-capitalism

Anarcho-capitalism is a relatively modern philosophy which emerged in the 1970s and 1980s, partly as a reaction against the increasing involvement of western governments in the regulation of capitalism. It has been associated with a movement known as **libertarianism**, which is an extreme form of conservatism whose main protagonist was Robert Nozick (1938–2002). Nozick proposed the transition to a society where the state should be shrunk to such a limited role that it would scarcely exist at all. Most laws would be abolished and replaced by a free society. We will pass over Nozick at this stage as he is

Key term

Libertarianism This refers to movements that believe in minimal government or even no government at all. This implies insistence on the widest possible freedom of individuals.

not normally described as an anarchist, though he shares many ideas with mainstream individualist members of the movement. The key figures in anarcho-capitalism are Murray Rothbard and David Friedman.

Rothbard actually coined the term anarcho-capitalism to describe his own philosophy. He claimed it was a synthesis of three other traditions:

- Nineteenth-century classical liberalism, which proposed a small, minimalist state.
- Nineteenth-century American individualist anarchism, as expressed by Henry Thoreau, Benjamin Tucker and Lysander Spooner. These individualists opposed the state on the grounds of its denial of individual sovereignty.
- The Austrian school of economics of the mid-twentieth century, which proposed completely free markets for goods, labour and finance, with little or no government regulation.

For Rothbard, economic freedom was a fundamental value, but it is in every way threatened by the power of the state. Put another way, he argued that political and economic freedom cannot be separated. The main aspect of the state he attacked was taxation. If we are entitled to everything we earn with our labour, then taxation becomes a form of institutionalised theft.

Michael Douglas starred as Gordon Gekko in the anti-capitalist film, *Wall Street*

In the film *Wall Street* (1987), the central character, a financial trader called Gordon Gekko, famously says, 'Greed is good.' He declares this at the peak of a period when neo-liberalism was at its height in the developed, capitalist world. What Gekko meant was that the pursuit of one's self-interest was both natural — an aspect of human nature — and good for economic growth generally. Capitalism relies upon the

Murray Rothbard (1926–95), the great contemporary American anarchist

free competition between self-serving individuals; this gives capitalism its incentives and its dynamism. This represents a typical view of human nature expressed by anarcho-capitalists. Rothbard expressed this idea thus:

> 'It's true: greed has had a very bad press. I frankly don't see anything wrong with greed. I think that the people who are always attacking greed would be more consistent with their position if they refused their next salary increase. I don't see even the most Left-Wing scholar in this country scornfully burning his salary check. In other words, "greed" simply means that you are trying to relieve the nature given scarcity that man was born with.' (*Man, Economy and State*, 1962)

Friedman concentrated to a similar extent to Rothbard on free-market economics. For Friedman, people are fundamentally economic animals (as opposed to social animals). We have an innate sense of entitlement, he argues, meaning that mankind is born with a belief that we are entitled to anything in nature as long as we have worked to gain it. To this robust defence of private property, Friedman adds that we must be free to enter into economic relations with others. This must be unregulated if it is to be mutually beneficial.

The state represents the enemy of this vision of an intensely individualistic world — its regulations prevent the natural outcome of competition between rational individuals pursuing their self-interest in an enlightened way. While liberals have adopted an optimistic view of human nature, anarcho-capitalists take a rational view — that it is natural for individuals to act in a self-interested way. As long as scarcity exists, self-interested activity will persist.

An anarcho-capitalist society may seem a frightening place. It is a social Darwinian world where only the fittest prosper. It does have its own sense of order, however. Free competition creates a kind of 'balance of interests'. Disorder is prevented because people have an interest in keeping such order. All the functions of the state in a free-market system can actually be provided by market forces, by individuals and private firms. As long as there is a demand for them, the market will supply a solution. In this way such services as health, education, social care and law enforcement will come about without a state to provide them.

Anarcho-capitalists take a relatively simple view of economics. The world is a competitive place — that is perfectly normal as scarcity and competition exist in the natural world where the fittest will progress and the weak will suffer. Free-market competition is also healthy because it creates incentives and therefore promotes innovation and growth. State interference in the economy cannot be justified as it is a denial of what is natural. It is not only the state that is the enemy of free-market capitalism; trade unions and powerful monopoly companies also inhibit free competition. However, anarcho-capitalists assume that monopolies will eventually be dissolved in the face of free competition.

Activity

Explain, in no more than 200 words, how anarcho-capitalists believe that capitalism could operate without a state.

Debate 4

Is anarchism merely an extreme form of liberalism?

Yes

- Both anarchists and liberals place individual liberty at the centre of their belief system.
- Both anarchists and liberals see the state as the potential enemy of individual liberty.
- Both have adopted an optimistic view of human nature, believing that mankind can potentially use freedom for good ends.
- Anarcho-capitalism can be seen as an extreme form of liberalism.

No

- Anarchists insist on the abolition of the state, while liberals see the state as the guarantor of liberty.
- Liberals broadly support free-market capitalism, while most (not all) anarchists oppose capitalism.
- Liberals see property ownership as natural, while most (not all) anarchists propose common ownership of property.
- Most liberals see inequality as natural, while most anarchists wish to promote absolute equality. However, anarcho-capitalists share with liberals a belief in natural inequality.

Key term

Autonomy In the context of individualist anarchism and nihilism, autonomy is the state to which individuals should aspire. It implies no artificial hindrance to one's thoughts or actions. Each individual can achieve autonomy only if the state and moral or social constraints are removed.

Egoism

It goes almost without saying that the egoists see human nature in similar terms to the anarcho-capitalists — it is based on self-interest and the desire for complete personal **autonomy**. For the egoists like Stirner, people see themselves as the centre of their own universe. This kind of solipsism leads people to believe that any kind of social intercourse is a threat to their freedom and individuality. The state must be abolished because it is a denial of the individual's autonomy.

The egoist anarchists who would deny even the existence of society may be described as nihilists. The nihilists criticise the anarcho-communists on the grounds that they see mankind as fundamentally sociable and so wish to see post-state society in terms of the existence of some kind of communes. Mankind is not naturally sociable, they argue, but is naturally individualistic. Max Stirner's concept of a union of egoists was not really a society but a collection of individuals held together by their common desire to serve their own interests. In this sense the egoists have much in common with the more modern philosophy of existentialism. Existentialists see the meaning of our existence only in terms of our ability to impose our will upon the world. They see themselves as artificially restrained by social ties just as much as the egoists and nihilists did.

The egoist conception of economic life is very much associated with the accumulation of property. We all have a drive to obtain possessions and, having obtained them, to retain them. Stirner's startling assertion that our relationships with other people are purely self-interested is expressed in this extract from his best-known work, *The Ego and His Own* (1844).

> 'Where the world comes in my way — and it comes in my way everywhere — I consume it to quiet the hunger of my egoism. For me you are nothing but my food, even as I too am fed upon and turned to use by you. We have only one relation to each other, that of usableness, of utility, of use.'

Egoism and its associated philosophy of nihilism are perhaps the most extreme forms of anarchism that have existed. However, as we have seen above, anarchism is a rich and varied tradition. Indeed, for many commentators, it is not a single ideology but a collection of different movements and philosophies with only one idea in common: the abolition of the state.

Summary: key themes and key thinkers

	Human nature	The state	Society	The economy
Max Stirner	We are fundamentally self-interested egoists.	The state is the complete denial of our egoism and individualism.	Society of any kind restrains. We must be completely self-reliant.	The accumulation and retention of property is our main economic motivation.
Peter Kropotkin	People are sociable and prefer collective activity.	The capitalist state must be destroyed by revolution and replaced by a voluntary system of independent, self-governing communities.	The commune should be the basis of society. Communes were to be small, independent, internally democratic units.	Capitalism was to be replaced by the communist system of small units which should, as far as possible, be self-sufficient.
Mikhail Bakunin	We are fundamentally social animals and productive work characterises our humanity.	The state is the servant of capitalism. Both the state and capitalism must be destroyed by revolution.	He proposed a federal system and the abolition of national boundaries. Federations of workers would cooperate and not compete with each other.	The market system of exchange was to be abolished and replaced by exchange based on the true value of labour and goods.
Pierre-Joseph Proudhon	We are characterised by our productive abilities and creativity as producers.	The state is oppressive and must be abolished, though possibly by peaceful, democratic means.	His theory of society was known as mutualism. People are bound together by economic and social relations which are mutually beneficial.	People should be divided into independent productive units, trading with each other on a mutually beneficial basis.
Emma Goldman	Stressed the need for individual liberty. The desire for freedom is fundamental to mankind.	The state is only one source of oppression and denial of liberty. Religion and property ownership are equally oppressive.	She proposed a society where all people would be treated as equal. She campaigned for economic, gender and racial equality in society.	A violent opponent of capitalism, she was more concerned with liberty than with economic justice, but was fundamentally a communist.

Tensions within anarchism

As we have seen, anarchism can hardly be described as one single ideology. It is very much a collection of movements and philosophies that has the abolition of the state at its heart. There are also tensions between anarchists. By tensions we mean here fundamental differences between different types of anarchism. We can see these tensions within four key areas.

- **Human nature:** the main schism here concerns the issue of whether people are basically socially minded or whether they are individualists. Anarcho-communists such as Kropotkin and collectivists like Bakunin see people as social animals who prefer to achieve their goals collectively. It is for this reason that they propose the replacement of the state by new communities which are on a smaller scale, are not based on nationhood and are voluntary. The voluntary nature of communities in their vision is what separates them from the state. States are coercive and imposed upon people, while free communities involve no element of force or power. Individualist anarchists, meanwhile, insist that mankind's principal motivation is a desire for individual liberty. For them, any kind of social organisation should be opposed on two grounds: first, that it is unnatural and second, that it removes individual sovereignty. The most extreme example of this belief is nihilism, but the anarcho-capitalists share a belief in the restoration of a world of economically independent, self-interested individuals.

  There are also distinctions in how much anarchists see mankind as perfectible. William Godwin was an optimist in this respect, as was Rousseau, though the latter was less confident and so proposed the existence of a supreme ruler until such time as an enlightened people could come to govern themselves. Most anarchists remained relatively open-minded about human nature. They largely confined themselves to the belief that once corrupt societies and government were abolished, the human condition would naturally improve and a new form of moral society would ensue. The exception were the egoist philosophers, such as Sorel, and the anarcho-capitalists, who cared little for individual morality, instead seeing people as self-interested and motivated by the pursuit of their own interests.

- **The state:** the need to abolish the state unites all anarchists. However, this does not mean they all see the state in the same light. Nor do they share identical views on how the state should be abolished. If we consider the relationship between capitalism and the state, we see an important distinction. While most anarchists stress the relationship between the two in terms of a partnership whose purpose is to suppress individual liberty and exploit people as producers and consumers, anarcho-capitalists see the state as the enemy of free-market capitalism. In the end both groups would abolish the state, but their reasons for doing so differ greatly.

  Anarchists are assumed to be violent revolutionaries who would bring down the state by force and by attrition. This is a valid assumption in most cases. However, some anarchist thinkers varied from this position. There have been four alternatives to the revolutionary position. The first, led by Godwin, is that the dissemination of morality and the creation of a moral society will make the state irrelevant. It would, under these circumstances, simply wither away. The second, exemplified by Proudhon, is that the state could be gradually abolished by democratic means. If anarchist ideas could gain popularity, the state might be simply voted out of existence. The third alternative was shared by individualist anarchists, mostly in the American tradition, such as Thoreau, Spooner and Warren. Rather than abolish the state, they proposed, individuals should simply withdraw from society and manage their own affairs autonomously. The state would then become irrelevant. Fourth, Mahatma Gandhi, who demonstrated anarchist tendencies in his struggle for Indian political and economic independence, insisted on non-violence. State property could be attacked, but not people.

- **Society:** it is in their conceptions of a just and free society that anarchists are perhaps most at odds with each other. There is a clear schism between collectivist anarchists who see human beings in terms of society and community, and individualist anarchists who see social organisation as a threat to the individual. As we have seen, all anarchists claim that their vision will create order, but they differ greatly on how to achieve it. On the 'social wing' stand such great figures as Kropotkin, Bakunin, Malatesta and Reclus, all of whom wish to create a natural society in place of the coercive state. On the other wing stand a variety of individualist thinkers, including those who would have individuals withdraw from society, notably Thoreau, as well as those who envisage a new order where individuals are free to compete with each other and to pursue their self-interest. Stirner from the nineteenth century and modern anarcho-capitalists, such as Rothbard, stand on this ground.

- **The economy:** anarchists tend to fall into two categories in their consideration of a new economic order. These can be briefly characterised as cooperation versus competition. There is unanimity among most anarchists (with the exception of anarcho-capitalists) that capitalism needs to be destroyed and replaced. The question has been 'replaced with what?' Mutualism was perhaps the most common solution to how a post-capitalist world might work. This involved forms of cooperation which would guarantee that the exchange of goods and labour took place to the mutual benefit of both parties to any transaction. Goods and labour would be assigned a true intrinsic value rather than the value placed on them by the free market. For others, however, exchange would involve some sort of process of negotiation between the parties. Bakunin's version of federalism proposed this kind of arrangement. The outcome might be as equally just as in mutualism, but the process would be different.

  But we must return to anarchist conceptions of human nature to determine where they stand on economic life. There is a basic distinction between those who see mankind as fundamentally social, in which case self-sufficiency and cooperation apply, and those who see mankind in terms of individualism, in which case negotiation or competition becomes natural and appropriate.

Conclusion: anarchism today

As a full-blown political ideology, anarchism scarcely exists today. There are some important libertarian and anarcho-capitalist thinkers who have some influence on the political system, especially in the USA, but none of them proposes the complete abolition of the state, merely its reduction to a minimum. They are anarchists only in that they wish to see the restoration of a high degree of individual autonomy and to take away most of the state's regulation of society. The conservative libertarian Robert Nozick still has his adherents and they still seek to persuade Americans that the future should lie with the minimal state. In his great work, *Anarchy, State and Society* (1974), Nozick summed it up thus:

> 'Our main conclusions about the state are that a minimal state, limited to the narrow functions of protection against force, theft, fraud, enforcement of contracts, and so on, is justified, but any more extensive state will violate persons' rights not to be forced to do certain things, and is unjustified; and that the minimal state is inspiring as well as right.'

But even though anarchism is in hibernation as a political movement, its spirit lives on. This can be seen in two particular areas of radical political thought. The first lies with the ecology movement. Some deep ecologists have suggested that the only way in which the environment can be saved for future generations is if capitalism is dismantled and industrialisation halted and if people return to a simpler way of life, preferably in small-scale communities. Certainly the ideas of radical economist E.F. Schumacher (1911–77), whose slogan, 'small is beautiful', became popular in the 1960s and 1970s, echo those of Kropotkin from a century earlier. Schumacher still has many disciples within the ecology movement.

The second area of thought lies with various contemporary anti-capitalist social movements. The activists associated with the Occupy movement (which opposes the excesses of capitalism and the financial system), for example, often associate capitalism with the modern state and seek to undermine both in the interests of the creation of greater equality and a more natural way of life.

However, the principal contribution of anarchism, in all its forms, to political thought lies not in its practicality or any possibility that its aims may be realised but in its root-and-branch critique of contemporary capitalist society and the growing power of the modern state.

The Occupy movement opposes the excesses of capitalism

Further reading

Five classic works of anarchist thinkers are:

Pierre-Joseph Proudhon. *What is Property?*

Peter Kroptkin. *Anarchism*.

Henry Thoreau. *Walden*.

Robert Wolff. *In Defense of Anarchism*.

Murray Rothbard. *Man, Economy and State*.

Important works about anarchism include:

Gurein, D. (2006) *No Gods. No Masters*, AK Press.

Marshall, P. (1992) *Demanding the Impossible*, HarperCollins.

Woodcock, G. (1962) *Anarchism*, World Publishing.

Exam-style questions

The following questions are similar to those in examinations set by Edexcel (Pearson) and AQA.

Edexcel (24 marks) or AQA (25 marks):

1 To what extent does anarchism differ from fundamentalist socialism? You must use appropriate thinkers you have studied to support your answer.

2 To what extent does anarchism have a coherent view of human nature? You must use appropriate thinkers you have studied to support your answer.

AQA only (25 marks):

3 With reference to the thinkers you have studied, analyse and evaluate why anarchists insist on the destruction of the state.

4 Analyse and evaluate the relationship between anarchism and utopianism with reference to the thinkers you have studied.

Index

A

Abbey, Edward 168, 170
Acton, Lord 21, 169
Adam Smith Institute 37, 70
Adenauer, Konrad 64
Ali, Tariq 94
altruism **153**, 155
anarchism 149–87
 anarchism today 186
 collectivist anarchism 172–77
 core ideas 152–71
 economy 165–67, 176, 185
 exam questions 187
 human nature 153–58, 172, 184
 individualist anarchism 177–82
 key themes and thinkers 183
 liberalism 16, 154, 170, 181
 origins 150–52
 socialism 163, 166, 171, 177
 society 162–64, 173, 176, 185
 the state 158–61, 164, 184–85
 tensions within 184–85
 types 171–82
 utopianism 168–71
anarcho-capitalism 152, 156, 161,
 164, 167, 177, 178–81, 184
anarcho-communism 151, 152,
 156–58, 168, 172–74, 184
anarcho-syndicalism 174–76
androgyny **125**, 141
anti-clericalism 159
anti-permissive policies **70**
Asquith, Herbert 32
atomism **71**

Attlee, Clement 101
authority **54**, **159**
autonomy **181**

B

Babeuf, François-Noel 84
Bakunin, Mikhail 90, 151, 154, 156,
 158–60, 162–63, 165, 183–85
Beauvoir, Simone de 129, 130,
 137, 145
Benn, Tony 88, 102, 106, 111, 113
Bentham, Jeremy 26, 27, 28
Bernstein, Eduard 105, 106,
 107, 113
Beveridge Report 32, 37
Bismarck, Otto von 61, 62
Blair, Tony 41, 110, 111, 113
Blond, Phillip 78
Brandt, Willy 107, 108
Brown, Gordon 110, 111, 113, 117
Burke, Edmund 24, 44, 47–49,
 51–53, 55–56, 58–62, 67,
 75–76, 78
Butler, R.A. 64, 68

C

Cameron, David 37, 41, 78, 80
Camus, Albert 130
Canning, George 59, 60, 61
capitalism
 anarchism 161, 163–67, 173–
 74, 176, 179–80, 185, 186
 conservatism 56, 57, 63, 69
 definition **88**
 feminism 125–26, 128, 133,
 134, 142, 143, 147

 liberalism 16, 25, 39
 socialism 88–89, 91, 93–94,
 99, 106–09, 112–13, 117–18
Castro, Fidel 97, 118
changing to conserve 44, **45**
China 40, 97, 99, 118
Chomsky, Noam 175
Christian democracy 64–65
Christianity 10, 13, 49, 52–53
class **86**, 94, 142
class consciousness **92**
classical liberalism 22–30
classical Marxism 91–93
classical revisionism 106–07
collectivisation **174**
collectivism 31, 32, 89, 116, 166
collectivist anarchism 90, 151,
 152, 156, 164, 165, 168,
 172–77, 184–85
common ownership **88**
communes 156, 158, 163, 166,
 169, 172, 175
communism
 anarchism 151, 156, **157**, 172–74
 conservatism 63
 definition **91**
 socialism 91, 93–99, 103–04
conservatism 43–81
 anarchism 170
 and capitalism 69
 Christian democracy 64–65
 conservatism today 77–80
 core ideas 47–57
 economy 56–57, 76
 exam questions 81

human nature 47–50, 76

key themes and thinkers 75

and liberalism 10, 37, 42

New Right conservatism 67–74

origins 46–47

politics of pragmatism 67

and socialism 47, 63, 77, 78

society 50–53, 76

the state 54–56, 76

tensions within 76

traditional conservatism 57–64

types 57–74

Corbyn, Jeremy 42, 99, 117, 118

Crenshaw, Kimberlé 131

Crosland, Anthony 59, 64, 86, 107–09, 113, 115, 116

cultural feminism **141**, 142

D

Darwin, Charles 27, 136, 157

democracy 30, 34, 39, 160, 173

democratic centralism **96**

democratic socialism 99–102, 104, 116

developmental individualism 27, **28**, 29

dialectic **92**

difference feminism 129, **138**, 146

direct action **175**

direct democracy **160**, 173

discrimination 35, 128, 133, **137**, 143

Disraeli, Benjamin 61, 62, 65, 87

Donne, John 85

Dworkin, Andrea 139

E

early classical liberalism 22–25

eco-feminism 142

ecology movement 186

economic liberalism **15**

economy

anarchism 165–67, 176, 185

conservatism 56–57, 76

definition 7

feminism 133–34

liberalism 15–16, 25, 39

socialism 88–89, 116

egalitarianism 63

ego **153**, 155, 177

egoism 154, 155, 177–78, 181–82

egotistical individualism **14**

Eisenstein, Zillah 141

empiricism **51**

enabling state **32**

Engels, Friedrich 86, 91–93, 94, 106, 114, 133, 142

Enlightenment 10–11, 13, 24, 41, 46–48, 83, 84, 150, 153

environmentalism 129

equality feminism 129, **138**, 146

equality of opportunity **20**, **133**, 135

essentialism **123**

Euro-communism 103–04, 113

European Union (EU) 34, 39, 42, 65, 78–80, 102, 128

evolutionary socialism 94, 101, **102**, 105

existentialism 130, 182

F

Fabian Society 99, 100, 101, 106

fascism **63**, 65

Fawcett Society 147

federalism 163, **164**, 185

female genital mutilation (FGM) 147

feminism 120–48

core ideas 123–34

cultural feminism 141–42

economy 133–34

exam questions 148

feminism today 147–48

human nature 123–27

key themes and thinkers 145

liberal feminism 135–38

liberalism 24, 36

origins 121–23

the personal is political 126–27

post-modern feminism 144

radical feminism 138–42

sex and gender 123–26

socialist feminism 142–43

society 128–32

the state 127–28

tensions within 145–46

types 135–44

Firestone, Shulamith 125, 127, 134, 139–41

first wave feminism 122, 135

foundational equality **19**, 21, 33, 87

Fourier, Charles 84, 91

Frankfurt School 104, 106, 115

fraternity **85**

French Revolution 11, 19, 24, 46–48, 51, 57–59, 61

Friedan, Betty 19, 35–36, 38–39, 124, 130, 135, 137

Friedman, David 156, 164, 167, 179, 180

Friedman, Milton 37, 57, 70

Fukuyama, Francis 40, 116, 117

fundamentalist socialism **91**, 92–105, 113, 115, 116

G

Gamble, Andrew 74

Gandhi, Mahatma 185

gender
   definition **124**
   feminism 123–26, 128, 131, 139, 141, 144
   liberalism 36
gender equality **137**
Giddens, Anthony 107, 110–13, 115, 116
Gilman, Charlotte Perkins 122, 135, 136, 145
Gilmour, Ian 73
Glasman, Maurice 79
Godwin, William 150, 151, 154, 158, 159, 184
Goldman, Emma 152, 160, 167, 169, 173, 183
government **150**
government by consent 17–18, 22–23, 32, 40, 41, 160
Gramsci, Antonio 103, 106
Green, T.H. 31, 32
Greer, Germaine 127, 139, 140, 141

H
Hanisch, Carol 126, 127, 134
harm principle **18**, 29, 36
Hayek, Friedrich von 32, 33, 37, 39, 57, 67, 70, 72
Hegel, Friedrich 92
hierarchy **52**
historical materialism **92**
Hobbes, Thomas 12, 14, 48–50, 54, 66, 75, 78
Hobhouse, L.T. 31, 34
Hobsbawm, Eric 84
Hobson, J.A. 31
Hogg, Quentin 64, 68
Hollande, François 99, 117
hooks, bell 131, 132, 145
Horkheimer, Max 104

human imperfection **47**
Hyndman, Henry 107

I
individualism 14–16, 18, 29, 78, 166
individualist anarchism 151, 152, 156, 164, 177–82, 185
insurrection **175**
intersectionality **131**, 132, 144

J
Jefferson, Thomas 25, 37
Judaeo-Christian morality 52–53, 54, 64
Jura Federation 157, 164

K
Kennedy, John F. 35
Keynes, John Maynard 32, 39, 107, 108, 109
Keynesian economics 57, 63–64, **108**
Kristol, Irving 70, 74
Kropotkin, Peter 90, 151, 154, 156–58, 160, 164–65, 172, 174, 183–85

L
Labour Party 45, 77, 79, 89, 100, 102, 110–11, 116–17
laissez-faire capitalism **22**, 25, **56**, 62, 88, 89
legal equality **19**, **137**
Lenin, Vladimir Ilyich 93, 95, 96, 98, 106, 113, 157
Leninism 93–99
liberal democracy 9, 30, 34, 160
liberal feminism 121, 124–25, 126, 135–38, 146, 147
liberalism 9–43
   anarchism 16, 154, 170, 181

   classical liberalism 22–30
   and conservatism 10, 37, 42
   core ideas 13–21
   economy 15–16, 25, 39
   exam questions 43
   human nature 13–14, 16, 39
   liberalism today 40–42
   modern liberalism 30–36
   origins 10–12
   and socialism 10, 15, 32–33, 83–85, 87, 114
   society 14–15, 39
   the state 16–21, 39, 40
   tensions within 39
   types 22–38
liberal state 16–20, 160–61
libertarianism 72, **178**
liberty 23, 30–31, 156, 158
limited government **20**
Livingstone, Ken 160
Lloyd-George, David 32
Locke, John
   anarchism 153
   conservatism 48, 68
   liberalism 11–13, 15–17, 19, 22, 36, 38–40, 42
Luther, Martin 10
Luxemburg, Rosa 93, 95, 97–98, 105–06, 113–14, 116

M
Macmillan, Harold 63, 67, 68
Malatesta, Enrico 159, 164, 172, 185
Mandelson, Peter 111
Mao Tse-tung 97, 113
Marchais, George 103
Marcuse, Herbert 104
Marx, Karl 61–62, 84, 86, 90–94, 98, 105–07, 113–16

Marxism
  anarchism 151, 163, 171
  classical Marxism 91–93
  definition **91**
  feminism 125–26, 134, 142
  Marxism–Leninism 93–99
  one-nation conservatism 61
McKinley, William 169
mechanistic theory **11**
Miliband, Ralph 94, 104–05, 113
Mill, John Stuart 13–15, 18, 26–30, 34, 38–39, 122, 135
Millett, Kate 125, 139, 140, 141, 145
minimal state **25**
Mitchell, Juliet 125
modern liberalism 30–36, 39
Montesquieu, Charles-Louis 23
Mussolini, Benito 63
mutualism **165**, 166, 172–74, 185

N

Napolitano, George 103
nation-state 55–56, 61–62, 65
Nechaev, Sergei 178
negative liberty **23**, 25, 29, 37, 39
neo-conservatism 70, 73, 74
neo-liberalism 6–7, 37–39, 57, 70, 73–74, 179
neo-Marxism 104–05
neo-revisionism 110–13
New Labour 41, 77, 111, 113, 117
New Right conservatism 38, 49, 53–54, 56, 57, 67–74, 76
Nietzsche, Friedrich 155
nihilism **155**, 178, 182, 184
noblesse oblige **52**
Norman, Jesse 78
normative view **51**
Nozick, Robert

anarchism 72, 178, 186
conservatism 49, 53, 56, 66, 67, 75, 76
New Right conservatism 70, 72, 73

O

Oakeshott, Michael 49, 51, 52, 66, 67, 75, 76
Occupy movement 186
one-nation conservatism **61**, 62
orthodox communism 93–99, 116
otherness 130, **137**
Owen, Robert 84, 91

P

Paine, Thomas 19
Pankhurst, Emmeline 122
Paris Commune 163
parliamentary socialism 94, 101, 102, 105
paternalism **52**, 53, 59
patriarchy **124**, 125, 127–29, 132, 135, 137–41, 146, 147
Paul, Alice 122
Peel, Robert 59, 60, 61, 67
philosophical anarchism 150, 152
Pitt, William 59
Podemos 108, 117
political equality **137**
Popper, Karl 37
positive freedom 30, **31**, 35, 39
post-feminism 144
post-modern feminism 131, 132, 144
power **158**, 169
private judgement **151**, 154
private sphere **126**, 127
progressive view **51**

property 15, 53–54, 83, 106, 142, 161–62, 167, 170
Proudhon, Pierre-Joseph 158, 159, 165, 166, 173, 183, 184
public sphere **126**, 127

Q

Quinton, Anthony 73

R

race 36, 131
radical feminism 121, 125, 127–28, 137, 138–42, 146, 147
Rand, Ayn 49, 53, 56, 70, 71, 75, 76
Rawls, John 31, 32, 33, 38, 39, 87
Reagan, Ronald 38, 57, 69
Reclus, Elisée 172, 185
reformists **138**
reserve army of labour **133**
revisionist socialism **105**, 106–13, 115–17
revolutionary socialism 93, 95, 97, 101, 105, 113
Rocker, Rudolf 170, 175, 176
Roosevelt, F.D. 32
Rothbard, Murray 152, 156, 164, 167, 179, 180, 185
Rousseau, Jean-Jacques 18, 46, 84, 150–51, 153, 160, 184
Rowbotham, Sheila 133, 134, 143, 145
Russia 40, 93, 118, 159

S

Sanders, Bernie 10, 42, 117
Sartre, Jean-Paul 130
Schmidt, Helmut 107, 108
Schröder, Gerhard 110, 113
Schumacher, E.F. 186
Schuman, Robert 64, 65

Scruton, Roger 65, 70

second wave feminism 123, 124, 130

sex **123**, 124–26

sexism 36, 131, 140, 147

sexuality 127, 141, 143, 144

Shaw, G.B. 99

Shore, Peter 108

Smiles, Samuel 26–27

Smith, Adam 15, 16, 25, 37, 39, 56, 58

social class 86, 92, 94

social contract **18**

social Darwinism 27, 157, 172, 173, 180

social democracy 107–08, 110

socialism 82–119

    anarchism 163, 166, 171, 177

    and conservatism 47, 63, 77, 78

    core ideas 85–90

    democratic socialism 99–102

    economy 88–89, 116

    exam questions 119

    feminism 134

    human nature 85, 115

    key themes and thinkers 114–15

    and liberalism 10, 15, 32–33, 83–85, 87, 114

    Marxism–Leninism 93–99

    origins 83–84

    revisionist socialism 105–13

    socialism today 116–18

    society 85–88, 115

    the state 90, 116

    tensions within 115–16

    types 91–114

socialist feminism 125, 127, 133, 134, 142–43, 146, 147

social justice 31, 32, **87**

social liberalism **35**, 36

society

    anarchism 162–64, 173, 176, 185

    conservatism 50–53, 76

    definition 7

    feminism 128–32

    liberalism 14–15, 39

    socialism 85–88, 115

solidarity **172**

Sorel, Georges 155, 158, 174, 175, 184

Soviet Union 65, 96, 99, 116, 175

Spencer, Herbert 27

Spooner, Lysander 177, 179, 185

Stalin, Joseph 96

the state

    anarchism 158–61, 164, 168, 169, 172–73, 176, 180, 184–85

    conservatism 54–56, 76

    definition 7, **158**

    feminism 127–28

    liberalism 12, 14, 16–21, 25, 31–33, 39, 40

    socialism 90, 116

state of nature 12, **16**, 17

Stirner, Max 151, 153–55, 177, 181–83, 185

Sturzo, Luigi 64

suffrage 27, 28, 34, 122, 135

suffragette movement 122, 135

supranationalism **65**

syndicalism **174**, 175, 176

Syriza 99, 108, 117

T

Taylor, Harriet 122

terrorism 41, 77

Thatcher, Margaret 38, 57, 67, 69, 73

Thatcherism **57**, 74

third wave feminism 144

Third Way 110–13, 116

Thoreau, Henry 151, 158, 167, 177, 179, 185

Tories **59**, 60

traditional conservatism 57–64

transitional liberalism 27, 29

Trotsky, Leon 96, 97, 113

Trump, Donald 41, 79

Tucker, Benjamin 179

tyranny of the majority 26, 27–28, 29, 34, 173

U

United Kingdom (UK) 55–56, 67, 80

United Kingdom Independence Party (UKIP) 41

United States of America (USA) 55–57, 68

utopianism **168**, 169–71

utopian socialism **84**, 91

V

Voltaire 18, 23, 46, 56, 159

W

Warren, Josiah 167, 177, 185

The Wealth of Nations (Smith) 15, 25

Webb, Beatrice 59, 89, 100, 101, 106, 113, 115, 116

Webb, Sidney 99–100, 101

Whig Party 46, 59

Wollstonecraft, Mary 23, 24, 36, 38, 121–22, 135

women's rights 121–23, 135, 137

Wordsworth, William 46